First World War
and Army of Occupation
War Diary
France, Belgium and Germany

5 DIVISION
Divisional Troops
28 Brigade Royal Field Artillery
and Belgian Artillery Regiment
1 August 1914 - 9 July 1915

WO95/1532

The Naval & Military Press Ltd
www.nmarchive.com
Published in association with The National Archives

Published by

The Naval & Military Press Ltd

Unit 10 Ridgewood Industrial Park,

Uckfield, East Sussex,

TN22 5QE England

Tel: +44 (0) 1825 749494

www.naval-military-press.com

www.nmarchive.com

This diary has been reprinted in facsimile from the original. Any imperfections are inevitably reproduced and the quality may fall short of modern type and cartographic standards.

© Crown Copyright
Images reproduced by permission of The National Archives, London, England, 2015.

Contents

Document type	Place/Title	Date From	Date To
Heading	28th Bde R.F.A. (Became A.F.A. 2 Army) Aug 1914-Dec 1916 And Belgian Arty Regt Feb-Jly 1915		
Heading	WO95/1532/1		
Heading	5 Division Troops 28 Brigade RFA 1914 Aug-1914 Dec		
Heading	28th Brigade R.F.A. August 1914.		
Heading	War Diary Of 5th Division 28th. Brigade RFA From Aug 17th 1914 To Aug 31st 1914 Vol I		
War Diary			
War Diary	Dundalk	07/08/1914	07/08/1914
War Diary	Belfast	07/08/1914	07/08/1914
War Diary	Irish Channel	18/08/1914	18/08/1914
War Diary	English Channel	19/08/1914	19/08/1914
War Diary	Havre	20/08/1914	21/08/1914
War Diary	Bavai	22/08/1914	23/08/1914
War Diary	Dour	24/08/1914	24/08/1914
War Diary	3/4 Mile W of Bry.	25/08/1914	26/08/1914
War Diary	Le Cateau	26/08/1914	30/08/1914
War Diary	Jaulzy	31/08/1914	31/08/1914
War Diary	St Quentin	26/08/1914	27/08/1914
War Diary	Noyon	28/08/1914	28/08/1914
War Diary	Pontoise	29/08/1914	29/08/1914
War Diary	War Diary Of 28th Bde. R.F.A. Ammunition Column. 5th Division. From Aug 5th. 1914. To Aug 31st 1914 (60th Dates Inclusive) Volume I		
War Diary	Dundalk	05/08/1914	16/08/1914
War Diary	Belfast	17/08/1914	19/08/1914
War Diary	Rest Camp Havre	21/08/1914	21/08/1914
War Diary	Landrecies	22/08/1914	22/08/1914
War Diary	Bavai	22/08/1914	22/08/1914
War Diary	La Rosiere	23/08/1914	23/08/1914
War Diary	Dour	23/08/1914	24/08/1914
War Diary	Bois de Boussu	24/08/1914	24/08/1914
War Diary	Small Plateau 800 N.E Of R In Dour Ref Map	24/08/1914	24/08/1914
War Diary	Belgium Mons 7a	24/08/1914	24/08/1914
War Diary	Under Cover of Hedge in Field 150th W of Main St Waast-Jenlain road 1/2 m. W. N.W. of Wagneries.	25/08/1914	25/08/1914
War Diary	Near Reumont	26/08/1918	26/08/1918
War Diary	S. Side of Reumont Le Cateau Au road about the R in Reumont	26/08/1914	26/08/1914
War Diary	About 10. m. from Reumont	26/08/1914	27/08/1914
War Diary	St Quentin	27/08/1914	27/08/1914
War Diary	Ollezy	27/08/1914	28/08/1914
War Diary	Farm Called Le Meriquin	28/08/1914	29/08/1914
War Diary	Jaulez	29/08/1914	30/08/1914
War Diary	Near Le Petit Marmont	30/08/1914	31/08/1914
War Diary	Nanteuvilly	31/08/1914	31/08/1914
Heading	28th Brigade R.F.A. September 1914.		
War Diary	War Diary Of 28th Brigade R.F.A. 5th. Division From Sept. 1st To Sept. 30th 1914 Vol II		

War Diary		01/09/1914	03/09/1914
War Diary	Bouleurs	03/09/1914	03/09/1914
War Diary	Tournan	05/09/1914	06/09/1914
War Diary	Favieres	06/09/1914	06/09/1914
War Diary	Villeneuve Le Comte	07/09/1914	09/09/1914
War Diary	Mortcerf	07/09/1914	07/09/1914
War Diary	Mouroux	08/09/1914	08/09/1914
War Diary	Champtortel	09/09/1914	10/09/1914
War Diary	Chezy-En-Orxois	11/09/1914	11/09/1914
War Diary	Billy-Sur-Ourcq	12/09/1914	12/09/1914
War Diary	Chacrise	12/09/1914	13/09/1914
War Diary	Mont De Soissons Farm	14/09/1914	30/09/1914
War Diary	Extract from letter from D.R. Peel to Mrs Peel Capt R.A. Jones R.F.A.		
War Diary	123rd Battery, R.F.A. August To December 1914		
Heading	War Diary 123rd Battery R.F.A. August To December 1914		
War Diary		01/08/1914	01/08/1914
War Diary		27/08/1914	30/12/1914
Heading	5th Div. R.F.A. 28th Brigade Aug-dec 1914		
Heading	5th. Division 28th Brigade R.F.A. 1-31.12.14 Vol V		
War Diary		30/10/1914	02/11/1914
Heading	War Diary Of 28th Brigade RFA 1-31 October 1914 Vol III		
War Diary		01/10/1914	14/10/1914
War Diary	Essars	15/10/1914	15/10/1914
War Diary	Gorre	16/10/1914	18/10/1914
War Diary	Festubert	19/10/1914	31/10/1914
Heading	War Diary Of 28th Brigade R.F.A. Nov. 1st-30th 1914 Vol IV		
War Diary	Strazeele	01/11/1914	01/11/1914
War Diary	Croix De Poperinghe	02/11/1914	02/11/1914
War Diary	Kemmel	03/11/1914	03/11/1914
War Diary	Lindenhoek	04/11/1914	30/11/1914
Heading	War Diary 28th Bde R.F.A. December 1914 Vol V		
War Diary		01/12/1914	11/12/1914
War Diary	Lindenhoek	13/12/1914	31/12/1914
Miscellaneous			
Miscellaneous	5th Div R.A. 28th Brigade. Jan-Dec, 1915		
Heading	5th Division 28th Bde. R.F.A. 1-31.1.15. Vol VI		
Heading	War Diary 28th Brigade R.F.A. January 1915 Vol VI		
War Diary	Lindenhoek & Neuve Eglise	01/01/1915	31/01/1915
Heading	Copy of Letter from Toni	06/01/1915	06/01/1915
Miscellaneous			
Heading	5th. Division. 28th Bde R.F.A. Vol VII 1-28.2.15		
War Diary	War Diary 28th Brigade R.F.A. February 1915 Vol VII		
War Diary	Lindenhoek & Neuve Eglise	01/02/1915	14/02/1915
War Diary	Lindenhoek	15/02/1915	28/02/1915
War Diary	28th Bde: R.F.A. Vol VIII 1-31.3.15 5th Division		
War Diary	War Diary Of 28th Brigade R.F.A. 5th Division Vol. VIII From 1st March-31st March 1915.		
War Diary	Lindenhoek	01/03/1915	31/03/1915
Heading	5th Division 28th Bde R.F.A. Vol IX April 1915		
War Diary	Lindenhoek	01/04/1915	09/04/1915
War Diary	Ypres	10/04/1915	30/04/1915
Heading	5th Division 28th Bde. R.F.A. Vol X 1-31.5.15		

War Diary	War Diary. 28th Brigade R.F.A. 5th Division From 1st to 31st May 1915 Vol X		
War Diary	Ypres	01/05/1915	31/05/1915
Heading	5th Division 28th Bde R.F.A. Vol XI. 1-30.6.15		
War Diary	War Diary 28th Brigade R.F.A. From June 1st To 30th 1915		
War Diary	Ypres	01/06/1915	30/06/1915
Heading	5th Division 28th Bde. R.F.A. Vol XII From 1st To 31st July 1915		
Heading	War Diary 28th Brigade RFA 5th Division July 1-31 1915 Vol 12		
War Diary		01/07/1915	31/07/1915
Heading	5th Division 28th Bde RFA Vol XIII August 15		
Heading	War Diary 28th Brigade RFA 5th Division August 1915 Volume 13		
War Diary		01/08/1915	31/08/1915
Heading	5th Division 28th. Bde R.F.A. Vol XIV. Sept 15		
Heading	War Diary 28th Bde R.F.A. 5th Division September 1915 Volume 14.		
War Diary		01/09/1915	30/09/1915
Heading	5th Division 28th. Bde. R.F.A. Oct & Nov Vol XV		
War Diary	War Diary 28 Bde RFA. 5th Divn October 1915 Volume 15		
War Diary		01/10/1915	31/10/1915
Heading	War Diary November 1916 28th Bde R.F.A. 5th Division Volume 16		
War Diary		01/11/1915	30/11/1915
Heading	5th Div. War Diary Division 1916 28th Brigade R.F.A. Vol XVI		
War Diary		01/12/1915	31/12/1915
Heading	123rd Battery, R.F.A. January to December 1915		
Heading	War Diary 123rd Battery R.F.A. January To December 1915		
War Diary	123 Battery R.F.A.		
Heading	5th Division 28th Bde R.F.A. January To December 1916		
Heading	War Diary 28th Bde R.F.A. January 1916 Vol XVII		
War Diary	01011916	01/01/1916	31/01/1916
Heading	War Diary 28th Brigade R.F.A. February 1916 Vol XVIII		
War Diary		01/02/1916	29/02/1916
War Diary	Arras	02/03/1916	24/06/1916
War Diary	Beaumetz	24/06/1916	20/07/1916
War Diary	Montauban	21/07/1916	31/07/1916
Heading	28th Brigade Royal Field Artillery August 1916		
Miscellaneous	A Form. Messages And Signals.		
War Diary	Montauban	01/08/1916	31/08/1916
War Diary			
Heading	28th Brigade R.F.A. September 1916		
War Diary		01/09/1916	22/09/1916
War Diary	Bussy les Daours	06/09/1916	22/09/1916
Heading	28 Bds		
War Diary		01/10/1916	14/10/1916
War Diary	Le Touret	16/10/1916	31/12/1916
Heading	123rd Battery, R.F.A. January to 13th May 1916		

Heading	War Diary 123rd Battery R.F.A. January To 13th May 1916		
Miscellaneous			
Heading	WO95/1532/2		
Heading	5th Div R.A. Belgian Artillery Regt 10th Febry July 1915		
Heading	War Diary of Belgian Artillery Regiment attd 28th Divn from Feb 10th to March 31 1915		
War Diary		10/02/1915	31/03/1915
Miscellaneous	Appendix No I		
Map			
Heading	A.G. The Base War Diary Belgian Artillery Regt Attd 28th Divn		
Map	Appendix III		
Heading	28th Division in Dist apparently attached 5th Division Belgian Artilery Regt Vol II 1-30.4.15		
War Diary		01/04/1915	24/04/1915
War Diary	Vlamertinghe	25/04/1915	30/04/1915
War Diary	Appendix IV O.C. Balgian Art.		
War Diary	Provisional Belgian Artillery Regt App V		
Miscellaneous	Appendix VI Provisional Ragt of Belgian Artillery		
Miscellaneous	Appendix VII		
Miscellaneous	Appendix VIII		
Heading	War Diary Belgian Artillery Regt attd 5th Divn		
Heading	5th Division Belgian Artillery Regiment Vol III 1-31.5.15		
War Diary	Vlamertinghe	01/05/1915	31/05/1915
Map	Appendix X		
Map	Appendix IX		
Miscellaneous	Appendix XI Belgian Artillery D.S.C. 154 11/5/15		
Miscellaneous	Fl Regiment d'Artillerie Appendix XII		
Map	Appendix XII 7th Belgian Art Reg Attd 5th Divn		
Map	Appendix XV front of 5th Divn M.G. H.Q 2nd Line		
Heading	5th Division Belgian Artillery Rub Vol IV 1-30.6.15		
Heading	War Diary June 1st-30th 1915 For 7th Belgian Field Artillery Regt Also 5th Divn		
War Diary	010615	01/06/1915	30/06/1915
Heading	5th Division Belgian Arty Regt Vol V 1-31.7.15		
Heading	War Diary		
War Diary		01/07/1915	26/07/1915
War Diary	Centre Group	27/07/1915	27/07/1915
War Diary	App XVII B.B. 51 9/7/15	09/07/1915	09/07/1915
Map			
Miscellaneous	App XIX	28/07/1915	28/07/1915
Miscellaneous	App XX R.A. Left Group	30/07/1915	30/07/1915
Miscellaneous	App XXI Left Group Bde 179 31.715	31/07/1915	31/07/1915
Map			

5TH DIVISION

28TH BDE R.F.A. (Became A.F.A. 2ⁿᵈ Army)
AUG 1914-DEC 1916
AND
BELGIAN ARTY REGT
FEB-JLY 1915

WO 95/15321

5 DIVISION TROOPS

28 BRIGADE RFA

1914 AUG — 1914 SEPT
~~DEC~~

Box 1532

5th Divisional Artillery.

28th BRIGADE R. F. A. ::: AUGUST 1914.

5 DIVISION TROOPS

28 BRIGADE RFA

1914 AUG — 1914 SEPT DEC

Box 1532

5th Divisional Artillery.

28th BRIGADE R. F. A. ::: AUGUST 1914.

CONFIDENTIAL 121/1082

WAR DIARY

OF 5th Division.

26th Brigade RFA

from Aug 17th 1914 to Aug 31st 1914

Part I

WAR DIARY
INTELLIGENCE SUMMARY

This War Diary begins on Aug. 17th indeed In the first dec of mobilization. This is due to the fact that the late Adjutant of the Brigade did not start the diary. It has been compiled since.

G.A. Sanders
Major R.F.A.
Cmdg 28th Brigade R.F.A.

Army Form C. 2118.

WAR DIARY
or
INTELLIGENCE SUMMARY
(Erase heading not required.)

Instructions regarding War Diaries and Intelligence Summaries are contained in F. S. Regs., Part II. and the Staff Manual respectively. Title pages will be prepared in manuscript.

Hour, Date, Place	Summary of Events and Information	Remarks and References to Appendices
DUNDALK Monday Aug. 17. 2 a.m.	Brigade HQ and B Sub-Section Bde Am. Col. leave Dundalk in 1st train at 2 a.m. Remainder of the Brigade & Column & No 2 Sub. Div. Am. Col. entrain at intervals of an hour, the last train leaving at 12 noon.	
BELFAST 4.30 6.10 am	First train arrives at BELFAST. March through town to YORK DOCK. Start Embarking at once on SS MESABA. All troops on board by about 1, & boatload consists of Headquarters, 122 Battery, half 123 Battery and the Brigade Am. Column.	R/G
5.30 pm	Move off from the dock.	
IRISH CHANNEL TUESDAY AUGUST 16	Nothing of interest occurs. Perfect weather	R/G
ENGLISH CHANNEL WEDNESDAY AUG. 19.	Arrive outside HAVRE at about 4:30 p.m. & wait for tide. Move slowly through the docks at 7 pm and get alongside quay at about 9.30 p.m. Commence disembarking at once. Horses all taken out first. Vehicles all on shore by about 5 am; the half Brigade	
HAVRE THURSDAY AUG 20	then marches to a rest camp about the town, about 5 miles away and arrives at 7.15 am	R/G

Army Form C. 2118.

WAR DIARY
or
INTELLIGENCE SUMMARY
(Erase heading not required.)

Instructions regarding War Diaries and Intelligence Summaries are contained in F. S. Regs., Part II. and the Staff Manual respectively. Title pages will be prepared in manuscript.

Hour, Date, Place	Summary of Events and Information	Remarks and References to Appendices
HAVRE THURSDAY AUGUST 20.	Move from Rest Camp at 12 mn. (Aug 20/21) to entrain at HAVRE station.	
FRIDAY AUG. 21.	Arrive at station at 3 a.m. HQ. & 122 Battery share 1 train. 123 Battery (being joined by ½ other half # which has just landed) entrain at different station.	# S.S. CALEDONIA, with half 123"Bty + 122" Bty on board, arrive in dock about 6 p.m. 20". RMT
6 a.m.	leave HAVRE. # 124 Battery, in a separate train, leave HAVRE about 9 a.m. Route via ROUEN (water & feed horses + hot coffee for the men) AMIENS (5 min. stop) & ST. QUENTIN. Bde HQ, 122 and 123 Batteries detrain at LE CATEAU station at about 11 p.m., Bivouack just beside the station and march off at 6 a.m. 124 Battery detrain at LANDRECIES at about 1 a.m., and, after a 2 hours halt, march towards BAVAI. arriving in bivouack about 3 p.m.	RMT
SATURDAY AUG. 22. BAVAI.	@ FORET DE MORMAL. Bivouack is 1½ m. S.W. of BAVAI. Main body of brigade arrive at about 4.30 p.m. Route via W. edge of	RMT

Army Form C. 2118.

WAR DIARY
or
INTELLIGENCE SUMMARY
(Erase heading not required.)

Hour, Date, Place	Summary of Events and Information	Remarks and References to Appendices
BAVAY SUNDAY AUG. 23	March from bivouack at 5 a.m. through HOUDAIN and ATHIS. Arrive at DOUR at 9 a.m., halt for an hour at the edge of the town. Then ordered into billets at	Cross the BELGIAN frontier about 7 a.m. Water rises
DOUR	MARLIERE farm (122 By & Bde Am Col) to Crossroads ½ m. N.W. of MARLIERE). Orders received at 1 a.m. from G.O.C. RA to reconnoitre & take up entrenched positions extending from Bois DE BOUSSU Eastwards.	Final positions:— 122 By - 4 m S.E. of CHAMP DES SARTS 123 By - 300× N. of un Bois DE BOUSSU 124 By - at S of Bois DE BOUSSU PMS
2 p.m.	Receive Move out of bivouack at once & get into positions by about 4 p.m. At 5 p.m. 124 By is ordered to advance to close support of Infantry near THULIN via BOUSSU, but movement is sent back again by GOC 14th Inf. Brigade, & reoccupies original position.	
MONDAY AUG. 24 DOUR	Brigade is ready to open fire at dawn. Heavy firing; 28th Brigade does not fire much. 124 did not open fire.	

Army Form C. 2118.

WAR DIARY
or
INTELLIGENCE SUMMARY
(Erase heading not required.)

Instructions regarding War Diaries and Intelligence Summaries are contained in F. S. Regs., Part II. and the Staff Manual respectively. Title pages will be prepared in manuscript.

Hour, Date, Place	Summary of Events and Information	Remarks and References to Appendices
MONDAY AUG 24		
11 am	Orders received to retire. One section ^ for battery left to cover withdrawal of the infantry.	123 Bty + section B 124 Bty got separated from the brigade + remain so till the brigade gets into bivouac S. of LE CATEAU on the night of Aug. 25/26.
	Brigade ^(less sections of 123 Bty) complete marched via WIHERIES + ATHIS + GUSSIGNIES to a position about 1/2 a mile of the B in BRY and came into action before dark. Bivouacked there with 3rd Cavalry Brigade + 108th Heavy Battery, R.G.A.	No infantry escort anywhere near this bivouack. RMP
TUESDAY, AUG. 25. 3/4 mile W. f BRY.	(4 am) Marched at dawn via St WAAST, BAVAY, N edge of FORET DE MORMAL, ENGLEFONTAINE, CROIX and halted off road about a mile N. of the ½ m N. in MONTAY.	Enemy shelling HOUDAIN as the column moves along ST WAAST-BAVAI road. 28th Bde in the rearguard of the Division.
About 3 pm	Came into action about 1/4 N. of this and began digging in.	Covering position to prevent enemy shelling bivouack S. of LE CATEAU.

Army Form C. 2118

WAR DIARY
or
INTELLIGENCE SUMMARY
(Erase heading not required.)

Instructions regarding War Diaries and Intelligence Summaries are contained in F. S. Regs., Part II. and the Staff Manual respectively. Title pages will be prepared in manuscript.

Hour, Date, Place	Summary of Events and Information	Remarks and References to Appendices
11.30 pm	Brigade bivouacked 3/4 N.E. of REUMONT. after being withdrawn hurriedly just before sunset from the position N. of LE CATEAU.	Very bad block in MONTAY village. No lights of any sort to help & no one to direct the various units. This caused between 2 & 3 hours delay. RAS
WEDNESDAY AUG. 26. 3.30 a.m.	Moved out of bivouack into position action a mile and a half N. of LE CATEAU. 122 & 123. 500 yards apart facing N.E. 124 on their left facing N.W. See Appendix.	

WAR DIARY
or
INTELLIGENCE SUMMARY.
(Erase heading not required.)

Army Form C. 2118.

Hour, Date, Place	Summary of Events and Information	Remarks and references to Appendices
AUGUST 26. 1914 LE CATEAU	Appendix – "LE CATEAU" The following accounts have been written of the battle by Battery Commanders. **122 Battery** Entrenched 5 a.m. about 1 m. W. of LE CATEAU under orders of G.O.C. 13th Inf. Bde. Engaged enemy's infantry advancing from N. with good effect at ranges from 2400 to 1300 yds. Enemy's guns never found our range but throughout the day we were under rifle fire from a wooded spur about 600 yards on our right front. About 2.30 p.m. Capt Jones brought up limbers + 2 machine guns from the same spur opened on the battery. Capt Jones + 6 men were killed + 2/Lt. Macleod + 14 men wounded, + about 20 horses killed within a minute. Only 3 guns succeeded in limbering up, of which one had to be abandoned soon after, the horses being shot. About 4.30 p.m. the remaining section took up a position West of MAUROIS to cover the retirement + fired on German infantry advancing W. of REUMONT at about 1500 yards range. Later the section retired + marching most of the night	

WAR DIARY
or
INTELLIGENCE SUMMARY.
(Erase heading not required.)

Army Form C. 2118.

Hour, Date, Place	Summary of Events and Information	Remarks and references to Appendices
LE CATEAU AUG. 26. 1914.	rejoined the remainder of the Brigade S. of ST. QUENTIN on the following day. 123 Battery. At daybreak the latter took up a position 1 m. W. of LE CATEAU & ½ m. South of the CAMBRAI – LE CATEAU road and entrenched. Battery opened fire on a hostile battery coming into action. Battery came under fire itself & Major Bayley telephone wire was cut by a shell. Major Bayley then came down from his observing station to the battery. The latter remained in action for some hours under a heavy shell fire. Casualties :- Major Bayler & 2Lt Spencer, Mr B.S.M. & 2 Sergeants wounded: an 9 Bomb. killed & 15 gunners wounded or missing. About 2 pm B.C. ordered men to retire. The guns were disabled, wounded men were carried to the rear	RMB RMB

WAR DIARY
or
INTELLIGENCE SUMMARY.

(Erase heading not required.)

Army Form C. 2118.

Hour, Date, Place	Summary of Events and Information	Remarks and references to Appendices
LE CATEAU AUG. 26. 1914	12 Battery moved out of bivouack about 3.30 a.m. on 26th August. Took up position 1½ m. W. of LE CATEAU facing N.W. under heavy fire from several German batteries which enfiladed us. Were obliged to turn guns round with drag ropes on the open. Brought 4 guns round facing N.E. opened fire on advancing infantry and guns. Very much impeded by rows of trees on high road on our front. Section control ordered. Casualties in detachment heavy. Lieut Capt Browning (killed) & 13 killed & wounded (including 3 Sergts) Remained in action till ordered to withdraw detachments about 2 pm but time is uncertain. The teams had previously been ordered to withdraw owing to shell fire. The latter retired in groups without the guns, assembling at place near ST QUENTIN about 10 or 11 pm the same evening.	

Army Form C. 2118.

WAR DIARY
or
INTELLIGENCE SUMMARY
(Erase heading not required.)

Instructions regarding War Diaries and Intelligence Summaries are contained in F. S. Regs., Part II. and the Staff Manual respectively. Title pages will be prepared in manuscript.

Hour, Date, Place	Summary of Events and Information	Remarks and References to Appendices
SUNDAY AUG 30. 2.30 a.m.	Halt for 3 hrs. Officers read at CARLEPONT. March via B. ST. MARD, RUE DU VAL to ATTICHY.	
1.30 p.m.	2 hrs. halt. Move into bivouack on River AISNE 3/4 mile E of 124 Bty. G/R CHADWICK drowned while bathing and buried there.	R.H.S
MONDAY AUG. 31. JAULZY. 7.50am	March to renewed via CROUTOY, ST. ETIENNE, PIERREFONDS MORIENVAL, FRESNOY LA RIVIERE to bivouack 1/2 mile N. of CREPY-EN-VALOIS, arriving 5 p.m.	5th Divisional Artillery all bivouacked close together. R.H.S

Army Form C. 2118.

WAR DIARY
or
INTELLIGENCE SUMMARY
(Erase heading not required.)

Instructions regarding War Diaries and Intelligence Summaries are contained in F.S. Regs., Part II. and the Staff Manual respectively. Title pages will be prepared in manuscript.

Hour, Date, Place	Summary of Events and Information	Remarks and References to Appendices
12 M.N. Aug. 26.27 ST. QUENTIN	Weather hitherto perfect turns wet and cold. Some Officers and men rejoin teams and 1st line wagons; marched via ROUPY, G.P. SERANCOURT, ST. SIMON, OLLEZY into bivouack 1/2 mile N. of EAUCOURT where rest of Brigade join up about 4 p.m.	124 detached bivouack for 1 hour near CLASTRES and rejoin at bivouack about 4 p.m. P.M.
THURSDAY, AUG 27		
FRIDAY, AUG. 28. 5 a.m.	Brigade marched with division via CUGNY, VILLESELVE, BERLANCOURT, GUISCARD and halted about midday at NOYON.	
2 p.m.	After two hours halt march via PONTOISE into bivouack at LE MERIQUE FERME arriving about 4 p.m. 3rd & 5th Divisions are bivouack'd all round.	
SATURDAY, AUG 29. PONTOISE	Day of rest. Troops addressed by Genl. FERGUSSON. Receive orders to move about 6.30 p.m.	P.M.
7 p.m.	Brigade marches with division near CUTS and	

Confidential.

$\frac{121}{1083}$

War Diary

of.

28th Bde R.F.A. Ammunition Column.

5th division

From Aug 5th 1914.   To Aug 31st 1914

(Both dates inclusive.)

Volume I.

Army Form C. 2118.

WAR DIARY
or
INTELLIGENCE SUMMARY.
(Erase heading not required.)

Instructions regarding War Diaries and Intelligence Summaries are contained in F. S. Regs., Part II. and the Staff Manual respectively. Title pages will be prepared in manuscript.

Hour, Date, Place	Summary of Events and Information	Remarks and references to Appendices
Aug 5th DUNDALK.	1st day of mobilisation. The B'ds Head Quarters Staff packed with Ammun 18 Ammun wagons 18 pr – 7 S.A.A. Carts 3 G.S. wagons S.A.A.	I arrived about 8 pm found at this time
6 am. Aug 6th DUNDALK.	2d day. Continued packing wagons etc. Nucleus of men supplied by batteries. B.S.h. middleton arrived late this night.	Nucleus consisted of 20 all ranks. W B.S.h & Q.M.S.
Aug 7th Sunny	3rd day. Finished packing wagons. Issued & started marking harness, fitting into complete sets. Put up horse lines after moving vehicles into field. 2 Cohen arrived late. It is annoying from ATHLONE.	The set of marking tools only delayed this very much. At this point the need for men made itself felt. Before they could hardly have been in the way.

Army Form C. 2118.

WAR DIARY
or
INTELLIGENCE SUMMARY.
(Erase heading not required.)

Instructions regarding War Diaries and Intelligence Summaries are contained in F.S. Regs., Part II. and the Staff Manual respectively. Title pages will be prepared in manuscript.

Hour, Date, Place	Summary of Events and Information	Remarks and references to Appendices
6 a.m. Aug 8th 1914 DUNDALK.	4th day. Finished drawing harness but not matching. Drew forage & supplies wagon. Reservists arrived mid-day. Told off into sub-sections. Appointed Corls. Staff etc. Drew blankets etc.	Still no Q.M.S. nor 2nd Subaltern. The Q.M.S. ought to be present from P.S. day. B.S.M. not necessary till men arrive.
same. Aug 9th	5th day. Issued harness to men. Marched. Paid out.	
Aug 10th	6th day. Horses started to arrive. Day spent team-ing. Began pup-arming 0.1810 — D.418 A.O.64	This was no pay Sergt for the column and y-ng of the No 1. (a Sergt) had not had experience I should have had the very greatest difficulty in having them completed.

[?]

Army Form C. 2118.

WAR DIARY
or
INTELLIGENCE SUMMARY.
(Erase heading not required.)

Instructions regarding War Diaries and Intelligence Summaries are contained in F.S. Regs., Part II. and the Staff Manual respectively. Title pages will be prepared in manuscript.

Hour, Date, Place	Summary of Events and Information	Remarks and references to Appendices
5. am. Aug 10th 1914.	7th day. Horses completed. Trained and harness fitted. Shoeing started. Horses marked. A.q. N.F. S.F. Q.M.S. arrived this evening. N° (1) (A survician	Practically every horse which came to the Column required to be Shod. (Many came without shoes) or to be re-shod. Questions re married establishment present age all of (m. Column on formation. Decided by O.C. Bde. ages up to 35 yrs. Read. 50 % Sergts 4 % Rank + file
Some Aug 12th	8th day. Drill & dun under Section Commanders. Paid out. harried nolls A.7./03 etc sent to the A.S. at the base.	
Aug 13th to Aug 15th DUNDALK.	9th to 12th Column shaking down into working order. Drill adv. each day under Section Commanders. Re arranging horse etc.	

Army Form C. 2118.

WAR DIARY
or
INTELLIGENCE SUMMARY.
(Erase heading not required.)

Instructions regarding War Diaries and Intelligence Summaries are contained in F.S. Regs., Part II. and the Staff Manual respectively. Title pages will be prepared in manuscript.

Hour, Date, Place	Summary of Events and Information	Remarks and references to Appendices
11.30 pm Aug 16th DUNDALK.	Advised to entrain. C sub at 2 am with H.Q. At B. Entrainions at 3 am. D & E at 4 am.	High trucks for general typical continental cars. Why don't English Rys. have special ramps? Flies certainly had not.
5 am Aug 17th BELFAST.	Arrived BELFAST. Detained until 7am. Found B sent already in ship. The rest of Column was entrained by 9.30 am. YORK DOCK around 7 am. on S.S. HESABA.	
	Left docks 5.30 pm. H. Qs 122nd Batty + half of 123 Batty also on board. Ship.	The 2nd hrse decks was very difficult to get into owing to steepness of ramp(?) but I suppose this was normal to understand.
Aug 18		
Aug 19th	Arrived at HAVRE 6.30 pm. Got alongside quay 9.30 pm. Started disembarking. Finished disembarking horses by 12.45 midn. Vehicles not till 4.30 am. Marched 5 miles and arrived in camp 7.30 am.	J.T.

WAR DIARY or INTELLIGENCE SUMMARY.

Army Form C. 2118.

(Erase heading not required.)

Hour, Date, Place	Summary of Events and Information	Remarks and references to Appendices
3.15 am Aug 21st Rest Camp HAVRE	Left camp to entrain. Started entraining at POINT 8. at 6 am. Train left at 9 am.	Entrained from ground by means of special ramps with clean attachment. Very easy being merely a matter of pulling. I like trucks better than horse boxes as they enable horses to be watered & looked after in the train than English. Water good, station good, plentiful.
2.30 am Aug 22nd LANDRECIES.	Detained outside by party of try. hosted 4.30 am. Arrived & went into bivouac just short of town.	
3 p.m. Aug 22nd BAVAI	Marched off for DOURI.	
5 am Aug 23rd BAVAI	Turned off main road & went into bivouac at LA ROSIÈRE by order of Staff Officer.	
11.45 am.		

WAR DIARY or INTELLIGENCE SUMMARY.

Army Form C. 2118.

Instructions regarding War Diaries and Intelligence Summaries are contained in F.S. Regs., Part II. and the Staff Manual respectively. Title pages will be prepared in manuscript.

(Erase heading not required.)

Hour, Date, Place	Summary of Events and Information	Remarks and references to Appendices
12.30 mid-day Aug 23rd 1914 LA ROSIÈRE	Left Am Col in bivouac & went to find position in which Batteries were entrenching to protect position for Am. Col.	Position was concealed by houses on N side & a large entrenchment on the other. A valley in front which there was water. Also water in the houses.
6 p.m.	Am Col moved by rain of Regt to B in BOIS DE BOUSSU.	
9 p.m. Aug 23. DOUR.	Am Col went into bivouac just off road at B in BOIS du BOUSSU	
3.30 a.m. Aug 28th 1914, DOUR.	Moved off to take up position selected for Am Col. Sent orderlies to 122, 123, 124 Batteries. Sent to TYLER forward with 3 J.A.A.S.C.V. to fill up Inf B— Do — (the 14th) which was opposite a line WASMES — — BOIS du BOUSSU — RY WORKS — BOIS du BOUSSU	
	Position of Batteries 122nd Batty 200° N. of M in CHAMP des SAIS 123rd — True N of "70" N of V in BOIS de BOUSSU 124th — In readiness at BOIS du BOUSSU	
6 a.m. BOIS du BOUSSU		

WAR DIARY or INTELLIGENCE SUMMARY

Army Form C. 2118.

Instructions regarding War Diaries and Intelligence Summaries are contained in F.S. Regs., Part II. and the Staff Manual respectively. Title pages will be prepared in manuscript.

Hour, Date, Place	Summary of Events and Information	Remarks and references to Appendices
5 a.m. Aug. 24. Small plateau 800 N.E. of R. in DOUR. Rgt hgt. BELGIUM. MONS 7a.	The Bn Col took up the above position. O'Sullivan got into touch with the three batteries of the Brigade + with 14th Bty. At 12 noon 23rd Am Col bivouacked at LA ROSIÈRE until 6.30. Then moved to BOIS DE BOUSSU + bivouacked there with horses in till 2 a.m. 24th when took up position in wagon.	See previous remarks about position. Inside small ring contour ½ m NNE of R. in DOUR just off S. edge of 2nd class road.
10.20 a.m. 24 Aug. Same.	Received orders to replenish all 2nd Arty units + proceed to ATHIS. Did so. 28th Bty on arrival at ATHIS was ordered to ETH + BRY. Took 4 position to be in readiness to supply them with Am.	The whole were clear up against a line of high with trees + would not have been so easy to load up. Contrs at foot of slope might 250 yds away in stream.
12.30 mid-day Same Same		
6.15 p.m. Aug 24. Under corn of ridge in field 150' W of main S.WAAST- JEMLAIN road. ½ m W.N.W. of WAGNERIES. Aug 25. 4.30 a.m. Same place	Ordered to retire to LE CATEAU by flank guard of III rd Division. Got cut off by flank guard of III rd Division — in etcid with it. Eventually worked across country W and Rejoined V Division about 5 km short 150th rear of 28th Bde of E of BREUMONT. Went into bivouac with rear of 28th Bde.	First heavy showers of rain experienced. J.J.J.

Army Form C. 2118.

WAR DIARY
or
INTELLIGENCE SUMMARY.
(Erase heading not required.)

Instructions regarding War Diaries and Intelligence Summaries are contained in F.S. Regs., Part II. and the Staff Manual respectively. Title pages will be prepared in manuscript.

Hour, Date, Place	Summary of Events and Information	Remarks and references to Appendices
3.30 am Aug 26th (26th) near REAUMONT	B attery moved out of bivouac and entrenched themselves. 122. 123. 112h slightly separated in a line facing N.E. on the N side of the REAUMONT — LE CATEAU road about 1m from REAUMONT. (approx only)	Wrote in + found in the bivouac field. Water quite good & plentiful. hot & mess inventory things.
6.30 am.	The Am. Col. moved into next field + formed up in column of route round the field close again it the hdges. Heavy battery came into action in dip 100x N of position of Am.Col. in howitzer battery about ½ m N.E. All batteries engaged. 2Lt TYLER went with 3 S.S.W. to 14th Inf Bde Amm's Brigade Reserve. Lt COKER took 3 18 fdr Am Wagons to 122. 3 uuu to 124. 2 to 123. Three S.A.A. carts sent to 14th Inf Bde	heitter the heavy battery nor the howitzers were located a piece with'l after the retirement had begun about 3 pm.

J.T.

WAR DIARY or INTELLIGENCE SUMMARY

Army Form C. 2118.

Hour, Date, Place	Summary of Events and Information	Remarks and References to Appendices
Aug 26th S. side of REUMONT — LE CATEAU road about ½ R in REUMONT	The 14th Iny Bde Ammn Reserve cuts stood by after this retired behind REUMONT. A slight stampede of teams and a few vehicles occurred about ½ E along the main road, but was easily checked. Brigade Maj TAILYOUR collected the limbers of the 122 and 124 Batteries and led them into a dip just N of the REAUMONT — LE CATEAU road about ½ m.E. of REAUMONT. He then rode forward to see if Col CAMERON, Captain JONES of the 122 Batty came back and let his teams up to the guns. Two out of six guns men got away (not as they hooked in, but had been put out of action previous to this 124 & 123 batteries <s>were</s> had been completely silenced <s>some time before</s> [illegible]	This was caused (where by a few gunners coming down to the wagon line & saying the order had been given to the detachments to leave their guns & save themselves. This was as far as I could see no real panic. A few of the teams were pretty easily stopped & reformed.

977

Army Form C. 2118.

WAR DIARY
or
INTELLIGENCE SUMMARY.
(Erase heading not required.)

Instructions regarding War Diaries and Intelligence Summaries are contained in F.S. Regs., Part II. and the Staff Manual respectively. Title pages will be prepared in manuscript.

Hour, Date, Place	Summary of Events and Information	Remarks and references to Appendices
About 10.30 pm Aug 26ᵗʰ about 10 m. from BEAUMONT (?)	Both batteries were enfiladed & rather taken unawares actually from the rear by gun and rifle fire, and it was found impossible to continue serving them or to bring up teams. The 5ᵗʰ Division was began to fall back along the main Le CATEAU — ST QUENTIN road and covered by the fire of the heavy battery & 8ᵗʰ(?) Howitzer Brigade. Went into bivouac in a heavy stubble field.	Two of not three (gun in cert one of them) of the guns of the 122 had received direct hits & were completely out of action.
I consider that getting into and out of this hill took more out of horses & men than the day's march straight on another 7 or 8 m.
2.15 am Aug 27ᵗʰ Same place.	Started off again, owing to heavy ground and uphill start the greatest difficulty was found in moving wagons.	Rain had fallen and softened the ground & it was also in a gain up slope.
Thur? Aug 27ᵗʰ ST QUENTIN	Arrived and passed straight through to OLLEZY	I think this must have been by the F¹⁶⁶ de Sacre just S. of R. m. BEAUVOIR
J.J.

WAR DIARY or INTELLIGENCE SUMMARY

(Erase heading not required.)

Army Form C. 2118.

Instructions regarding War Diaries and Intelligence Summaries are contained in F. S. Regs., Part II. and the Staff Manual respectively. Title pages will be prepared in manuscript.

Hour, Date, Place	Summary of Events and Information	Remarks and References to Appendices
3 p.m. Aug 27th OLLEZY	Arrived & went into bivouac just S. of Ry. 14th Inf Bde camped opposite. About 7.30 received from H.Q. - all is quiet you will remain in bivouac the night.	Several German spies were shot here in the camp. Thank God not us.
3 am Aug 28th OLLEZY	Received order through 14th Inf Bde to move at once stating Point E of QUIGNY at which point Am Col arrived at 4.55 am. Joined the main Column.	Water scarce and it took about 1 hr to get horses all watered; about ½ m from bivouac
1.55 am		Watered ?tch.
11.30 am	Arrived at PONTOISE when we were halted in the town until 1.30 p.m.	
3 p.m. + Farm called LE MÉRIQUIN	Went into bivouac near farm house about ½ midway between LA POMMERY and PONTOISE. 28th Bde part of Supply Section + those of two other Brigades came into same area.	Water scarce + some way off. I am almost certain this was the farm.
5.30 am Aug 29th Same place	About to resume march.	

Army Form C. 2118.

WAR DIARY
or
INTELLIGENCE SUMMARY
(Erase heading not required.)

Instructions regarding War Diaries and Intelligence Summaries are contained in F. S. Regs., Part II. and the Staff Manual respectively. Title pages will be prepared in manuscript.

Hour, Date, Place	Summary of Events and Information	Remarks and References to Appendices
About 3 pm. Aug 29th JAVLEZ	Bivouacked with 28th Bde on banks of R. D'AISNE	Men looked refreshed, properly fed which did them a lot of good.
About 7 am. Aug 30th JAVLEZ	Resumed march.	
About 4 pm. Aug 30th near LE PETIT MARMONT	Arrived went into bivouac. The Heavy battery, 28th Bde were also in this bivouac. Also 27th Bde R.F.A.	Water good but very scarce. In a large farm.
5 am Aug 31st Same place	Outpost line engaged by German Cav + Hy in motor cars. Column resumed march.	Horses not watered before starting. I think this action really put an end to all hopes the Germans may have had of a distance.
About 5 pm. Aug 31st NANTEUILLY	Bivouacked in front of roads J. not S. of town, with 28th Bde. Infantry came in later quite pleased with themselves.	I am not at all certain of the name of this town.

J.T.

5th Divisional Artillery.

28th BRIGADE R. F. A. ::: SEPTEMBER 1914.

CONFIDENTIAL

$\frac{121}{1063}$

WAR DIARY OF

28th Brigade RFA
5th Division.

From Sept. 1st to Sept. 30th 1914.

Vol II

Army Form C. 2118.

WAR DIARY
or
INTELLIGENCE SUMMARY
(Erase heading not required.)

Instructions regarding War Diaries and Intelligence Summaries are contained in F. S. Regs., Part II. and the Staff Manual respectively. Title pages will be prepared in manuscript.

Hour, Date, Place	Summary of Events and Information	Remarks and References to Appendices
TUESDAY Sept. 1 About 7 a.m.	Brigade moves through CREPY and halts just S. of railway. After short halt moves on through ORMOY, halting there for about an hour, and, after a slow march with many halts,	
5 p.m.	bivouacks S.W. of NANTEUIL.	
WEDNESDAY Sept. 2. 4 a.m.	Brigade moves via SILLY-LE-LONG, OGNES, OISSERY, ST. SOUPPLETS, CUISY to LE PLESSIS L'EVEQUE and bivouacs there about	
10.30 a.m.	Fighting section of 122 Battery sent out on outpost with 14th Inf Brigade	
8.10 p.m.	Ordered to retire again, and Brigade (less section) moves to CHARNY where is joins up with the 4 Bde Am. Column of the Divisional Artillery. Move on, after an hours halt to southwards to ROUTE NAT.LE N° 3, turn eastwards	
THURSDAY Sept 3 6 am	and bivouack for 3 hours 1 m. N. of TRILBARDOU. 28th Bde + Column march via ESBLY + CRECY to about 1 m. E. of FERROLLES - halt from about 11:30 to 2:30 pm.	

Army Form C. 2118.

WAR DIARY
or
INTELLIGENCE SUMMARY
(Erase heading not required.)

Instructions regarding War Diaries and Intelligence
Summaries are contained in F. S. Regs., Part II.
and the Staff Manual respectively. Title pages
will be prepared in manuscript.

Hour, Date, Place	Summary of Events and Information	Remarks and References to Appendices
Sept 3. 3.30 pm	On the road. March then resumed, turning back through the eastern edge of CRECY to bivouack at BOULEURS.	
FRIDAY Sept 4. BOULEURS.	Orders received that the Division is to rest as much as possible. Nothing done during the main part of the day. Lt-Col. E.C. Cameron decides to go sick as he is feeling very unfit, and is taken into hospital.	
7 pm.	28th Bde & the 4 Bde Ammn. Columns move together to CRECY - half an hour - resume the march via to VILLENEUVE LE COMTE. Park off the road for about 2 hours just E. of this village, then on through TOURNAN	Section 122 Bty remains in bivouack till 10 pm when it marches with the Division.
SATURDAY Sept 5 TOURNAN 2.15 a.m.	to bivouack beside COMBREUX CHATEAU, close to this town. Remain in bivouack all the day and that night. 122 Bty's fighting section rejoining the brigade at 7 am.	Pte.
SUNDAY Sept 6. TOURNAN 6.30 am	The Brigade receives orders to move forward again in a general advance, travelling with the Brigade Am. Col. in rear of the main body of the 5th Division ; 122 Bty. March to FAVIERES. Section with the main body. Then where we parked from about 11 a.m. to 2 p.m.	Pte. Dismounted Park & 120 men & 44 wagons leave the Park join Baggage train.

(9 26 6) W 257—976 100,000 4/12 H W V

Army Form C. 2118.

WAR DIARY
or
INTELLIGENCE SUMMARY.
(Erase heading not required.)

Instructions regarding War Diaries and Intelligence Summaries are contained in F.S. Regs., Part II. and the Staff Manual respectively. Title pages will be prepared in manuscript.

Hour, Date, Place	Summary of Events and Information	Remarks and references to Appendices
FAVIERES – 2 pm SUNDAY SEP. 6.	On to VILLENEUVE LE COMTE, arrived about 4 pm. No further orders reach the Brigade, the village is full of 4th Division troops, so we bivouack just off the road at 7.30 pm.	RHE
MONDAY SEP. 7. 11 am VILLENEUVE LE COMTE 1 pm	Continue the advance through the FORET DE CRECY to MORTCERF: park outside the village on the Eastern side for 2½ hours	
MORTCERF 3.30 pm	Ordered to advance Eastwards towards COULOMMIERS. Route via FAREMOUTIERS & TRESNES to MOUROUX. 28th Brigade + Am. Columns bivouack for the night at LA BELLE IDÉE, 2½ m. W. of COULOMMIERS.	RHE
TUESDAY SEPT 8. 6.30 am MOUROUX	March via COULOMMIERS, BOISSY LE CHATEL, ST. GERMAIN & DOUE. Parking for about 2 hours at St GERMAIN + 1½ hours at DOUE. Ordered to bivouack at MARDY, but when there about an hour, fresh orders are received to advance via ST CYR & ST OUEN to CHAMPTORTEL. Bivouack there.	RHE

Army Form C. 2118.

WAR DIARY
or
INTELLIGENCE SUMMARY.
(Erase heading not required.)

Instructions regarding War Diaries and Intelligence Summaries are contained in F.S. Regs., Part II. and the Staff Manual respectively. Title pages will be prepared in manuscript.

Hour, Date, Place	Summary of Events and Information	Remarks and references to Appendices
WEDNESDAY SEP. 9. CHAMPTORTEL	Remain in bivouack all day, while the 5th Division tries to force the passage of the MARNE RIVER. Bivouack here for the night.	Inf. reinforcements arrive pass us for 5th Division [Subalty & clothes arrived] PH?
THURSDAY SEP. 10. CHAMPTORTEL 6. am	Advance through SPACY & MERY, along N. bank of the MARNE to MONTREUIL. Halt for 3 hours; Town blocked with troops. Then straight on Northwards through DHUISY, GERMIGNY, GANDELU (1 hours halt) to bivouack beside the road ½ m. S. of CHEZY-EN-ORXOIS	
FRIDAY SEPT. 11 CHEZY-EN-ORXOIS 7.45 am.	Move off just before 8 o'clock through DAMMARD, PASSY, MARIZY-ST-GENEVIEVE (1 hour's halt) & MARIZY-ST-MARD. It	3rd & 5th Division troops billetted in this village. PH?
2:30 pm	now starts to rain heavily & continues till we get into bivouack. 5n through CHOUY to BILLY-SUR-OURCQ.	
5 pm	Bivouack for the night in the same field as most of the Divisional Artillery.	PH?
SATURDAY SEP. 12 BILLY-SUR-OURCQ	March at 7 am via ST. REMY (where we are halted for about 2 hours) through HARTENNES towards CHACRISE.	
12 noon	Halt at left of hill about ½ m. south of this village for	

(9 26 6) W 257—976 100,000 4/12 H W V
79
3298

Army Form C. 2118.

WAR DIARY
or
INTELLIGENCE SUMMARY.
(Erase heading not required.)

Instructions regarding War Diaries and Intelligence
Summaries are contained in F.S. Regs., Part II.
and the Staff Manual respectively. Title pages
will be prepared in manuscript.

Hour, Date, Place		Summary of Events and Information	Remarks and references to Appendices
SATURDAY SEPT. 12. CHACRISE	2:30 p.m.	2½ hours. Then move till the head of the brigade is just in CHACRISE. It now settles down for the night. It steadily wet.	
	5 p.m.	Two hours more halt. Then move on 400 yards and	
	8 p.m.	halt till after dark. Ordered to billet in Mercillage for the night, leaving the	14th Inf. Bde already billeting in Mercillage. R.H.B
SUNDAY SEP. 13 CHACRISE	5:30 am	carriages in the streets + unhooking the horses. Continue the advance, moving through NAMPTEUIL-SOUS-MURET towards SERCHES. Halt at MONT DE SOISSONS farm for ±	
	2 p.m.	Move 500 yards to the flank after being seen by a hostile aeroplane. Bivouack where we are.	R.H.B
MONDAY - Sep. 14 MONT DE SOISSONS FARM		Wet morning. Do not move from our bivouack all day. The Division is trying to get across the river AISNE + drive the enemy from his very strong position the other side.	R.H.B
TUESDAY Sept. 15.		No change. Fighting section of 122 Battery lose a gun which falls into the river AISNE when crossing a pontoon bridge at VENIZEL.	R.H.B

79/3298

Army Form C. 2118.

WAR DIARY
or
INTELLIGENCE SUMMARY.
(Erase heading not required.)

Instructions regarding War Diaries and Intelligence Summaries are contained in F.S. Regs., Part II. and the Staff Manual respectively. Title pages will be prepared in manuscript.

Hour, Date, Place	Summary of Events and Information	Remarks and references to Appendices
MONT DE SOISSONS FARM. WEDNESDAY 16th Sep.	Very wet night. No change. Part of 6th Division arrives + reinforcements of officers for 5th Div.	PtS
THURSDAY 17th	Major Sanders & Peel, with fighting section, rejoin the Brigade. We are told that 6 guns are on their way up from railhead for the Brigade and are ordered to form 2 four-gun batteries. Weather turns cold. No change in the situation.	PtS
FRIDAY 18th Sept.	3 mobilized sections (with 6 18lbr guns etc) arrive at 1pm but sent away again at once to the 3rd Division. Change position & bivouac 500 yards more northwards. General Situation much the same.	PtS Dismounted park of 28th RBde rejoin the Brigade.
SATURDAY 19th Sept	Very wet night. No change	PtS
SUNDAY 20th	Rain in the night, bitterly cold day. No change Voluntary Church Parade	PtS
MONDAY 21st	No change - still cold showers	PtS
22nd	No change. weather unknown	PtS

WAR DIARY
or
INTELLIGENCE SUMMARY.
(Erase heading not required.)

Army Form C. 2118.

Instructions regarding War Diaries and Intelligence Summaries are contained in F.S. Regs., Part II. and the Staff Manual respectively. Title pages will be prepared in manuscript.

Hour, Date, Place	Summary of Events and Information	Remarks and references to Appendices
MONT DE SOISSONS WEDNESDAY SEPT. 23.	No change. Good weather. 3 6 guns (3 mobilized Sections) arrive for the brigade at 3 p.m.	Capt. Lord Arbuthnot Lieut W Anchor Armytage Clery
THURSDAY 24th Sept	The Brigade is organised into 2 4-gun batteries and details. The batteries known as "A" Battery & "B" Battery are commanded by Capt. Gillman & Maj. Kinsman respectively.	arrive with Maguire one attached to 28th Bde. Any Maj. Sedgwick Capt. Crofton Capt North Brown Lieut Armytage } posted to 28th Bde 2nd Q.14 2 Lieut Clery Any Any
FRIDAY 25th	No change. Major Sedgwick + Capt M. Crofton join the Brigade in the evening.	
SATURDAY 26th	No change. Maj. Sedgwick posted to "A" Battery.	
SUNDAY 27th - 4 am	Orders received to be ready for action at once, as enemy are reported advancing over Condé bridge	
6.30 am	News received that alarm was false.	
8 am	More that 200 men extended dig gun pits + replacements for several batteries about 2 miles E. & W. of MONT DE SOISSONS. No change.	Pte
MONDAY 28th Sept	Continue with & digging gun emplacements for second line of defence. No change.	Major I M Wilson posted to 28th Regt. Pte Pte
TUESDAY 29th Sept	No change.	

Army Form C. 2118.

WAR DIARY
or
INTELLIGENCE SUMMARY.
(Erase heading not required.)

Instructions regarding War Diaries and Intelligence Summaries are contained in F. S. Regs., Part II. and the Staff Manual respectively. Title pages will be prepared in manuscript.

Hour, Date, Place	Summary of Events and Information	Remarks and references to Appendices
MORT DE SOISSONS WEDNESDAY 30th Sept.	The brigade still carries on with digging. Move bivouack at 12.30 pm to 1A SIEGE farm (1 m. South of COUVRELLE). No change. Weather very good.	Major L M Wilson joins the Brigade. RHS

(9 26 6) W 257—976 100,000 4/12 H W V 79/3298

letters Capt R.A. Jones R.F.A.
about

P.A. Lecateau
File

Extract from letter from D. R. Peel to Mrs Peel
dated Sept 20th 1914.

I have just got your letter dated Sept 9th. I evidently was not very clear about the guns – In our battery we only got two away, only two teams lined, or part of them, one was mine, the other MacLeods. The latter behaved splendidly & although shot through the arm & his two lead horses, lead drivers dead, he unhooked the lead horses & got on the centres himself (driver killed) & drove the gun out of action – His own horse had been shot. He may get the V.C. & will certainly get a French decoration "Chevalier d'honneur" for which the French have called for names amongst us. One of Lutyens Sergeants got a gun away with my other team which I told you never reached me – I was the furthest two guns from where the teams were coming up, the way being so blocked to my gun for that team by so many dead horses & teams lying in the road, that the head driver wheeled to his left & took the nearest gun which was Lutyens. Both MacLeods teams – who was on the left of course got to him first, one was completely shot up & the other I

of our battery out of the chaos of riderless horses & scattered wagons, it was all over the place. We finally got together the two guns & ammunition wagons & the Major & Lutyens went into action again with them as rearguard, wasn't it splendid of the Major — As a matter of fact they got nothing to fire at, but that does not alter the fact. I finally caught a riderless horse & tried to collect our remaining 10 wagons & men which were all mixed up with the retreating force until 3 a.m next morning — They were all together by 4 a.m. It was an awful night. The 6th Division which had taken the whole brunt of the attack & suffered nearly 6,000 casualties were no longer a fighting force. The regiments were all mixed up & were streaming down the road in batches all night, many wounded amongst the guns & transport.

"Account of "Le Cateau" Aug 26th 1914

2

have told you about — Both teams of Lutyens lay in a heap — My other team was splendid & got to one of my guns where the Major (Onslow) found it & it fell in a heap — Major Kinsman & Major Bayley's batteries were under such awful fire that they did not try to bring the teams down at all & so lost all their guns. The 5th Division lost 31 out of 74 guns that day, the others being mostly Major Nutter & Henning's Brigade (Kildare they went for D.B.) Jimmy Thorburn when Ap was killed wanted to send down more teams but the general stopped him as it was useless under such awful fire — When the 123 battery detachments were withdrawn Capt Gilman with Rainy went back to pick up the wounded, the latter looked about for his Major & finally found him lying wounded in some turnips, he got him on to a horse & carried him back to safety. He will also probably get something. Both the other batteries went some time before us leaving their guns. The Red Cross picked up our battery wounded but am not quite sure, because when I got back to the rear Lutyens & I tried to collect what remained

28th Bde. R.F.A.
5th Div.

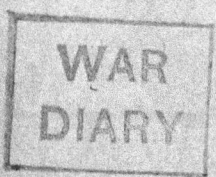

123rd BATTERY, R.F.A.

AUGUST to DECEMBER

1914

War Diary

123rd Battery R.F.A

August To December 1914.

August 1914

In 1914 the Battery was stationed at Dundalk. On August 4th 1914, about 4.0 a.m. the order to mobilize reach'd the Battery. By August 13th the mobilization was complete.

Aug 17th The Battery left Dundalk on Monday Aug. 17th in two trains and embarked right half Battery on the "Mesaba" & the left half on the "Caledonian" at Belfast.

Aug. 20th The Right half Battery arrived at Havre on Thursday Aug. 20th and disembarked that night, proceeding to the rest camp.

The officers of the Battery were
Maj. G.R. Bayley R.F.A.
Capt. A.G. Gillman
Lieut R.B. Miller
2/Lt E.A. Spencer
2/Lt R.W. Autobus

The staff Sergts were B.S.S.Maj. Beach
           B.Q/S. Belcher
           Staff Sgt. Farr. Saunders.

The Total Strength was
     5 Officers
     186 Men
     176 Horses.

August 1914

Night Aug. 20th - 21st
The left half Battery arrived at Havre & disembarked.

The disembarkation was a difficult operation because the order of loading had not been satisfactorily arranged. Some of the XXVIII Bde Am. Col. & the 121st By had been loaded above the Battery vehicles.

Aug. 21st The disembarkation was completed by 3.0 am & the Battery then marched to the Station and entrained. At 6 am the Battery left in one Train travelling via Rouen & Amiens, disembarked the same evening at Le Cateau station and bivouacked in the Station Yard.

Aug. 22nd The Battery marched to Bavai

" 23rd " " " to Dour and bivouacked but was turned out at once to prepare a position which was occupied in the evening.

August 1914

The Battle of Mons. Aug. 23rd & 24th

The position occupied by the Battery was Sth of Bois du Bossu about 2 miles N.E. of Dour, with 114th Battery on the left and 122nd Battery on the right, and close to the infantry firing line. The position in action was covered from view by a high Railway embankment on which the BC's observation post was.

The surrounding country was a mass of Coal Pits & close to the immediate front which was a level plain thickly wooded with many small villages.

Aug. 24th. The Battery received its baptism of fire.

About midday fire was opened upon German infantry in close column preceded by dense lines which were first observed about 1000 yards away.

Orders to retire reached the battery so only some 60 rounds were fired at the infantry. The fire was believed to be very effective.

The retirement was conducted

August 1914

under heavy fire from German Field Artillery was safely carried out. The total casualties being only 2 horses wounded.

The Battery retired via Dour, to a rearguard position near Athis at about 3-30 p.m.

At about 4-30 p.m. orders to retire to Bavai Saint Waast & bivouacked in the dark about 9 p.m.

Aug. 25th The Battery marched about 3-30 p.m. to Le Cateau and went into bivouac about 2 miles S.W of that place.

The Battle of Le Cateau
August 26th 1914

The Artillery of the 5th Division Expeditionary Force was placed approximately as follows (reference France 1/80,000 Sheet 13 Cambrai)

15th Brigade R.F.A about ¼ mile N. of F— in Font de Noriette

28th Brigade, West of the St Quentin Road (except 122 Battery which was East of that road) about 300x

August 1914

South of the S. in Pont des Quartre Veaux.

27th Brigade west of St Quentin Road behind the left of the 28th Bde.

8th Brigade separated one Battery to each infantry Brigade.

The infantry (13th Brigade) in front of the XXVIII Brigade RFA lay on the road Le Cateau – Inchy, the firing line being from 500ⁿ to 600ⁿ in front of the line of guns.

The 123rd Battery was placed 200ⁿ S. of letter S. in Pont des Quatre Veaux facing N by E.

The position was in the open and on the forward slope of an incline 500ⁿ at least forward of the crest-line. Cover was effected by a line of poplar trees on the Le Cateau – Inchy road at a distance of 500ⁿ to 800ⁿ.

The cover proved quite ineffectual except to make observation of fire difficult.

The position in fact proved to be thoroughly unsound.

August 1914

The Battery was in position about 8.0 am. & entrenched under unaimed rifle fire.

The enemy were at that time holding the village of Le Cateau.

The 122nd Battery was placed about 300 y distant on the right rear of the 123rd Battery facing due N. The observation station was 200 x to the right front. The 124th Battery was 100 x in rear of the left flank of the 123rd facing approximately N.W. i.e. nearly at right angles to the line of fire of the 123rd.

As far as the 123rd Battery was concerned the action opened by the Battery engaging a German B⅔ moving into action on the ridge lying N of the SOLESMES - LE CATEAU road.

No effect was observed before the hostile battery got under cover of the ridge.

By this time the BC's observing station had been moved back

August 1914

to a point behind the battery on the Le Cateau – Trois Villes road, where the Brigade HQ's was, with the HQ of the 13th Inf. Brigade.

The second target engaged about 9.30 a.m. was infantry advancing from the above mentioned ridge.

About this time the hostile guns commenced firing at the Battery & one of the first shells cut the BC's telephone wire.

The B.C. shortly after came to the Battery.

It was about this time that 2/Lieut Spencer was wounded the first casualty.

The Battery now remained without firing for a period as observation from the battery was bad. The shell fire began to be serious & several casualties occurred. No 2 gun in action (C Subsection) was struck on the sights & the whole detachment killed or wounded. This gun was not in action again.

August 1914

At the same time, Major Bayley was wounded and Capt A.J. Gillman took command of the Battery.

It was then about 10·0 a.m. Capt Gillman finding that he could not see from the Battery went out to the left front about 200 y & fought the battery from there.

The targets engaged were only infantry targets. About 10·11·0 a.m. it became necessary to move the left & centre sections from their entrenchments in order to fire toward the N.W. because the infantry on the left having fallen back the left flank of the battery became exposed. Fortunately the German infantry did not press their attack.

In this operation the guns of the centre section (A & B in barracks) fell into their detachment pits, consequently by 11 a.m. only 3 guns of the Battery were in action.

August 1914

All this time the battery was under intermittent fire from guns & field Howitzers, which at times was very heavy & always accurate.

About midday an effort was made to bring off the guns of the XXVIII Bde. The horses of the 122nd Battery came up but only two guns were brought off.

It then became apparent that the position was hopeless.

The Battery continued in action firing slowly, only the left section being now in action, until about 2·0 p.m. when the order to abandon the guns was given.

The officers and men of the Battery retired behind the ridge in rear taking all those wounded who were not mortally hit with them.

Before retiring the guns were rendered unserviceable.

The 124th Battery had already abandoned their guns & it was through the BC of this Battery who was in the pits of the 123rd Battery

August 1914

that Capt. Gillman received the advice to abandon the guns.

The left section of the 125th Bty were the last 2 guns of the ~~XXVII~~ Bde R.F.A. to continue firing.

The total casualties amounted to
2 Officers
The B.S. Major
9 Sergeants
16 NCO's & Men.

By this time the whole division was withdrawing towards St Quentin in some disorder.

The teams of the right section got separated from the remainder of the teams.

The wreck of the battery was collected in the evening of the 27th August 1914 at OLLEZY.

Captain Gillman was awarded the Military Cross on 1st January 1915.

B.S.M. Beard was awarded the Russian order of St George 3rd Class 25.6.15.

August 27th — Oct 5th

The men & teams & such vehicles as remained took part in the retirement of the Army to TOURNAN.

On one or two days some 16 men formed a mounted rifle section to work with the rearguard.

The remains of the Battery advanced with the 5th Division (attached to the Ammunition Column) in the advance to the Aisne, and were thus present at the Battle of the Marne & the Battle of the OURCQ.

The Brigade was in reserve at Mont de Soissons farm during the Battle of the Aisne.

6 Guns arrived & two composite Batteries were formed but did not go into action as such.

The XXVIII Brigade thus formed left the Aisne on Oct 1st with the rest of the V Division.

Oct. 1914

"The Brigade was reorganized on Oct 5th while halted in billets at VEZ near VILLERS COTERETS

The 123rd Battery was officered as follows

    Major F.R Seagurok R.F.A. (RQO)
    Capt A.C Gillman
    Lieut R.B Miller
    2 Lieut R.H Aubrous

    BSM   Durant
    BQMS Belcher
    S Sergt Ferris Sanders.

On this day Sergt McBride & Corpl S.S. Lucas of the Battery were gazetted to commissions as Lieut R.F.a.

Oct 6th   Marched to Gilocourt, every effort at this time was made to conceal the March from Aerial observation. Marching was done at night & the Bivouacs put among trees.

Oct 7th   Oct. 7th – 12th 1914
         Marched to LE MEUX entrained at
10 pm.

Oct 8th Detrained 2.0 pm at PONT REMY
         Marched to CAOURS to rejoin Brigade HQ.
Marched again 10.0 pm to GUESCHART going
into billets about 2.0 AM

Oct 9th   Marched at 6.0 pm via St Pol to
          OSTREVILLE.

Oct 10th In billets at OSTREVILLE

Oct 11th Marched at 7.0 AM, the first daylight
march for 10 days to FOUQUERE near
Bethune.

Oct 12th Marched about 5.30 AM to BEAUVRY
the 131 Battery was brought into action in
support of the 13th Infantry Brigade south
of the Canal D'Aire with its left on the
Canal and its right covered by the
French Troops attacking VERMELLI. Late
in the evening the 123rd came into action
firing against CUINCHY. The Brigade bivouacked
in the BEAUVRY ANMEGIUNI ROAD

Oct 13th   Oct 13th 1914

The 123 & 124th Batteries came into action about 6.0 A.M. close to the Beauvrey Annequin Road about the N N in Annequin with observation stations in the Coal dumps of FOSSE No 9 De BETHUNE. The 123 Battery came into action north of the road firing by compass bearing in the direction of CUINCHY. About 7.0 AM the battery was moved to the south of the Road.

The Battery was placed just S of the J in FOSSE No 9 De BETHUNE, the B.C's Observation station was the old coal dumps 100x S.E of the last E in FOSSE No 9 De BETHUNE.

The Zone to be covered by the battery was from a point just south of the M in CAMBRIA to FONT. DES MARCHAIS.

Later in the day the Battery received orders to plaster the ground around the NCHY of CUINCHY and LA BASSEE Station & also the NCHY of GIVENCHY LA BASSEE the Battery fired about 800 rounds that day

The position of the battery was never discovered by the Enemy and though the B.C's post was shelled there were no casualties.

The battery withdrew to billets west of BEAUVREY about 6 pm.

Oct 14th   Oct 14th - 15th 1914

The battery was in action in the same position by 4.30 AM.

There was heavy firing all day & in the evening the XXVIII R.F.A & 65th (Howitzer) Battery supported the attack of the French at VERMELLES.

For this the British Artillery received the thanks of the French in a very complementary order.

A very heavy German counter attack was made in the evening.

At 6.30 pm the battery marched to ESSARS & billeted

The battery fired about 1000 rounds.

Oct 15th

The XXVIII Bde was ordered to go into reserve. Batteries to take 4 hours tours of Duty.

About 10 pm during the tour of Duty of the Battery, Orders were received to send a Battery forward to assist the XV Bde R.H.A who were holding the line from the canal near GIVENCHY to FESTUBERT.

Oct 16ᵗʰ–17ᵗʰ 1914

The Battery turned out at once, and was in action by 4.30. at a point close to the X roads 800 X. west of F. in FESTUBERT, the B.C's observation post was in a Haystack just S of FESTUBERT (Ch) with that of the O.C. 52ⁿᵈ Bty R.F.A. which was in action a little further EAST.

Only 20 rounds were fired.
The zone fired upon was from CHᵀᵀᴱ Sᵗ ROCH to Northern end of GIVENCHY.
Returned to Billets 5.30
No Casualties

Oct 16ᵗʰ

The Battery was in action by 5.30 am but did not open fire as there was a dense fog & very little fighting.
Returned to Billets about 4.30
Casualties NIL

Oct 17ᵗʰ

The Battery was in position of Verdunes close to its old position at 5.30 am.

The Infantry having reoccupied GIVENCHY and the line CHᵀᵀᴱ S ROCH – CANTELEUX and also the Village of Violaines it became necessary to find more advanced positions; an observation station, to fire on the line LORGIERS – VIOLAINES was found close S. of the second S. in the Quinque Rue.

Oct 18th – 19th 1914

The Battery position was just N.W. of the
4 Roads at La Quinque.

Almost immediately the Battery was
ordered to fire on the Zone 1. of Violaines to
Northern outskirts of La Bassee, firing had
to be principally from the map.

The Infantry were attacked principally
from the factory near the 1 of Violaines &
there was heavy firing.

The Battery fired about 800 rounds

Returned to Billets about 5.30 pm
close to Battery position

Casualties Nil

Oct 18th.
Battery in same position. Action
similar to previous day expended about
600 rounds.
Casualties. Nil.

Oct. 19th.
Moved battery to close up to observing
Station. Same targets. Expended about 200Rds
Casualties. Nil.

In Evening reconnoitred new position close to Rue
De Ouvert.

Oct 20th   Oct 20th 1914

Battery in action close to & in Rue de Ouvert, B'ys position close to front - zone to be covered N.W. edge of La Bassée, also ordered to fire on factory near & in Violaines. Infantry demanded support all along the front. Very heavy Artillery fighting.

The Battery expended 1500 Rounds.

Lieut Aukobus who was out as forward reconnoitring Officer was unable to get in message.

Withdrew to billets at about 8.30 p.m. Late in the afternoon the Germans shelled the Rue Douvert. Late in the evening they again opened fire, and continued a heavy shrapnel fire, their shells falling directly over the centre of the Battery. Unfortunately when searching behind the Battery they put 4 or 5 shells into the teams, 3 men were wounded, all slightly & 12 horses hit of which 5 were killed or destroyed in consequence.

In the Battery one man was hit by a splinter.

Casualties Men 3
            Horses 12.

Oct 21st.   Oct 21st 1914

The Battery was in action by 5·30 a.m. but the position was moved some 200 yards to the North, still under cover of the same swell of ground on account of the incident of the day before.

There was less heavy firing during the day.

Lieut Antrobus who went out as forward reconitering Officer, did good work especially in locating the German trenches in front of La Bassée & two hostile batteries.

About 2·0 pm the observation post of the B.Cs. of the 123 & 52nd Batteries was shelled, one man of the 52nd was killed & the Hay Stack set on fire, fortunately good cover had been made by the B.C. Staff

The Germans then carefully searched with field Howitzers the position which the Battery had occupied the previous day.

Rounds Expended 800
Casualties Nil

The Battery was ordered to remain in action all night. Lieut Mullins with 12 men was left with the guns & the Battery returned to billets about 8·0 pm.

Night Oct. 21-22. Oct 21-22 1914

A heavy German attack was made about 10pm & the Battery turned out. Lieut Miller opened fire towards La Bassée, the action of the Battery contributed in no small measure again to the failure of this attack.

About 4.0 am on the 22nd another attack was made, again the Battery opened fire and was later informed that the German advance from La Bassée was checked. As the 123rd Battery was the only one to open fire at the time, it was clearly due to this fire, that the attack in this quarter failed.

By 4.30 am it was clear that the Germans were in Violaines from which point the left flank of the Battery was completely exposed.

Major Sedgwick therefore decided to withdraw; before the movement had been completed, orders to do so were received, and the Battery withdrew to Festubert.

Oct 22nd.   Oct 22. 1914

The Battery was ordered to re occupy its old position at La Quinque Rue. This was found to be too exposed, so the Battery went into action in its old pits just N.W of the X roads at La Quinqua Rue.

Observation Stations close by, the Objections fired upon, were
1/ Trenches & Horses in front of the N.W Corner of Violaines
2/ Infantry near 1 in Violaines
3/ Eastern portion of Rue de MARAIS
4/ Beau Puits
Firing was heavy most of the day

Lieut Autrobus by going forward to etc ave of the Manchester Regiment on 3 occasions obtained very useful information

The Battery went into Billetts near the Brasserie in the Rue de Caillou about 7.20 p.m.
Casualties Nil
Ammunition Expended 1200 Rounds

Lt Antrobus mentioned in despatches June 1915.

Oct 23-24. 1914

Oct 23rd
The Battery was ordered into reserve, to billets, at the East e in Rue de Béthune.

It was shelled out of this by the 8" German Howitzer (Black Maria) shortly after it was ordered to remain in readiness but did not advance.
Casualties nil.
Billetted at 4.30pm in Gorre.

Oct 24th
Ordered to remain in reserve at Gorre, but about midday orders were received to go into action to cover the right of the 11th Infantry Brigade.

The Battery went into action at a point close to the S. in Rue des Charattes, observing Station of B.C. just south of E. in Rue de Bois, objectives farm + localities at ranges from 2300 to 3700 bearing from 105 to 120 from the battery position.

Also farms just South of QU in La Quinque Rue.
Only a few rounds were fired to get the line.
Casualties nil.

Oct 30th 1914

Whilst in this position the Battery remained in action night & day.

Every night the Germans made attacks & the Battery opened fire.

No properly defined targets were visible, firing was done to pre-arranged ground in front of Infantry

Advanced reconnoitring Officers could see but little & could get no information back because of shortage of telephone Equipment

The Battery was in the same position from Oct 24th to Oct 30th inclusive

Rounds Expended 2500.
Casualties. 1 Driver hit in the Wagon line by a spent bullet.

On Oct 30th An Aeroplane bomb was found Corpl Dalton very foolishly endeavoured to discover its mechanism. The fuse exploded & wounded Corpl Dalton & Br Shackery. Corpl Dalton died next day of his wounds.

On the night of Oct 29–30th the Infantry of the 3rd & 5th Divisions were relieved by the Infantry of the Indian Division.

Nov. 1-3. 1914

On night of Oct 30-31st the Artillery arrived T at dawn. Oct 31st, the position of the Battery was occupied by the 19th Battery R.F.A. (Major C.R. Buckle)

The 28 Brigade marched via LOCON & MERVILLE to reserve near ST'RADEELE

Nov. 1st The Brigade moved about 1.30 pm to via Bailleul a point on the Belgian Frontier close to Locres.

Nov 2nd Halted in Billets

Nov. 3rd Marched at 5.15 am via CROIX ae POPERINGHE to KEMMEL. Here the Brigade halted, and the B.C. went forward to reconnoitre a position between WULVERGHEM and MESSINES. the line here was held by the British Cavalry, with French Cavalry on the left & the 4th Division on the right.

Finally the Battery came into action just west of the LINDENHOEK - NEUVE EGLISE Road, a little south of LINDENHOEK, B.C. Observation Station in front, east of Road. Objective MESSINES - WYTCHEARTE ridge as far as Km. Stone 4 north of MESSINES.

Nov 4-12. 1914

The French Cavalry were reported as likely to attack MESSINES in the evening.

Nov. 4th 5th 6th 7th 8th 9th 10th in action in same position.
The French Cavalry attack was daily expected, but did not come off, the Battery remained in action day & night.

Nov 11th
In Camp in reserve.
A retrenched position was prepared 300 yards behind.

Nov 12th
In action in same position.
The Battery remained in the same position till the 18th when it had two days rest, and then went into a position a little further forward. The arrangement at this period was that four Batteries, those of the XXVIII Brigade & a R.H.A. Battery took four days in a position near Lindenhoek, 2 days in a forward position near WULVERGHEM & two days rest.

On Nov 5th Lieut Curteis joined the Battery & took charge of the Centre section.

Nov. 12 - Dec. 11. 1914

The Horse Artillery Battery left the Area & then the three Batteries had a routine, 48 hours in action at LINDENHOEK, then 48 hours at WULVERGHEM, & then 48 hours in retreat.

There was some shelling every day. The Germans generally shelled the ridge near LINDENHOEK, the forward battery at WULVERGHEM was regularly shelled, also the B.C's observing station on the ridge in front of MESSINES.

Officers were allowed to go on leave & Capt Cullinan & Lieut Miller went, also one N.C.O. Sgt Sago. Dec 8th leave was stopped, the battery's billet at this period, was a farm on the Dranoutre, Lindenhoek road 1000x East of DRANOUTRE. There were no casualties, the billets were made fairly comfortable, the weather was very bad in December & there was a cold snap in November of 4 or 5 days duration.

Dec 11th
The Battery moved to WULVERGHEM position

Dec. 11-13th 1914

This position had been close to WULVERGHEM in the Valley of the DOUVE River the wet weather made the place impossible, the pits were deep in mud & water, the position was therefore moved to a point about 400x S. and a little East of NEUVE EGLISE

The observation Station was a cottage was 400x in front of the battery where also were H.Q. Infantry Brigade & 27 Artillery Brigade.

Thence a wire ran to a forward Station on the WULVERGHEM - MESSINES road about 300x from the infantry firing line & 600x from the German trenches, the Battery maintained this position until December 19th when it was withdrawn to its old billet near DRANOUTRE & went into reserve.

Dec 13th

One Section with Lieut R.B Miller was detached & joined the 65th (How) BRFa near LINDENHOEK.

A. Section of the 65th (How) Bg was attached to the 123rd Battery.

Dec. 13-19. 1914

On Dec. 13th an attack was made by the French South of YPRES, and the 4th British & 3rd British Corps, east of PLOEGSTREET. & ARMENTIERES. on the German line.

The role of the Battery was to watch & cover the front of 13th Infantry & 2 Batt. 14 Infantry Bdes. from Point 76 to the MESSINES Road.

The 65th (How) Battery & attached Section 123rd had the same role.

During the 13th the Battery was ordered to fire on the S.E. corner of WYTSCHAETE wood but otherwise took no part in the attack it role being purely defensive.

A few rounds averaging 150 daily were fired at the various localities occupied by the Germans & at their trenches.

From Dec 14th to 19th no event of importance occurred, Telephone communications with the B.C. at the forward observing station was maintained without great difficulty although the wire was temporarily interrupted every day by shells striking the wire

Dec 19-26. 1914

The interruption was generally close to the Observing Station which was shelled every day, particularly heavily on the 13th 18th & 19th.

The Work of the Battery Staff
  B⁰ Mann
  B⁰ Jefferys
  B⁰ Luillett.
During this week was highly satisfactory

Dec 20th to 23rd the Battery was in reserve.

Dec 23. The Battery went to the LINDENHOEK position (Dec 25 Christmas Day) the Battery returned to its position at NEUVE EGLISE, a night attack was expected but did not materialize

Dec 26th Was bright & clear & the B.C. at the forward position observing station saw the extraordinary spectacle of German & British Soldiers walking about on the space between the lines, the Battery held this position until Dec 28th when it went back to reserve. During these days not a rifle shot was fired along the front, though the artillery fired occasionally, the forward observing station as usual receiving much attention.

Dec 28. 1914 – Jan 6. 1915.

Dec 28th The Battery withdrew to reserve.

Dec 30th To position at LINDENHOEK

Index..............

SUBJECT.

5TH DIV.

No.	Contents.	Date.
	R.F.A. — 28TH BRIGADE — AUG-DEC, 1914 — Dec 1916	

121/3688

5th Division

28th Brigade R.F.A.

Vol V. 1 — 31.12.14

Army Form C. 2118.

WAR DIARY
or
INTELLIGENCE SUMMARY.
(Erase heading not required.)

Instructions regarding War Diaries and Intelligence Summaries are contained in F.S. Regs., Part II. and the Staff Manual respectively. Title pages will be prepared in manuscript.

Hour, Date, Place	Summary of Events and Information	Remarks and references to Appendices
FRIDAY OCTOBER 30th	Situation on our immediate front remains in the afternoon the IX Brigade concentrated and sent forward to Rennes	
SATURDAY 31st	Handed over to XV Bde & Battn. all ready by 7 a.m. Marched via BETHUNE — OBINGHEM — HINGES — MERVILLE — VIEUX BERQUIN — ST HAZEELE — ROUGE CROIX. Put into billets at 8 p.m. Staff arrived to 13th Infantry Brigade.	
SUNDAY 1st	Paraded at 2 p.m. via MOOENACKER — METEREN — BAILLEUL — CROIX DE POPERINGHE — marched to 7th Outskirts Park arrived in billets by 6.30 p.m.	
MONDAY 2nd	No change. Fine bright day. Cold.	

CONFIDENTIAL

War Diary
of
28th Brigade RFA
5th Division
1 – 31. October 1914

121/1818

Vol II

Army Form C. 2118.

WAR DIARY
or
INTELLIGENCE SUMMARY.
(Erase heading not required.)

Instructions regarding War Diaries and Intelligence Summaries are contained in F.S. Regs., Part II. and the Staff Manual respectively. Title pages will be prepared in manuscript.

Hour, Date, Place	Summary of Events and Information	Remarks and references to Appendices
THURSDAY OCT. 1ST	No change. Weather good.	
FRIDAY 2nd	Weather good. Left LA SIÈGE Farm at 9 p.m. arrived NEUVILLE ST JEAN 12.30 a.m. Marched via MONT DE SOISSONS Farm — NAMPTEUIL — MURET — DROIZY.	Ordered to park guns & put horse lines under cover, our of sight of aeroplanes
SATURDAY 3rd	Weather good. Left NEUVILLE SITEAN at 7 p.m. Marched via HARTENNES. Arrived TIGNY 8 p.m.	
SUNDAY 4th	Weather good. Left TIGNY 6 p.m. Marched via LONGPONT — CORCY — FLEURY — VILLERS-COTTERÊTS — LARGNY — VEZ. Arrived 5 a.m.	Held up for 2 hours by motor transport, one of the little caught fire causing delay
MONDAY 5th	Weather good. No change	
TUESDAY 6th	Left VEZ at 4 p.m. bivouacked at BELLIVAL 7 p.m. Slight drizzle began at 8 p.m.	
WEDNESDAY 7th	Left BELLIVAL 8 a.m. Marched via GILOCOURT — ORROUY — BETHISY-ST-MARTIN — VERBERIE — LE MEUX. Arrived at LE MEUX H.Q. & 124 Battery at 3 p.m. Commenced entraining 6.30 p.m. finished by 9.30 p.m. 123 Battery started at 10.15 p.m.. 122 Battery commenced entraining 10.30 p.m. to COMPIEGNE where entrained	Halted for two hours at VERBERIE to water & feed. 122 Battery proceeded independently

(9 29 6) W 2794 100,000 8/14 H W V Forms/C. 2118/11.

Army Form C. 2118.

WAR DIARY
or
INTELLIGENCE SUMMARY.
(Erase heading not required.)

Instructions regarding War Diaries and Intelligence Summaries are contained in F.S. Regs., Part II. and the Staff Manual respectively. Title pages will be prepared in manuscript.

Hour, Date, Place	Summary of Events and Information	Remarks and references to Appendices
THURSDAY OCT. 8th	Detrained H.Q. & 124 Battery at PONT REMY. Commenced at 6.30 a.m. finished at 9.30 a.m. Left Station at 11.30 a.m. Marched via BELLANCOURT — VAUCHELLES — CAOURS. Got into billets at 4 p.m. Received orders to move on to GUESCHART. Started 10 p.m. Marched via CAOURS — MILLENCOURT — AGENVILLERS — GAPENNES — NOYELLE-en-chaussée — GUESCHART. Arrived at billets 1.30 a.m.	Map. AMIENS SHEET 12. " ABBEVILLE " 11 " ARRAS " 7 122 B.C. marched separately to H.Q. GUESCHART from ABBEVILLE
FRIDAY OCT 9th	Ready to move 2.30 p.m. Marched 4.30 p.m. via GENNE-IVERGNY — QUEUX — HAUT MAISNIL — GALAMETZ — WILLEMAN — OEUF — RAMECOURT — ST POL — OSTREVILLE. Got into billets by 8.30 a.m. after a halt for 2 hours by the roadside one mile WEST of RAMECOURT.	123 R.G. joined H.Q. & 124 at CAOURS. H.Q. Dismounted party carried H.Q. on motor lorries.
SATURDAY OCT 10th		
SUNDAY OCT 11th	March with the 5th Division at 7 a.m. via MONCHY-BRETON — LA THIEULOYE — DIÉVAL — OURTON — DIVION — BRUAY — LA BUISSIERE — HESDIGNEUL — FOUQUIERES-LEZ-BETHUNE. The Division was halted when the Brigade reached this point. The Brigade was attached to the 13th Infantry Brigade who were told off as 2nd Corps reserve, but Lt. RAINY'S Section 124th Bty ordered to take up positions	5 guns & 14 wagons with teams join brigade at OSTREVILLE

Forms/C. 2118/11.

Army Form C. 2118.

WAR DIARY or INTELLIGENCE SUMMARY.
(Erase heading not required.)

Instructions regarding War Diaries and Intelligence Summaries are contained in F.S. Regs., Part II. and the Staff Manual respectively. Title pages will be prepared in manuscript.

Hour, Date, Place	Summary of Events and Information	Remarks and references to Appendices
SUNDAY OCT 11th (Cont)	but did not come into action. Brigade ordered to billet where it stood at FOUQUIÈRES	13th Inf Brig. with 25th By RFA brought in to fill up a gap.
MONDAY 12th	Ordered to be ready to move at 10.30 a.m. Started at 11.30 a.m. via BETHUNE – BEUVRY. Halted at cross-roads ½ mile North of A in ANNEQUIN. 124th Bty went into action by the E of ANNEQUIN at 1 p.m. in action all day. 122nd Bty came into action NORTH of road on cross roads referred to at 5 p.m. Bombardment of position. Batteries covered ground between AUCHY & VERMELLES	Western French left at CAMBRIN & the CANAL 800ˣ North, on the NORTH bank of which were the mobile English wing of the 2nd Corps. VERMELLES strongly held by the Germans with machine guns.
TUESDAY 13th	All three Batteries in action by 5 a.m. VERMELLES heavily shelled & set on fire in places but held all day by Germans. Very heavy firing all day over the same front. Batteries moved back after dark to 1 mile west of BEUVRY. In villes by 4 p.m.	This held up our Infantry EAST of CAMBRIN. BRIG. GEN HICKIE away 13th Inf Bde.
WEDNESDAY 14th	March at 3.30 a.m. & take up positions of yesterday VERMELLES again 600ˣ EAST heavily bombarded & German Infantry Trenches West of CAMBRIN located & shelled effectively by Ank. Batteries withdrawn after dark & march via BEUVRY – LE QUESNOY to ESSARS. In billets by 9 p.m.	On the 13th asked K.C.O. to convey thanks to the 28th Bde for its assistance rendered to 13th Inf. Bde. On the 14th G.O.C. 21st French Corps personally thanked Sir HORACE SMITH-DORRIEN asking him to remain the same for its support.

Forms/C. 2118/11.

Army Form C. 2118.

WAR DIARY
or
INTELLIGENCE SUMMARY.
(*Erase heading not required.*)

Instructions regarding War Diaries and Intelligence Summaries are contained in F.S. Regs., Part II. and the Staff Manual respectively. Title pages will be prepared in manuscript.

Hour, Date, Place	Summary of Events and Information	Remarks and references to Appendices
TUESDAY OCT. 13th	Copy of Memorandum from G.O.C. 13th Infantry Brigade.	
	"The Brigadier General requests Major Sanders Commdg 28th Brigade R.F.A. to convey to the officers N.C.O.'s & Men of his brigade in his own name & that of his command in the 13th Infy. Bde their appreciation of the assistance accorded to the Infantry by the Gunners today. He will have much pleasure in bringing this good work to the notice of the Divisional General."	
	From 13th Infantry Brigade.	
WEDNESDAY OCT 14th	Special 5th Divisional Artillery orders 14th October 1914.	
	"This evening the G.O.C. 2nd French Corps visited the G.O.C. 2nd Corps & expressed to him personally his gratitude for the assistance rendered to him today by the Artillery of the 5th Division. General le Maistre expressed his admiration for the accurate shooting which, notwithstanding the advance of the French troops until Kain by fragments only a short distance in front of Kain, to gain enfilade ground. He added that according to reports given him by his own Staff Officers the fire of the Howitzer Battery had been particularly effective. Sir Horace Smith Dorrien has desired that his compliments should be conveyed to the units who were engaged in supporting the French advance in;— The 28th Brigade R.F.A & the 65th Howitzer Battery; and the General Officer Commanding is confident that all ranks of the 5th Divisional Artillery will share his pride & pleasure at the compliment paid to them."	

Sd. C.W. Bartholomew
Brigade Major
5th Divisional Artillery

Army Form C. 2118.

WAR DIARY
or
INTELLIGENCE SUMMARY.
(Erase heading not required.)

Instructions regarding War Diaries and Intelligence Summaries are contained in F.S. Regs., Part II. and the Staff Manual respectively. Title pages will be prepared in manuscript.

Hour, Date, Place	Summary of Events and Information	Remarks and references to Appendices
THURSDAY OCTOBER 15 ESSARS	March at 6 am 2 miles to GORRE village, and go into billets. Brigade now in reserve under orders of 5th Div. Artillery. 123 Battery placed under orders of O.C. 15th Bde RFA and moved at 12.30 pm into action south of FESTUBERT. Nothing further happens all day.	
FRIDAY OCTOBER 16 GORRE	Rather foggy day. Brigade remains in Billets. 123 Bty in action all day but does not fire a shot.	RHB Lt-Col SANDYS posted to the Brigade RHB RHB
SATURDAY OCTOBER 17	Brigade still in reserve, remains in Billets. 123 Bty advance to the L. of LA BUNRQUE RUE, + billets there at night.	
SUNDAY OCTOBER 18	Brigade moves at 6 am to just West of FESTUBERT village, and parks all day just off the road. Moves into billets at 5 pm in farms just close by. 123 Bty advances 1000 yards eastwards to a new position.	PHB
MONDAY OCTOBER 19 FESTUBERT	In Billets all day. 123rd Bty in action by the RUE D'OUVERT. Slight enquyte in the afternoon at enemy trench.	HA
TUESDAY OCTOBER 20th	123rd Bty in action in same place. 122nd Bty went into	

Army Form C. 2118.

WAR DIARY
or
INTELLIGENCE SUMMARY.
(Erase heading not required.)

Instructions regarding War Diaries and Intelligence Summaries are contained in F.S. Regs., Part II. and the Staff Manual respectively. Title pages will be prepared in manuscript.

Hour, Date, Place	Summary of Events and Information	Remarks and references to Appendices
TUESDAY OCT. 20th (cont.)	action at 2 p.m. Also attached to 15th Bde R.F.A.	Lt. Col. W. Sandys Lt. Col. 15th Bde R.F.A.
	122nd Bty in action in front South of FESTUBERT	H/a
WEDNESDAY 21st	No change	Major Sandys
THURSDAY 22nd	The Brigade is attached to 13th Infantry Bde 122nd & 123rd Btys. Major Wilson joins 27th Bde R.F.A. came back under the Colonel's orders. On morning of 22/23rd a	Major Wilson 27th Bde R.F.A. 3 drivers 123rd Bty wounded
	Infantry force from entrenched position at VIOLAINES.	H/a 4 horses killed 4 wounded
FRIDAY 23rd	123rd Bty goes into reserve. 124th Bty comes into action near the Brewery. 122nd Bty withdraws to RUE DE L'EPINETTE	65th Bty (How.) 18th & 28th Bde Major Humphrey's Ammunition wounded H/a
SATURDAY 24th	B.C.'s observing from Brewery billets sent by Black hauis a look B.C.'s were obliged to keep changing the positions of their batteries as they were galloped away by sprees & fire heavily shelled by Black haus the day. They were mostly H.A. Epc Newbuy 124th Bty wounded by bombs from aeroplanes	
	to haystacks near RUE DE L'EPINETTE. 122nd Bty in action North of RUE DU BOIS. 124th Bty in action North of BREWERY ROAD & about 300 x in rear of it. Two sections of 123rd Bty brought into action at 1.30 p.m. East of 122nd Bty. After dark one gun of 124th Bty under Lt RAINY was brought up behind the Infantry line West of FESTUBERT & fired against horses of LA QUINQUE RUE at 8.45 p.m. H.Q. moved back to GORRE	

(9 29 6) W 2794 100,000 8/14 H W V   Forms/C. 2118/11.

Army Form C. 2118.

WAR DIARY
or
INTELLIGENCE SUMMARY.
(Erase heading not required.)

Instructions regarding War Diaries and Intelligence Summaries are contained in F. S. Regs., Part II. and the Staff Manual respectively. Title pages will be prepared in manuscript.

Hour, Date, Place	Summary of Events and Information	Remarks and references to Appendices
SUNDAY OCTOBER 25th	Slight rain during previous night. 124th Bty withdrew to near RUE DE L'EPINETTE	HC
MONDAY 26th	One section from each battery withdrawn before daylight & sent to rest & refit to LES CHOQUAUX for 48 hours. 124th Bty moved back about 600 yds along the RUE DU BOIS & Sonk ? in B.C. 124th Bty observed from a "workman" about 25 feet up the tree.	HC HC Peel gets his jacket & goes to "C"
TUESDAY 27th	No change. Weather became wet	HC
WEDNESDAY 28th	No change. Rain. During night of 28th/29th associated in repulsing attack on right half of 14th Infantry Brigade on our left.	HC
THURSDAY 29th	During the morning continued firing on front of 14th & 14th 9th Bde. In the afternoon turned on to our own front. During the night of 29/30th four attacks were made on our immediate front at 8.30p.m., 12 midnight, 3 a.m., & 4.30a.m., the enemy in the afternoon or night took four small fire trenches.	The 13th Infantry Bde were displeased with the effect of our fire better during HC

(9 29 6) W 2794 100,000 8/14 H W V Forms/C. 2118/11.

Army Form C. 2118.

WAR DIARY
or
INTELLIGENCE SUMMARY.
(Erase heading not required.)

Instructions regarding War Diaries and Intelligence Summaries are contained in F. S. Regs., Part II. and the Staff Manual respectively. Title pages will be prepared in manuscript.

Hour, Date, Place	Summary of Events and Information	Remarks and references to Appendices
FRIDAY OCTOBER 30th	Situation in our immediate front remains. In the afternoon the IX Indian Brigade relieved over our position. Received	Discs. Cpl Selleen, of 1208 R.E. was fatally wounded by an aeroplane bomb. B.C.Thankery was wounded at the same time.
SATURDAY 31st	Handed over to IX Bn & Battalion went by 7 a.m. Marched via BETHUNE — OBLINGHEM — HINGES — MERVILLE — VIEUX BERQUIN — STRAZEELE — ROUGE CROIX. Got into billets at 3 p.m. Btn. attached to 13th Infantry Brigade	

CONFIDENTIAL

121/2577 5th Division

WAR DIARY
of
28th BRIGADE.
R.F.A.

Nov. 1st – 30th 1914

Vol IV.

Army Form C. 2118.

WAR DIARY
or
INTELLIGENCE SUMMARY.
(Erase heading not required.)

Instructions regarding War Diaries and Intelligence Summaries are contained in F.S. Regs., Part II. and the Staff Manual respectively. Title pages will be prepared in manuscript.

Hour, Date, Place	Summary of Events and Information	Remarks and references to Appendices
NOVEMBER		
SUNDAY 1st		
STRAZEELE	Very fine day. Brigade ordered to move at 1:30 p.m. March via MOOLENAEKER and BAILLEUL. long detour in BAILLEUL owing to the town being very crowded with British & French troops. Continue the march to CROIX DE POPERINGHE village where the Brigade goes into billets. We are now in reserve under orders of 7th Inf Bde.	RMS
7 pm		
MONDAY 2nd	Nothing at all happens during the day. lovely weather. Remain in same billets	RMS
CROIX DE POPERINGHE		
TUESDAY 3rd	The Brigade marches at 5:30 am via LOCRE & halts South the head of the column in KEMMEL village at 7 am. The C.O. and Battery commanders spend sometime reconnoitring for positions East during this reconnaissance a good many of KEMMEL village & the Brigade sorts to drop in KEMMEL village & the Brigade has to move South. References in	
KEMMEL	KEMMEL - NEUVE-EGLISE road, but the ridge from WULVERGHEM is going 7.5 is under heavy shell fire. Brigade finally brought into action on a line roughly N.S. through KEMMEL, but 122 & 124 Batteries	(illegible) to OSTEND Sheet. Scale 100,000 map
3 pm	are moved again before they open fire. The Brigade is in action just before dusk, but 122 & 124 batteries are withdrawn for the night to billets.	Billets of the brigade on both sides of LINDENHOEK - DRANOUTRE road, about 1 mile behind the gun positions. RMS

(9 29 6) W 2794 100,000 8/14 H W V Forms/C. 2118/11.

Army Form C. 2118.

WAR DIARY
or
INTELLIGENCE SUMMARY.
(Erase heading not required.)

Instructions regarding War Diaries and Intelligence Summaries are contained in F.S. Regs., Part II. and the Staff Manual respectively. Title pages will be prepared in manuscript.

Hour, Date, Place	Summary of Events and Information	Remarks and references to Appendices
WED. NOV. 4th LINDENHOEK	In action ready to open fire by 6 am. The Brigade is now in action as explained in the margin. Foggy morning and the Bde. does not open fire till about noon. Heavy artillery fire by 13th Division in the afternoon which dies out before dark. Light rain in the evening. 124 Battery left in action during the night - others withdrawn.	122 Bty - 400 yds S.S.E in LINDENHOEK on W. side of KEMMEL - NEUVE EGLISE road. 124 Bty - 200 yds S.S.E. of 122 Bty. 123 Bty - 600 yds W.S.W. of figure 9 on the same road. [122mm observing from haystacks 200 yds E. of 124's guns 123 from a cottage 100 yds South of three haystacks] PAS
THURS. NOV. 5th	Brigade ready by 6 am. Fine sunny day. Very little shooting done by the Brigade, but there is very heavy artillery fire in the afternoon. The French guns beside us shooting as hard as they can. A peaceful day as far as the Brigade is concerned. 122 Bty out all night.	2d Lt. C.I. Curtius joins the Bde rto posted to 123 Bty. 2d Lt. J.C. Tipler from Ba Am Col is 122 Bty 2d Lt. Shier posted to Bde AC PAS
FRIDAY NOV. 6th	Ready by 6.15 am. Foggy. Fire a little at noon to support French attack. Hear that the Germans have got point 75 during the night. Very little else happens. Billets as usual - 123 Bty out.	Hear Maj Sanders is promoted Lt. col. Capt Croxton is promoted major Lt Cather is promoted Capt. Gazette 30th Oct. PAS
SAT. NOV. 7th	Inaction 6.30 am. Another foggy morning, turning into a dull day. Nothing of any interest happens - only just a little firing at odd times. 124 Bty. out all night.	Pas

(9 29 6) W 2794 100,000 8/14 H W V Forms/C. 2118/11.

Army Form C. 2118.

WAR DIARY
or
INTELLIGENCE SUMMARY.
(Erase heading not required.)

Instructions regarding War Diaries and Intelligence Summaries are contained in F.S. Regs., Part II. and the Staff Manual respectively. Title pages will be prepared in manuscript.

Hour, Date, Place	Summary of Events and Information	Remarks and references to Appendices
1914		
SUNDAY NOV 8th LINDENHOEK	Foggy cold morning. Only fire twice all day — at 11.45 & 12 noon. Nothune most all day. 122 Bty out for the night. 123 Bty in reserve.	2nd Lt Evans leaves the Bde to be A.D.C. to Gen. Headlam. dated Nov. 2. RAS
MONDAY Nov. 9th	Foggy but warmer. Fire, as usual, in searching areas under the direction of the G.O.C. R.A. Nothune of interest occurred. 123 on night duty — 124 Bty in reserve all day.	
TUESDAY Nov 10th	Very uneventful day; practically nothing to be seen, though a fair amount of searching is done. 122 in reserve. 124 out at night.	New R.S.M. Jones W.O. is posted 21st — dated 3rd Nov. RAS
WEDNESDAY Nov. 11th	Wonderfully good light today: a good deal of useful work registering is done. Reconnaissance for a Brigade position to support infantry second line is made by the C.O. in the morning. Work is strenuous. Pits dug and gun pits prepared in the afternoon. Wet evening. 123 in reserve for the day. 122 out for the night.	RAS
THURSDAY Nov 12th	Fine day & light continues good. Observation station shelled from 11 am to 12 noon, but no damage is done. Continue to search areas under Direction of 5th Div. Artillery. £124 in reserve for the day. 123 out at night. 50 r.b. shells drop in the neighbourhood of our billets during the night.	RAS

Army Form C. 2118.

WAR DIARY
or
INTELLIGENCE SUMMARY
(Erase heading not required.)

Instructions regarding War Diaries and Intelligence
Summaries are contained in F. S. Regs., Part II.
and the Staff Manual respectively. Title pages
will be prepared in manuscript.

Hour, Date, Place	Summary of Events and Information	Remarks and References to Appendices
FRIDAY NOV 13	Miserable wet day – very cold, and light bad. Very uninteresting generally. Little shooting done. Still raining in dark. 122 outer night 122 in reserve all day. By two shell near wo in the night in billets	BQMS M.J.R. WOOD 122 Bde gets a commission as 2nd Lt. RFA 2 men in 122 Bde wounded by promotion from 105th Heavy Bty. RWF Move the bullet is known on roads sort of & of DRANOUTRE. RWF
SAT. NOV. 14.	Practically no shooting going on. Cold morning – very welcome frost. Quiet afternoon. 123 Bde in reserve. 122 out for the night. One or two shells again drop near the billets	
SUN. NOV. 15.	A dreadful day – snow sleet frantically cold. Positions of 18 hostile batteries ascertained by aeroplane reconn- aissance yesterday, fire at some just South of WYTSCHAETE. Practically no other targets engaged: light very bad. 122 Bde in reserve 123 Bde on night duty	Change Bdrs – 122 Bdq ables to DRANOUTRE village hearing the dearly boulevards RWF
MON. NOV 16.	Very cold : nothing fired at except localised batteries under the orders of 14 Ind Bde (Gen Macdy), as this Brigade Bde took over the trenches in front of us after dark from the French. A good deal of firing take place in the earlier part of the night and there is a great deal of noise of battle etc behind the Allies trenches 122 B attm occupies after dark a forward position close to WULVERGHEM so as to be able to give close support to the Infantry	"E" Batter Bty RFA also attacked yesterday. F.O.C. Ref Bde. Taking up position S. of 124 Battery. Reporting from Same place on 123 Bty. RWF

Army Form C. 2118.

WAR DIARY
or
INTELLIGENCE SUMMARY
(Erase heading not required.)

Instructions regarding War Diaries and Intelligence Summaries are contained in F. S. Regs., Part II. and the Staff Manual respectively. Title pages will be prepared in manuscript.

Hour, Date, Place	Summary of Events and Information	Remarks and References to Appendices
TUESDAY NOV. 17 LINDENHOEK.	Cold bleak morning turning fine later. 129th (How.) Battery placed under orders of O.C. 26th Brigade, and comes into action a little South of 124th Battery. Fool of the KEMMEL-NEUVE-EGLISE road not much shooting done by us or the Germans at LINDENHOEK, but the 122nd Bty. in the advanced position is fired at off & on all day.	Col Sanders D.C. 122 Bty slightly wounded in the lee. RHE
WED. NOV. 18	Ice in the morning: bright sunny day. A fairly quiet day except that 122 Battery again got shelled a good deal. 122 Bty withdrawn after dark and come into reserve, their place being taken by 124 Bty. Frosty night.	RHE
THURS NOV 19	Weather ber. bad. Frozen the night and snow 8" and or all day. Bitterly cold. Practically no shooting done. Frost in the night.	Lieut Rainy wounded while in the infantry trenches observing for the Battery. RHE
FRI. NOV. 20.	Ground quite white & frozen: bright sunny day. Observing Station got shelled a little - no damage done. 124 Battery's Observing Station also shelled. 124 Bty withdrawn into reserve after dark, their relieves by 123 Bty. 122 into action again at LINDENHOEK also after dark.	Lt. CHARWORTH MUSTARD RFA came to brigade - posted to 124 Bty. RHE
SAT. NOV. 21.	Black frost in the night. Everything frozen solid. Lovely day. Enemy shell our infantry a good deal so we search for their batteries all along behind the ridge from MESSINES - WYTSCHAETE.	RHE

Army Form C. 2118.

WAR DIARY
or
INTELLIGENCE SUMMARY
(Erase heading not required.)

Instructions regarding War Diaries and Intelligence Summaries are contained in F. S. Regs., Part II and the Staff Manual respectively. Title pages will be prepared in manuscript.

Hour, Date, Place	Summary of Events and Information	Remarks and References to Appendices
SAT NOV 21 LINDENHOEK.	Observing stations on LINDENHOEK ridge are shelled a little, but there are several "blind" shells. "E" Batter withdrawn from the 25" Brigade group after dark and is replaced by I Battz	RAE
SUN. NOV. 22.	Another black frost. Quiet day - no excitement except a little shelling of surrounding stations & the trenches in front. German aeroplane brought down between our guns & the infantry own air men & a British airman in pursuit. Pilot & observer captured. After dark, I Battery goes to forward position at ——.	3 Officers sent forward after task to the various infantry headqrs to find out whether anything that would help our guns is obtainable. RAE NL. Lt. Geddoes joins the Brigade as Lt. PHILLIPS RAMC, who goes to 13th Field Ambulance. RAE
MON. NOV. 23	BEHIND WULVERGHEM and 123 Battery comes back into reserve. Misquite so cold. Quiet day. Germans appear to be done shooting. More "blind" shells every day; more than 80% are blind.	
TUES. NOV 24.	Distinctly warmer - a partial thaw. Batteries shooting searching fire as usual on and behind the WYTSCHAETE - MESSINES ridge wherever the German guns open fire on the trenches. 122 Bty goes to forward position of WULVERGHEM	35 shells only do shell which pass over the morning little. I Battery withdrawn from Can. Div. RAE
WED NOV 25	Warm & thawing. After amount of searching & swinging as yesterday and 129 (Howr) Battery fires on German trenches for night firing carried out.	Registration RAE

79
3298

Army Form C. 2118.

WAR DIARY
or
INTELLIGENCE SUMMARY

(Erase heading not required.)

Instructions regarding War Diaries and Intelligence Summaries are contained in F. S. Regs., Part II. and the Staff Manual respectively. Title pages will be prepared in manuscript.

Hour, Date, Place	Summary of Events and Information	Remarks and References to Appendices
TUESDAY NOV. 17 LINDENHOEK.	Cold bleak morning turning fine later. 122nd (How.) Battery placed under orders of O.C. 28th Brigade, and comes into action a little South of 124th Battery. E of the REMMEL-NEUVE-EGLISE road. Not much shooting done by us or the Germans at LINDENHOEK, but the 122nd Bty in the advanced position is fired at by WARDEN all day.	Col Sanders D.C. 122 Bty slightly wounded in the ear. RHP
WED NOV 18	Ice in the morning; bright sunny day. A fairly quiet day except that 122 Battery again got shelled a good deal. 122 Bty withdrawn after dark and come into reserve, their place being taken by 124th Bty. Frost night.	RHP
THURS NOV 19	Weather very bad. Frost in the night and snow storms on and off all day. Bitterly cold. Practically no shooting done. Frost in the night.	Lieut Rainy slightly wounded while in the infantry trenches observing for the Battery. RHP
FRI. NOV. 20.	Ground quite white & frozen; bright sunny day. Brigade Observing Station gets shelled a little - no damage done. 124 Bty withdrawn Battery's Observing Station also shelled. 122 Bty Into reserve after dark, being relieved by 123 Bty. 122 into action again at LINDENHOEK also after dark.	PAP Lt. CHADWORTH musters RFA joins brigade - posted to 124 Bty.
SAT. NOV. 21.	Black frost in the night. Everything frozen solid. Lovely day. Enemy shell our infantry a good deal so we search for their batteries all along behind the ridge from MESSINES - 'YWYTSCHAETE.	RHP

3298

(9 26 6) W 257—976 100,000 1/12 H W V

Army Form C. 2118.

WAR DIARY
or
INTELLIGENCE SUMMARY
(Erase heading not required.)

Instructions regarding War Diaries and Intelligence Summaries are contained in F. S. Regs., Part II. and the Staff Manual respectively. Title pages will be prepared in manuscript.

Hour, Date, Place	Summary of Events and Information	Remarks and References to Appendices
SAT. NOV 21 LINDENHOEK.	Observing stations on LINDENHOEK ridge also shelled a little, but there are several "blind" shells. The 25th Brigade group afterwards and is replaced by I Battery. "E" Battery withdrawn (from another flank front). Quiet day — no excitement except a little shelling of our observing stations & the trenches in front. German aeroplane brought down between our guns & the infantry; aviator & damage done by a British airman in pursuit. Pilot & aeroplane captured. After dark, "I" Battery goes forward into reserve.	RHG
SUN. NOV 22.	Brigade HQ WULVERGHEM and 12.3 Battery comes back into reserve. Not quite so cold. Quiet day — Germans appear to be doing nothing. More "blind" shells every day; more than 50% are blind.	3 Officers sent forward afterwards to the various infantry HQs giving to give suggestions about anything that would help our guns to assist. RHG Roome. Lt. GEDDOES joins the Brigade via Lt. PHILLIPS R.A.M.C., who goes to 14th Fd. Ambulance. RHG
MON. NOV 23	Distinctly warmer — a partial thaw. Batteries shoot searching fire as usual on and behind the WYTSCHAETE–MESSINES ridge whenever the Germans are seen in or the trenches. 12B Bty goes forward billets in WULVERGHEM.	As mere shell only to shell which pass over the trenches little. I Battery withdrawn into Fd. Dun. Div. RHG
TUES. NOV 24.		
WED NOV 25	Warm & raining. A few armoured searching & surgeons as yesterday and 12.9 (How) Battery fires on German trenches. Registration for night firing carried out	RHG

Army Form C. 2118.

WAR DIARY
or
INTELLIGENCE SUMMARY

(Erase heading not required.)

Instructions regarding War Diaries and Intelligence Summaries are contained in F. S. Regs., Part II. and the Staff Manual respectively. Title pages will be prepared in manuscript.

Hour, Date, Place	Summary of Events and Information	Remarks and References to Appendices
LINDENHOEK THURS. NOV. 26.	Snow all gone but everywhere is very muddy and soft. All batteries in action - none in reserve. Pompom Wolfganis 5" Div., which is under our orders to be thoroughly action against point 75 and is entrenched at the H.Q. LINDENHOEK. On exceptionally quiet rather foggy day. 123 Bk. does not fire a round at all. Bn goes to WULVERGHEM hollow after dark.	RMS
FRI. NOV. 27.	Dull weather. LINDENHOEK ridge is shelled in the morning + right hand (i.e. Southern) observation cottage nearly hit. No damage done to us. 65th (How.) Battery arrives at DRANOUTRE in the afternoon and is attached to the 28th Brigade. 122 Bk is in reserve. B. fairly quiet day.	RMS
SAT. NOV. 28	Fine and quite a quiet day; light for shooting also very good and a fair amount done whenever the Germans spewed. 124th Battery withdrawn from 28th Bde group before dawn and 65th RHA takes its place. After dark 123 Bk. relieves 124 Bk. the latter going into reserve.	Lt.Col. G.H. Sanders Maj. Gov. Kingsman } leave BAILLEUL at 5 a.m. for ENGLAND Capt. LA Cotter } for 7 days leave.
SUNDAY NOV 29.	Another fine day with fairly good light. German million do a good deal of shooting in a great many of their shells do not much. 28th Bde does not shoot much. 14th Inf. Bde	RSM Cox Sgt. Sage } goes to 7 days furlough LEFT ALSO

79 LINDEN

3298

Army Form C. 2118.

WAR DIARY
or
INTELLIGENCE SUMMARY
(Erase heading not required.)

Instructions regarding War Diaries and Intelligence Summaries are contained in F. S. Regs., Part II. and the Staff Manual respectively. Title pages will be prepared in manuscript.

Hour, Date, Place	Summary of Events and Information	Remarks and References to Appendices
LINDENHOEK. SUNDAY NOV. 29 (contd)	Handover 13th Inf Bde at 9 am. So the 28th Brigade now comes under the orders of the latter (Brig. Gen. Count Gleichen). 65th How. Bty does a little night firing at 7.15 pm at a German Sap & forward trench, hitting it with success. 123 Battery (in advance posn) shelled in the morning by German heavy artillery — no harm done.	R.H.S.
MONDAY NOV. 30th	Dull day as regards the weather. German heavy guns have fire on KEMMEL, LINDENHOEK ridge etc and our guns search for hostile artillery on & behind the MESSINES—WYTSCHAETE ridge. Nothing of any unusual occurs. 122 Bty moves forward to the WULVERGHEM position — 123 comes into reserve & Hy goes into action again.	R.H.S.

Army Form C. 2118.

WAR DIARY
or
INTELLIGENCE SUMMARY
(Erase heading not required.)

War Diary
26th Bde R.F.A.
December 1914

Vol. V

Army Form C. 2118.

WAR DIARY
or
INTELLIGENCE SUMMARY
(Erase heading not required.)

Instructions regarding War Diaries and Intelligence Summaries are contained in F. S. Regs., Part II. and the Staff Manual respectively. Title pages will be prepared in manuscript.

Hour, Date, Place	Summary of Events and Information	Remarks and References to Appendices
TUESDAY DEC 1st	Atmosphere very clear. Best view of MESSINES—WYTSCHAETE Ridge to date. 124th Bty in action on LINDENHOEK Ridge. 129th Bty in forward position. Fired as yesterday.	Rounds fired 171 H.E.
WEDNESDAY 2nd	Very good views again. Fired as usual in the afternoon. 124th Bty searched & registered likely Observing Stations. Woke up "Black Maria" who fired at Southern slopes of MONT KEMMEL	374 " H.E.
THURSDAY 3rd	Fine & clear. 124th Bty in advanced position 1230 & 1224 Btys at LINDENHOEK. Between 1.50 p.m. & 1.54 p.m. bombarded MESSINES—WYTSCHAETE Ridge; observed by H.M. The King from behind KEMMEL. 122nd Bty goes into reserve.	" 540 1 @ 9 m.S & 7 N.C.O's & Men sent to LOCRE to represent the Bde at the distribution of Honours Medals by H.M. The King. R.S.M. Cox got the D.C.M. H.E.
FRIDAY 4th	Rain on & off; fired as usual; very quiet day.	Rounds fired 570 H.E.
SATURDAY 5th	Rain & Snow all day; nothing doing	
SUNDAY 6th	123rd Bty in advanced position 122nd at LINDENHOEK cold frosty day. Turned to rain at night. Special Order of the Day by HIS MAJESTY THE KING	" 146 H.E.

Officers, Non-commissioned Officers and men,—

I am very glad to have been able to see my Army in the Field. I much wished to do so in order to gain a slight experience of the life you are leading. I wish I could have spoken to you all, to express my admiration of the splendid manner in which you have fought & are still fighting against a powerful and relentless enemy.

WAR DIARY
or
INTELLIGENCE SUMMARY

(Erase heading not required.)

Army Form C. 2118.

Instructions regarding War Diaries and Intelligence
Summaries are contained in F. S. Regs., Part II.
and the Staff Manual respectively. Title pages
will be prepared in manuscript.

Hour, Date, Place	Summary of Events and Information	Remarks and References to Appendices
	By your discipline, pluck & endurance, inspired by the indomitable regimental spirit you have not only upheld the traditions of the British Army but added fresh lustre to its history. I was particularly impressed by your soldierly bearing & cheerful appearance. I cannot share in your trials, dangers & successes, but I can assure you of the proud confidence & gratitude of myself & of your fellow countrymen. We follow you in our daily thoughts on your certain road to victory. GEORGE, R.I. December 5th 1914 General Headquarters. Appreciation by 2nd Corps Commander. Dear Smith-Dorrien, Sir Horace Smith-Dorrien told me last night that the bombardment of the MESSINES—WYTSCHAETE position on the day of His Majesty's visit by the 5th Divisional Artillery had been most effective. He stated that he had been much impressed by the accuracy of the fire, that every shell appeared to be exactly in the right place. I am sure you fellows will be glad to hear this. Well done! Yours ever John Headlam 6/12/14.	
MONDAY DEC 7th	Rain again. 128th Bty in advanced position obliged to move back 50 yards on account of bad state of the pits.	Bullets of 65th How. Bty of the 8th Bde R.F.A. att. to 28th Bde. shelled by Heavy Howitzer 3.30 P.m. 4 men Killed 2 wounded H.B.

Army Form C. 2118.

WAR DIARY
or
INTELLIGENCE SUMMARY
(*Erase heading not required.*)

Instructions regarding War Diaries and Intelligence Summaries are contained in F. S. Regs., Part II. and the Staff Manual respectively. Title pages will be prepared in manuscript.

Hour, Date, Place		Summary of Events and Information	Remarks and References to Appendices
TUESDAY DEC	8th	Rain. Nothing doing. Rounds fired 38	HE
WEDNESDAY	9th	Thick fog all day " 26. Howitzer Bty (65th) moved 700 yards South as to West of LINDENHOEK — NEUVE EGLISE road.	HE
THURSDAY	10th	124th Bty in forward position moved back to 600 yards East of NEUVE-EGLISE as the pits near WULVERGHEM were flooded. Rounds fired 64. Foggy. Rain	HE Centre of square K I(a) rg. BELGIUM (sense "G") Sheet 28 S.W.
FRIDAY	11th	Nothing doing. Foggy again. Rounds fired 58	HE

Army Form C. 2118.

WAR DIARY
or
INTELLIGENCE SUMMARY
(Erase heading not required.)

Instructions regarding War Diaries and Intelligence Summaries are contained in F. S. Regs., Part II. and the Staff Manual respectively. Title pages will be prepared in manuscript.

Hour, Date, Place	Summary of Events and Information	Remarks and References to Appendices
LINDENHOEK Sunday DEC 13th.	All batteries in action today. Lt. MILLER's section leaves the "NEUVE EGLISE" position and is brought into action very close by The 65th Battery RFA (Howitzer). Fine day: not much shooting, but registration of "point 74 ridge" carried out. 120th Bty RFA ordered to join the 28th Bde group, and is brought into action on the Eastern side of KEMMEL HILL.	Rep. BELGIUM ('B' series) Sheet 28 S.W. Bty position about ½ mile East of in F.A.O. extended to top armt & square F.S.a. Observation from cross roads in F.S.d. RMS
MONDAY DEC 14th	A very busy day. Attack by 3rd Division (on our left) and 16th + 32nd French Corps on a line running from MAEDELSTEDE FARM roughly NO/NW. 5th Div. Artillery esherate by bombard-the area round WYTSCHAETE WOOD. The MAEDELSTEDE FARM. Everything ready by 6.30 am. Preliminary series 7 to 7.45 am, first series 7.45 – 8.45 am, & then first series repeated every ½th hour till 3 pm, when preliminary series is repeated. Objectives – firstly "point 74" ridge, (b) the S. area of WYTSCHAETE ^ (3) W. edge of WYTSCHAETE wood. Answering German fire; and all artillery fire ceases after Midday. 28th Bde group fires nearly 3500 rounds in the day.	(C.16.d) 120, 122, the Bty under direct orders of Div. Artillery + Lt. Sandup. 123 Bty. & (now) 65th Bty (each with an attached section of Howitzer) under orders of 13th Inf Bde. Bombardment is entirely for Bty under Div. Artillery. There under IH only short aheques. Each of Div. arty batteries have 1 hr. of duty between 11-4 pm RMS
TUESDAY DEC 15th	Ready by 6.30 am as yesterday, and bombardment programme repeated. At 9am one bty (B) the 3 under Lt. Sandup orders) absent "of duty of a time. Between 11am + 4 pm one section of each battery fires for an hour at a time. Very little	

Army Form C. 2118.

WAR DIARY
or
INTELLIGENCE SUMMARY
(Erase heading not required.)

Instructions regarding War Diaries and Intelligence Summaries are contained in F. S. Regs., Part II. and the Staff Manual respectively. Title pages will be prepared in manuscript.

Hour, Date, Place	Summary of Events and Information	Remarks and References to Appendices
LINDENHOEK TUESDAY DEC 15th (contd)	Annoying hostile artillery fire. The fire of the allied attack not nearly so intense as yesterday. About 1500 rounds fired by the 26th Bde group. Weather fair – dull.	RMS
WEDNESDAY DEC 16th	An uninteresting day. Just a few registering rounds of our fire. A "Black Maria" shell dropped within 5 yards of the subaltern of 122nd Bty but no harm is done. The attack on WYTSCHAETE appears to be discontinued.	* 6" H.E. Howitzer shell. RMS
THURSDAY DEC 17th	Cold dry day. No shooting done except to register MAEDELSTEDE FARM, each battery being allowed a certain time for this purpose. No other event of any interest occurs.	Gen. HEADLAM overseeing officer from each battery at KEMMEL HILL windmill. RMS
FRIDAY DEC 18th	Cold day. Turning to rain in the afternoon. Fire not opened until 10 am, when MAEDELSTEDE FARM is bombarded. Bombardment repeated at 1 & 3 pm, & during the actually moments of schooling a very intense fire is kept up. Nothing else occurs.	Bombardment consists of 2 min. quick times, 10 min. interval, 3 min. Total time 15 min. Official time for starting fire in the morning changed to 7:15 am. RMS
SATURDAY DEC 19th	Dull weather. Nothing of interest occurs. After dark, 120th Bty rejoin the 27th Brigade, A. MILLER rejoins 123rd Bty which comes into reserve, and 12th Bty go to "forward" position.	2nd J.D JONES & M.J.R. WOOD RFA from Supernumerary. RMS

Army Form C. 2118.

WAR DIARY
or
INTELLIGENCE SUMMARY
(Erase heading not required.)

Instructions regarding War Diaries and Intelligence Summaries are contained in F. S. Regs., Part II. and the Staff Manual respectively. Title pages will be prepared in manuscript.

Hour, Date, Place	Summary of Events and Information	Remarks and References to Appendices
LINDENHOEK SUNDAY DEC 20th	Ready to open fire at 7.15 as usual. No shine occurs during the day — scarcely any fire at all.	Lt-Col Garsanders leaves the station whilst patrol home to England. Major Crofton 15th O.C. 122 Capt Thorburn " Capt in 122 } Change in the R.H. in Capt Coker O.E. Amm Col. consequence. Leave restarted from today. Lts Armytage, Duff & Attenboros go to England earlier in the morning. RHS
MONDAY DEC 21st	Dull weather, turning into a wet afternoon. Combined "shoot" at 9 a.m. all along our line, which is repeated again at 5.15 p.m. Infantry report results good. Nothing else done.	Major Crofton goes on "leave" RHS
TUESDAY DEC 22nd	Bad day with sleets & attempts at snow. We do just a little irregular shooting.	RHS 48 hour relief commences again
WEDNESDAY DEC 23rd	Very bad light all day. Some snow falls. Only shooting done is a few rounds fired by the Howitzers. After dark 122 Bty come into reserve, + 122 Bty goes to "forward" position. During the day, 14th Inf Bde take over our Brigade area from 13th Inf Bde	
THURSDAY DEC 24th	Weather better: cold & sunny after 11 a.m. Great deal of firing during the night + all down by the French to the morning of us. We don't take any part & scarcely fire at all.	RHS
FRIDAY DEC 25th	A first-rate day. Hard frost in the night + sunny morning. Dence fog comes on about 9 a.m., hiding everything. We fire about 20 rounds only during the day. Germans don't fire at all. 122 Bty comes into reserve after dark +124 goes to LINDENHOEK, 123 to ELZENWALLE	RHS

Army Form C. 2118.

WAR DIARY
or
INTELLIGENCE SUMMARY

(Erase heading not required.)

Instructions regarding War Diaries and Intelligence Summaries are contained in F. S. Regs., Part II. and the Staff Manual respectively. Title pages will be prepared in manuscript.

Hour, Date, Place	Summary of Events and Information	Remarks and References to Appendices
LINDENHOEK DEC. 26. SATURDAY.	Very hard frost in the night. Another day with practically no shooting, some to observation being impossible. Some snow in the afternoon.	R+S
DEC. 27. SUNDAY.	Cold raw day. No shooting by LINDENHOEK batteries, but a certain amount by 18 hr. & row. section at NEUVE EGLISE. Germans much more active than usual; shelling trenches in front of WULVERGHEM. After dark, 12+ B4, move to NEUVEEGLISE; 123 B4 come into reserve.	R+S
DEC 28 MONDAY.	Poor day, raining till about 4 p.m., and a strong wind blowing. Practically no shooting till 1 p.m. when all the guns of our "group" have a combined shoot, and another short shoot at 2.35 p.m. Nothing else occurs.	Hear Lt. Roving is posted to R.H.A. R+S
DEC 29 TUESDAY	A perfect frightful night; violent rain & wind. Storm. Tower of KEMMEL blown down; the country half under water. Only a few registering rounds fired during the day. 124 B4 and How. Sections have a night shoot at 10 p.m. roff to 15.	R+S
DEC 30 WEDNESDAY	Good day – sunny & fine, turning into a very cold afternoon. A couple of short shoots in the morning by the NEUVE EGLISE guns. Nothing else happens all day.	Lt. A. R. RAMEY leaves the Bde. to join the 14th Bde. R.H.A. R+S

Army Form C. 2118.

WAR DIARY
or
INTELLIGENCE SUMMARY
(Erase heading not required.)

Instructions regarding War Diaries and Intelligence Summaries are contained in F. S. Regs., Part II. and the Staff Manual respectively. Title pages will be prepared in manuscript.

Hour, Date, Place	Summary of Events and Information	Remarks and References to Appendices
LINDENHOEK DEC 31st THURSDAY	Cold day raining a little most of the time. A shot at 9.30 am another at 2.30 pm h NEUVE EGLISE guns; nothing else done all day.	Pps

WAR DIARY
or
INTELLIGENCE SUMMARY

Confidential

November	119	120	121
11	15		
12	56		18
13	50	(148)	
15	38	152	
		7	
16			70
17	24		
18		26	
19	12	75	8
21		5	
22		17	
		(20)	
23			
24	48		99
28		13	(56)
December			
1			5
2		62	
3	83	60	107
		126	
14	195		36
	115		
	130		
	87		
15	82		532
	(48)		
	144		
	452		
	(48)		
16	43		
17	172		
	(30)		
19	142		197
	(30)		
20			172
22	79	103	225
23	40		
24			114
25		76	
28		20	
29			50
31	121		

From
Sept. 5th to Dec 31st

$119 = 10,094$ rnds
$120 = 8,010$ " $+830?$
$121 = 7,895$ "
$25,999$

The above includes 576. High Explosive Shell.

← Brigade supplied with 380 rnds.

There is no record of expenditure of ammunition previous to September 5th, except that on August 24th the Brigade was supplied with 846 rounds.

WJOalun Lieut
RFA(RR)

	119	120	121
Sept			
5		39	
8	308	152	77
9		152	
13			152
			246
14	236		76
	303	300	458
15	77	152	304
	456	152	152
16	356		76
			152
17	228		
18	304	83	152
	76		
19	304	114	83
20	103	76	
21	111	131	
22	241	152	
23	44		38
24	35	152	
25		74	
26		76	
27		152	
30		76	
October			
1		76	
3	12		
6		304	
13	56	132	130
	152	152	
	135	286	
14	228	228	59
	116	81	76
			40
15	152	236	73
	88		76
	18		
17	207		60
			152
18	121	144	45
	315		152
	152		76
	208		228
			133
19	143		
	76		
26	152		

	119	120	121
October			
20	152		304
	164		
	118		
	152		
	302		
	152		
	88		
21		228	76
		152	152
		76	221
		152	
		152	
22		304	119
		76	151
		76	152
		152	228
		76	228
		228	151
		152	228
		228	
		48	
		46	
23	152		
	151		
27	113	102	186
	150		
28			139
29		152	130
		152	
		152	
30	198	126	
	46		
	50		
November			
1	34		91
2	56		72
3	75	75	
		152	
		75	
4	95	65	65
6	29	39	67
7	29	48	36
9	36		34
10	7	34	16

Index

SUBJECT.

5TH DIV.

No.	Contents.	Date.
	R.A. 28TH BRIGADE. JAN.-DEC., 1915	

121/4194

5th Division

28th Bde. R.F.A.

Vol VII. 1 — 31.1.15.

Army Form C. 2118.

WAR DIARY
or
INTELLIGENCE SUMMARY

(*Erase heading not required.*)

Instructions regarding War Diaries and Intelligence Summaries are contained in F. S. Regs., Part II. and the Staff Manual respectively. Title pages will be prepared in manuscript.

Hour, Date, Place	Summary of Events and Information	Remarks and References to Appendices
Confidential	WAR DIARY. 28th Brigade R.F.A. January 1915 Vol VI Wandres *Lieut. Colonel,* *Commanding 28th Brigade R.F.A.*	

Army Form C. 2118.

WAR DIARY
or
INTELLIGENCE SUMMARY
(Erase heading not required.)

Instructions regarding War Diaries and Intelligence Summaries are contained in F. S. Regs., Part II. and the Staff Manual respectively. Title pages will be prepared in manuscript.

Hour, Date, Place	Summary of Events and Information	Remarks and References to Appendices
LINDENHOEK and NEUVE-EGLISE FRIDAY JANUARY 1st	Dull clear day. Just a couple of shot-ghosts in NEUVE-EGLISE guns and a few rounds from the Austrians at LINDEN-HOEK is all that happens during the day. 124 goes into action after dark – 122 into reserve.	Capt A.G. Gillman + Lt. A.R. Rainy RHA awarded a "Military Cross" in New Year Honours. Lt. J.M. McCrae R.F.A. joins the Brigade and posted to Bde. H.Q. Col. 2Lt. C.E. Buxton R.F.A. joins the Brigade and posted to 124 Batter. RHQ Lt. L.G. Lutyens posted to R.H.A. "G" Battery. RHQ
SATURDAY JAN. 2nd	An uninteresting day. Just a little shooting done by NEUVE EGLISE guns.	
SUNDAY JAN 3rd	7.30 – 8 am. Combined shoot by 28th Brigade group on all parts of the German trenches. No more firing done by 10 for remainder of the day. WULVERGHEM shelled between 9 and 10 am. A bad day, turning into a wet afternoon.	RHQ 122 for instruction – 123 into reserve. Lt. CURTEIS leaves for ENGLAND on 6 days leave at 4 am RHQ
MONDAY JAN 4th	Rain and sleet in the morning. Light getting very bad and firing impossible. Advanced How. Section fires a few rounds. No one else does anything. 14th Inf Brigade leave this area at 4 pm. We come under the 15th Inf Bde.	
TUESDAY JAN 5th	Fairly good day: drier. Light very bad. Howitzers at LINDENHOEK fire a few rounds. No other batteries fire. WULVERGHEM and NEUVE EGLISE shelled by the Germans during the day. Otherwise nothing happens. After dark 123 Battery handed over to Lt-Col. DUFFUS & come under his command. 122 Bty at LINDENHOEK changes with No. 04 at NEUVE EGLISE.	Capt Thorlum + Lt Tyler start at 4 am on 5 days leave. RHQ

Army Form C. 2118.

WAR DIARY
or
INTELLIGENCE SUMMARY
(Erase heading not required.)

Instructions regarding War Diaries and Intelligence Summaries are contained in F. S. Regs., Part II. and the Staff Manual respectively. Title pages will be prepared in manuscript.

Hour, Date, Place	Summary of Events and Information	Remarks and References to Appendices
LINDENHOEK + NEUVE EGLISE WEDNESDAY - JAN. 6TH	A distinct improvement in the weather - a good day. Hardly any interval scuds; very little firing on either side.	2Lt. J.E. CLAYTON joins Bde. Hdgrs 15.1.2.34.
THURSDAY JAN 7TH	Bad weather again - raining & snowing most of the day. Just a few rounds fired by guns at NEUVE EGLISE. Nothing else happened. 122 Bty changed with 124 Battery after dark. 122 being now back at LINDENHOEK.	RAS
FRIDAY JAN. 8TH	Raining all night & very stormy; country still more flooded. A very quiet day.	RAS
SATURDAY JAN 9TH	Fine till 10:30 am - steady rain after that for the rest of the day. Only 9 rounds fired by the Bde group altogether.	RAS 122 & 124 Btys change positions afterwards.
SUNDAY JAN 10TH	Dry and fine. Combined shoot at 3 different hostile dumps. The day on enemy's trenches in our front & on roads & farms close to them. Very little hostile fire in reply; nothing else happened.	RAS
MONDAY JAN 11TH	A really good fine sunny day. Our gun fire considerably more than usual, as the light is good, and the enemy's guns are particularly active too. Hostile shrapnel done by one NEUVE EGLISE guns. 122 & 124 change positions.	Col. Sandys goes to England on 6 days leave in the evening. RAS

Army Form C. 2118.

WAR DIARY
or
INTELLIGENCE SUMMARY
(Erase heading not required.)

Instructions regarding War Diaries and Intelligence Summaries are contained in F. S. Regs., Part II. and the Staff Manual respectively. Title pages will be prepared in manuscript.

Hour, Date, Place	Summary of Events and Information	Remarks and References to Appendices
LINDENHOEK. + NEUVE-EGLISE		
JAN. 12 - TUESDAY.	Cold Heavy day. Howitzer Section (in square T.10.B.) got heavily shelled in the morning by German 6 inch How., but no damage is done. LINDENHOEK ridge E.100-7020 also shelled during the day. Very little fire by us.	Sect. of 65th Bde R.F.A. atta 28th Bde R.F.A. Ref. "Belgium & France" B senio sheet 28 S.W. (new square) R.H.S.
JAN 13 - WEDNESDAY	Warm, but steady rain practically all day. Thick fog. The Brigade group fires only 20 rounds. Quiet on our front, but heavy firing on some distance to the North all day.	R.H.S.
JAN 14 - THURSDAY	Fine day, with good light. We do a lot of registering during the day. 65th Battery do a good shoot on point 76, and 18 pounders fire on enemy's trenches all along our front. German artillery quiet. Windy night.	2/Lt. TYLER in the Inf. Trenches, observing. 2/Lt. BUXTON to England on 5 days leave. 2/Lt. R.W.L.FELLOWES joins the Bde. & is attached to 12th Bty.
JAN 15 - FRIDAY	Fine - light v. fair. Nothing of interest to record.	R.H.S.
JAN 16 - SATURDAY	Almost no firing by our guns. Germans shell NEUVE EGLISE & backward dressing station. 13th Bde take over our area from 15th Inf Bde in the afternoon. Raining after dark.	R.H.S.

Army Form C. 2118.

WAR DIARY
or
INTELLIGENCE SUMMARY

(Erase heading not required.)

Instructions regarding War Diaries and Intelligence
Summaries are contained in F. S. Regs., Part II.
and the Staff Manual respectively. Title pages
will be prepared in manuscript.

Hour, Date, Place	Summary of Events and Information	Remarks and References to Appendices
LINDENHOEK and NEUVE-EGLISE JAN. 17. — SUNDAY.	Quiet day. Cold and looking like snow. A few rounds fired + occasional shells at enemy's trenches from WULVERGHEM.	RJS
JAN. 18 — MONDAY.	Some snow in the night + snow fell on all day. Weather v. bad. Germans bombard our trenches heavily from 10.30 am till 2pm when their fire slackens. All our guns and now under Divisional Artillery open fire in return. Quiet for the rest of the day after 2pm.	*Lt Col D.I.A.H. on leave 4th Col Sankey returns from leave in meantime. Maj J. Griffith A.V.C. returns leave to England in accordance with Armies Order No.
JAN. 19 — TUESDAY.	Foggy day. New forward observing stations for Neuve-Eglise guns lined for the first time, and some regulation done by 12e Batterie. No one else fires and enemy quiet. Thaw.	RJS
JAN. 20. — WEDNESDAY.	Rather foggy and cold. Only 2 rounds fired altogether.	RJS
JAN. 21 — THURSDAY	Rain in the night and rain till and after during the morning. Only a few rounds fired. 112 By (NEUVE-EGLISE) champagne in battn. after tea.	RJS
JAN. 22 — FRIDAY.	Frost with ice during the night. Fine bright sunny day. Sky full of aeroplanes. Only a little shooting of the ordinary nature done, as day is rather foggy for observation.	RJS

Army Form C. 2118.

WAR DIARY
or
INTELLIGENCE SUMMARY

(Erase heading not required.)

Instructions regarding War Diaries and Intelligence Summaries are contained in F. S. Regs., Part II. and the Staff Manual respectively. Title pages will be prepared in manuscript.

Hour, Date, Place	Summary of Events and Information	Remarks and References to Appendices
LINDENHOEK – NEUVE-EGLISE		
JAN. 23. Saturday.	Fairly hard frost during the night. Another fine day, inclined to be foggy. A good deal of firing on both sides of our area, but our immediate front is pretty quiet. Forward observing officers again sent in trenches parallel to WULVERGHEM-MESSINES road, and some careful registration done by 122 Battery.	× L. Clery R.A.C.
JAN 24. SUNDAY.	Foggy. Impossible to see. Quiet day. Nil rounds fired.	
JAN. 25. MONDAY.	Cold, frosty – foggy. Nil rounds fired.	R.A.C. × Searchlights seen over our line from the German lines. Rear of Neuve Eglise Highland.
JAN. 26. TUES DAY.	Frost & ice in the night – cold day. Nothing much happens. Great preparations in the evening by the Infantry for possible surprise attack when the next 24 hours intolerable the Kaiser's birthday.	R.A.C. Major & A Tiltonville R. Barty has been awarded a D.C.M. R.A. Bty's guns at Lindenhoek moved back 350 yds W. (L6 T.3.0.) the early morning. R.A.C.
JAN 27. WEDNESDAY	Very cold. Weak, bitter day. Comparatively quiet though there is a certain amount of Artillery fire during the earlier part of the day. Forward observing officer again out for 122 Bty. (now permanently attached to remain at NEUVE-EGLISE)	× L. Tyler R.A.C.
JAN 28. THURSDAY.	Hard snow – cold – frost. A few rounds fired twenty registration and a few rounds Graft 76. Nothing of any interest occurred.	R.A.C.

Army Form C. 2118.

WAR DIARY
or
INTELLIGENCE SUMMARY
(Erase heading not required.)

Instructions regarding War Diaries and Intelligence Summaries are contained in F. S. Regs., Part II. and the Staff Manual respectively. Title pages will be prepared in manuscript.

Hour, Date, Place	Summary of Events and Information	Remarks and References to Appendices
LINDENHOEK & NEUVE EGLISE		
JAN 28. THURSDAY.	A hard & cold day with frost. Afterwards fired strength registration which was carried on thro' changing weather, the guns being founded shot to shot. Afterwards or Pl. 76.	P.H.S.
JAN 29 FRIDAY.	Hard frost - very cold indeed. Summing morning. 122 B.y. did a good deal of accurate registration. Return enemy inferred import. A little snow about 8.30 pm	Major Crofton informed Havre hit in a. Returned Havre ke to duty. 2 other casualties. P.H. 2/2 Can. Div. P.H.S.
JAN 30 SATURDAY.	Still cold. A little fine snow. Snow during the night. A very quiet day in every way.	P.H.S.
JAN 31 SUNDAY.	Some frost in the night. Snow in the morning, and light intermitable for shortime. Enemy's artillery fairly active between groups, do no rifle or M.G. fire at all during the day.	P.H.S.

R.H. Sudden Lieut. 28 n Gd. Dr.

Copy of letter from Tom
Jan. 6. 1915

Yesterday our Battery Sept.
Major Beach late of 123. gave
the officers & N.C.O's here an
account of his experiences. I
got hold of him afterwards
but did not get anything much
from him, partly because
there was not much time &
partly because I don't think
he really remembers much &
it is mostly reconstructed
from talks about it afterwards.
He was badly wounded himself
that day & must have had
an awful time, 5 days on a

wagon before a doctor saw him — a considerable distance. He takes
Major Somalen officer (Lieut) — that R. Shot saw a chance of
him with 10 China & it felt getting a gun away & decided
drawing. He luckily escaped to take the risks ought to have been
complication. rewarded i.e. 123+124 guns
he says he saw R. Shot his if have to smashed & attempt to get
the Turks. They had to come them away — wheels one ski: led
up a white road in full view 122 was — a slight loss of men
of the enemy & then turn M. out horses (24 feet or to Major S. J &
have, it was just as they turn was two B. their guns got
that the Germans opened on them escaped & say forward first out
with shrapnel shell he said of the enemy fire & then getting
the Germans had the range absolutely away. I gathered that the
he doesn't know anything about laties a railway embankment
a machine gun but says they near Huristi condemns. All were
may have been one on the of spent the night dying guns into
right flank. Where R. was. he in the Monday the Germans coming
was in the Egypt and saw it from in $\frac{1}{2}$ a word some 1200 yds on

in front in mass, marching as
though on parade — they opened fire
at 1000 yds & could see great
holes being made in their ranks,
finally they got to a canal in front
& began putting pontoons across
which were continually shot away
— finally they got across & the
28th Bgde had to retreat. I think
they were retreating all Tuesday
being covered by the guns of some
other Brigade & on Tuesday night
they got into some billets & were
told they would have a days rest,
but early Wed: morning they were
roused up & had to take up
their position, which owing to
the force of circumstances was
not very good & on Wed: began

firing at 500 yds before they abandoned their guns, while the rest of the Division were retreating. He confirms that they were very heavily outnumbered both by guns & infantry & speaks very highly of the Yorkshire Light Infantry as saving the situation at present Loos.

23rd Marched 5 A.M. reached DOUR
1 P.M. halted 2 hrs. Went on & occupied
position at BOUSSU BOIS. dug in.
Sent off 2 sections at 7.15 P.M. to support
13 & 14 Inf Bdes. Returned 12 midnight not
24th required. Principal task given to battery was to
shell BOUSSU if enemy advanced that
way. There had been heavy fighting on the
N-edge of the village on 23rd. Thank God the
Prussians did not advance this way the
village was full of women & children.
    Heavy fighting on right & left all morning
nothing happened on our front.
    Retired about 12.30 P.M. were lucky to get
away, retreat much exposed & was heavily
shelled just after we left.
    Took up various positions to cover retirement
but did not shoot. Bivouacked at ST WAAST
LAVALLEE at 8 P.M.
25 Marched at 2.40 A.M. to ROUMENT at
3 P.M.

A2
A96

121/4043

5th Division

28th Bde R.F.A.

Vol VII 1 - 28.2.15

Army Form C. 2118.

WAR DIARY
or
INTELLIGENCE SUMMARY.
(Erase heading not required.)

Instructions regarding War Diaries and Intelligence Summaries are contained in F. S. Regs., Part II. and the Staff Manual respectively. Title pages will be prepared in manuscript.

Hour, Date, Place	Summary of Events and Information	Remarks and references to Appendices
	War Diary 26th Brigade R.F.A. February 1915 Vol. VII	Wardup *Lieut. Colonel,* *Commanding 28th Brigade R.F.A.*

Army Form C. 2118.

WAR DIARY
or
INTELLIGENCE SUMMARY.
(Erase heading not required.)

Instructions regarding War Diaries and Intelligence Summaries are contained in F.S. Regs., Part II. and the Staff Manual respectively. Title pages will be prepared in manuscript.

Hour, Date, Place		Summary of Events and Information	Remarks and references to Appendices
LINDENHOEK & NEUVE EGLISE			
MONDAY	FEB 1st	Snow & frost with clear intervals. 124's Bty registered from KEMMEL & 65th Bty towards obs. stn. N34 points in vicinity of KRUISSTRAAT CAB'T.	
TUESDAY	" 2nd	Thaw set in with rain. Telephone communication with Infantry Trenches tested practically.	
WEDNESDAY	" 3rd	Rain on & off. Telephone communication tested, nothing unknown.	
THURSDAY	" 4th	Fine day. A few rounds on O/a. A few rounds on O/a.	
FRIDAY	" 5th	Beautiful Spring Day. Nothing unusual on our fronts.	
SATURDAY	" 6th	Fair & cold but due day. A little more firing than usual in support of Infantry.	
SUNDAY	" 7th	Dull day but no rain. No firing at all on the Brigade front.	
MONDAY	" 8th	Fine day, very clear. Visibility in O/a shelled by H/S 80 & 122.	15th & H/S 80. & 122.
TUESDAY	" 9th	Fine morning wet afternoon. Very little doing.	from 13th H/S
WEDNESDAY	" 10th	Fine day but hazy. Area received. Brigade relieved	
		124th M.O.W.E. 122 takes position at LINDENHOEK. 124th goes into to position in front of 65th & good road by 12.30 P.M. Dec 14th 1812.	2/Lt F.H.B. Bond H.F. Hall
THURSDAY	" 11th	Have See turned up with 122 's Bty gave them a few rounds for luncheon	joined & posted to 122 & 12.30 Bty
FRIDAY	" 12th	Very little shooting. Chung Table place at 6.30 p.m.	
SATURDAY	" 13th	Battery registered from no position when lights permitted	the respectively
SUNDAY	" 14th	Hazy & no moon. Fine afternoon. A little shooting. Rain oscil day. Battery continues where put—	

[signature]

Army Form C. 2118.

WAR DIARY
or
INTELLIGENCE SUMMARY.
(Erase heading not required.)

Instructions regarding War Diaries and Intelligence
Summaries are contained in F.S. Regs., Part II.
and the Staff Manual respectively. Title pages
will be prepared in manuscript.

Hour, Date, Place		Summary of Events and Information	Remarks and references to Appendices
LINDENHOEK			
MONDAY	FEB 15th	Morning cold. Afternoon sleet & snow. Batteries registered when possible	HQ
TUESDAY	" 16th	Fine sporting day. All four Batteries continued registering.	"
WEDNESDAY	" 17th	Cold wet day. Batteries continued registering when possible.	"
THURSDAY	" 18th	Fine spring day again. Batteries continued registering. Test messages sent from Infantry Trenches.	HQ
FRIDAY	" 19th	Fine day, more registration by Batteries	Honours
SATURDAY	" 20th	122nd & 124th Batteries fired along the ∞ allotted zones, returning young officer & in reply to German fire. Mont Kemmel message. 124th Bty went into reserve. 123rd came into action (6 guns). 65th Bty withdrawn	Lt. Col. W.R.M. Santey C.M.G. Lt. Col. G.H. Senter D.S.O. Lt. Col. F.C. Campbell C.B. Mentioned in Dispatches Lt. Col. W.R.M. Santey Lt. Col. G.H. Sanders Major G.R. Kinnaman
MONDAY	" 21st	Very foggy morning, dense in the afternoon. 65th Bty marched out North to join 28th Division. On afternoon 122nd Bty marched behind Pt 76 for a section of Field Guns which were giving trouble in KEMMEL Heavy fog all day. We only fire four rounds.	Capt. J. Thedrum Capt. Lord Alfred Browne Lt. R.H. Stadlet Q.M.S. Briggs H.Q. No 621702
TUESDAY	" 22nd		
WEDNESDAY	" 23rd	Frost at night, fog all the morning, cleared up afternoon 123rd Bty fired at Templeux	Sgt. Lee C.H. No 15806 Gnr Squires. A.H. No 25869
THURSDAY	" 24th	Frost at night. Snow all morning, mixed with rain & clear in afternoon 123rd Bty ordered to turn on to German trenches in front of Sector D. but could not fire till 4 pm owing to light. Snipers battery on Infantry 122nd Bty	HQ on 23rd k following information for a [illegible] Lt.R.Powell 22nd Bty
FRIDAY	" 25th	turned on to their German trenches. Shewed all night but thaw sets in under own. 123rd Bty fired at German trenches hoping to catch reliefs on the move between	2nd Lt. S.N. Burgess 124th Bty Lt. Capt. Bowles 124th Bty 2nd Lt. PSC Campbell Johnston 124th Bty
SATURDAY	" 26th	3.15 AM & 3.50 AM. During the day 122nd & 123rd Bties fired in course Frost at night. Fog all morning. Fine afternoon. Bty fired as usual. 122nd got on to Trench mortar about 4.30 pm 124th Bty's unoccupied	HQ All from 14th Divl Artn
SUNDAY	" 27th	position shelled heavily with light field guns shrapnel. Owing to news of supposed German attack 124th Bty ordered into action 122nd Bty withdrew into reserve. Battery fired as usual. This day. No attack.	HQ 15th Bde relieved by 84th " commanded
MONDAY	" 28th	Very fine morning, cloudy afternoon. Battery fired perfect eight. Battery fires an usual.	by Brig.gen. Bowles.

28th Bde: R.F.A.

Vol VIII 1 – 31.3.15
5th Division

Army Form C. 2118.

WAR DIARY
or
INTELLIGENCE SUMMARY.

(Erase heading not required.)

Hour, Date, Place	Summary of Events and Information	Remarks and references to Appendices
	War Diary of 28th Brigade R.F.A. 5th Division Vol. VIII From 1st March — 31st March 1915.	

Instructions regarding War Diaries and Intelligence Summaries are contained in F.S. Regs., Part II. and the Staff Manual respectively. Title pages will be prepared in manuscript.

WAR DIARY or INTELLIGENCE SUMMARY.

(Erase heading not required.)

Army Form C. 2118

Instructions regarding War Diaries and Intelligence Summaries are contained in F.S. Regs., Part II and the Staff Manual respectively. Title pages will be prepared in manuscript.

Hour, Date, Place	Summary of Events and Information	Remarks and references to Appendices
March 1st LINDENHOEK	Fine morning till 11am. Cloudy & cold after, with minor snow in the afternoon. 9.30 a.m. 124 Bty. our gunners taking out items free of them, light weigh at this time. Great communication extended between Battalion & their respective Battalion H.Q. Battalion fired no usual interzone fire day 123rd & 124th Btys fired on registration.	J/L
2nd	Pt 76.	J/L
3rd	Fine day. Batteries continued registering in intervals on Pt 76 from 7.15–7.45 AM 125th Bty light task in the morning but 80 rounds difficulty 4.7". fired on farms in N36d with 4.2" fired on Pt 76 & 124 Bty did a little wire cutting 4pm. 123rd & 124th Batteries continue registration. 124 also fired	J/L
4th		J/L
5th	on German trenches in front of KRUISSTRAAT CABT. in our own trenches opposite this front were being shelled. Fine day.	J/L
6th	123rd Bty change position 2 sections brought up to LINDENHOEK RIDGE 200 yards south of 122nd Bty position the other 124 Bty position, weather good. 122nd Bty came out of reserve in the afternoon. Both Batteries registered them glass the day. 124 Bty from just over Pt 76 on cossan there was very slight FRENCHMANS FARM shelled & set on fire	J/L

(73969) W4141–463. 400,000. 9/14. H.&J. Ltd. Forms/C. 2118/10.

WAR DIARY or INTELLIGENCE SUMMARY.

Army Form C. 2118.

(Erase heading not required.)

Instructions regarding War Diaries and Intelligence Summaries are contained in F.S. Regs., Part II and the Staff Manual respectively. Title pages will be prepared in manuscript.

Hour, Date, Place	Summary of Events and Information	Remarks and references to Appendices
LINDENHOEK		
March 7th	Reconnu. section 123rd Bty joined up. Our wire cutting Battery reported on about wire cutting. Zones with other officers in the forward trenches during the morning. Weather good. At 3.30 p.m. a combined shoot of 5th Division Gunners on Pt 76 ridge.	11th 83½ 2nd (Late eleventh) Bty. ... in sector C.O.E.
8th	Frosty morning. Batteries registering front rank and the weakened 200 yards above normal range to Spanbroekmolen. 3. P.M. Batteries carried out a wire cutting programme having a prearranged. Fine day at 8.10 A.M. Batteries carried out wire cutting as ordered by 5th Divl Arty. Fuzes regular & shoot appeared good.	He rejoined after seeing all officers of 14th Division New Army. He registered after as thought. They were 122 Bty Lt R. Poore 123 ~ 2nd Lt S.N. Bagley 2nd Lt C.A. ETT Brookes 124
9th	Fine day. From 7.30 A.M. the Batteries commenced a wire cutting shoot on the entanglements on Pt 76 with apparent good results. Infantry in two different trenches reported wire cut in front of them. Fuzes regular, shoot lasted one hour. Our wire cutting young officers were introduced as a gun returned from I.O.M.	2nd Lt R.S.C. Campbell Johnston 124 on the morning of the 9th. The following officers came to us from home to temporarily instruction 2nd Lt R.E. Costigan after 122 P.R. Pearce 123 W.E. Bardsley 124 J. McKenzie 124
10th	the afternoon young officers were introduced a gun returned from I.O.M.	

WAR DIARY or INTELLIGENCE SUMMARY.

Army Form C. 2118.
PECKHAM

(Erase heading not required.)

Hour, Date, Place	Summary of Events and Information	Remarks and references to Appendices
LINDENHOEK March 11th	Very bad light all day. In the afternoon a large wire cutting shoot was carried out under difficult circumstances. 124 Bty firing 120 rounds each. The forward observing officer of 123 gave a very good report of the shoot stating that the greater majority of their shells fell in the wire showing considerable damage to parapets.	
12th	An attack had been arranged for the morning but at 7.50 AM light was too bad for us to fire. The mist did not lift till 2 p.m. as wire was 9.30 p.m. registration commenced by 122 & 123 Batteries. Trench mortars were fired from N.W. of the 124 Bty. light was good tie to SPANBROEK Mill this went down again. Between 3.30 & 4.5 p.m. very heavy fire was maintained by 5th & 3rd Division artillery on wire & front trenches. At 4.10 p.m. when the enemy was tried to take place. We increased our range on to second line trenches facing S.E. & west of & keep. Wire cut by 122 marked X & cut by 123 V.8.Z.a 2 objective marked O-E on sketch in margin	

WAR DIARY or INTELLIGENCE SUMMARY.

Army Form C. 2118.

Hour, Date, Place	Summary of Events and Information	Remarks and references to Appendices
March 12th (cont)	From 3.50 to 4.10 pm 124 Battery had been enfilading main trench with a heavy rate of fire. At 4.10 pm they switched to the north & continued firing at the trench to the south of their first objective. Between 4.10 & 4.25 pm. 222 Battery recommenced a rapid rate of fire after which it slackened off till 4.55 when owing to a heavy fusilade of gun fire was intensified until the rifle fire slackened off at 5.10 pm. a slow rate of fire was then maintained till dark. The fire of 122 & 123 Batteries on the wire was not accurate. In the last five minutes of the 123 Bty were firing from 4.0 to 4.5 pm, fired 270 rounds from four guns two of which were out of action for the last two minutes. About 4.45 pm. the gunners obtained 124 Bty position with 8.2" Howitzer one man was wounded. Gr W. Kerrigan. 60987. Throughout the day there were two forward observing officers 2Lt Clark drawing from F trench & 2Lt Curtis from a mined bank behind E trench. HQs Communication with 2nd Curtis was ... ... Kit with Hepburn was good	

WAR DIARY or INTELLIGENCE SUMMARY.

Army Form C. 2118.

(Erase heading not required.)

Instructions regarding War Diaries and Intelligence Summaries are contained in F.S. Regs., Part II and the Staff Manual respectively. Title pages will be prepared in manuscript.

Hour, Date, Place	Summary of Events and Information	Remarks and references to Appendices
LINDENHOEK		
June 13th	The night was better today & the Barrage had been patched. Reconnoitre was conducted at 9 am. At 8/15 am a report was received from 2/ Antigens found in the barn behind E1 trench who went to find out what to find to our infantry in German front line trench. This was reported to Divl Artillery also brand in to schaafbert. At 2.15 pm 122 Bty registered on lines at 123. Bty at 4 pm did the same. Forward observation Officer reports fire very accurate. In the evening Bty returned to their former defensive zone.	In the evening Battle which had moved Hqrs forward for the attack returned to DRANOUTRE.
14th	Very bad sight again in the morning. A good light in the afternoon. Batteries registered. 122 Bty also fired at a point in the German parapet where Set Coys located a machine gun during the attack.	
15th	No firing all day. Bde under orders to move South of NEUVE EGLISE attn on instructions of 32nd Hy Bde (3rd Division) Bde & Battery commanders came out to take over our positions.	

A.9 H.& f.ide. Forms/C. 2118/10.

Army Form C. 2118.

WAR DIARY
or
INTELLIGENCE SUMMARY.
(Erase heading not required.)

Instructions regarding War Diaries and Intelligence Summaries are contained in F.S. Regs., Part II. and the Staff Manual respectively. Title pages will be prepared in manuscript.

Hour, Date, Place	Summary of Events and Information	Remarks and references to Appendices
LINDENHOEK		
January 16th	Weather dull but fine. 122 Bty fired at German trenches on Pt. 76. One man of 123 Bty wounded.	× Gnr Williams W. 9701 on 23rd
17th	11 a.m. "Cook's" arrived at Lou. At 2 p.m. the move was cancelled for to-day.	Lt H.F. Hall Gnrs 47469 Sgt Keene H.J. 31958 Gnr A. Banks. proceeded to BERTHEN to the School of Instruction for Trench Mortars. H.F.G.
18th	Light wind had all day. Batteries did not shoot.	
19th	Light wind again in the morning turning to driving sleet in the afternoon. Batteries did not open fire.	On 22nd Capt R.B. Miller left to join the Reserve Division. H.F.G.
20th	Snow during the night. Light wind good afternoon. 11 a.m. Batteries fired a few rounds to test Range, was found to be 100 yards longer than normal & cometated about 14 points + a 150	
21st	Perfect bright & very fine day. 124 Bty registered trenches north of SPANBROEK MOLEN	In the afternoon of 22nd the following officers left for Home.
22nd	124 Bty registered on trenches south of the Mill again the light being good. The day The brigade assumed a new front corresponding to the front of the 84th Inf. Bde. Bdy stretching from PECKHAM to the cutting on the WULVERGHEM-KRUISSTRAAT road. A fine day. 124 battery registered points in their new zone.	on a month of 22/23rd The following officers arrived for a tour as follows: Lt C.H.E. Wilson ack 122 2 Lt bt S. Amers 123 2 Lt R. Nicholson 124 C.M.G. H.F.G. Lt Col E. Mackworth ack ack Bourgnaties on the 23rd
23rd	Snow has fallen in the afternoon 122 & 123 Bty fired a few rounds in their zones.	

WAR DIARY
or
INTELLIGENCE SUMMARY.

(Erase heading not required.)

Army Form C. 2118.

Instructions regarding War Diaries and Intelligence Summaries are contained in F.S. Regs., Part II and the Staff Manual respectively. Title pages will be prepared in manuscript.

Hour, Date, Place	Summary of Events and Information	Remarks and references to Appendices
LINDENHOEK		
March 24th	Rain on & off all day. 122 & 124 Batteries did a little registering.	W. Major Reed R.A. acting for 5 days previous to 13th Bty through 25th
25th	Cold wet day. 122 fired a few rounds at "Snipers College" from which Germans have been firing at our Infantry.	H.Q.
26th	C.O.s fine day. Light wind. Range finder gallery. 124 registered.	H.Q.
27th	All three Batteries continued registering.	D/C
28th	Light magnificent again. Batteries registered & checked night lines.	H.Q.
29th	At 8.30 pm at request of Infantry 124 Bty fired on Germans. Their noise which had been causing some anxiety hitherto died out when.	
29th	Very cold fine day. 124 Bty fired a few rounds.	H.Q.
30th	Again very cold fine day. 122 & 124 Btys did a little registering.	H.Q.
31st	Fine day slightly warmer. 123 & 124 Btys did a little registering. 122 Bty did not fire. O.C. 123 Bty reconnoitred positions near FRENCHMAN'S FARM.	H.Q. Lt. C. Beddows R.A.M.C. promoted Captain 29/3/15

M Anduff
Lieut. Colonel,
Commanding 28th Brigade R.F.A

121/5"321

5th Division

15th Bde R.F.A.

Vol IX   April 1915

WAR DIARY or INTELLIGENCE SUMMARY

Army Form C. 2118.

Hour, Date, Place	Summary of Events and Information	Remarks and references to Appendices
LINDENHOEK April 1st	Very fine warm day. At 9.30 A.M. 122 opened fire on KRUISSTRAAT EMBT. 124 Bty fired on machine gun emplacement South of SPANBROEKMOLEN in German trenches. 122 & 123 did some registering as night zones were being altered. 122 & 124 Bty did a little registering. At 1.20 p.m. 124 fired in reply to Germans shelling F sector. A very fine warm day.	
2nd		
3rd	A cold wet day. 123 Bty did not fire. 122 Bty registered. 124 Bty fired at a machine gun emplacement fired by suspect patrol last night on the road South of PECKHAM.	
4th	Wet cold day. Batteries did not fire.	
5th	Wet cold day again. Batteries did not fire.	
6th	122 & 124 Btoes fired a little along their front. 124 Bty fired again along Kemmel in the German were wiring over infantry. A cold day.	
7th	A cold wet day. At 1 a.m. two actions were withdrawn from each of our Batteries to their places taken by 1st, 2nd & 3rd Btns of the 2nd Staffordshire Bde. 1st Bty registered in the morning along the front of 14 & 15 ridges as far as the right of E1 Mgr. 2nd Bty the front of E1 & E2. 3rd Bty registered in front of F2 & F4.	Germans fell up the left of the fourteen ridge towards E1 left during night of 2/3 rd. On the night of the 4th/5th the 3 & 4 2nd Bde began withdrawing from the trenches. The line & relief was Territorial Brigade. On the morning of the 5th the line & relief Bde took place. (wristband Bde) 122nd Bty was relieved by 2nd Bk. 123rd "" "" 1st "" 124th "" "" 3rd ""

Army Form C. 2118.

WAR DIARY
or
INTELLIGENCE SUMMARY.
(Erase heading not required.)

Hour, Date, Place	Summary of Events and Information	Remarks and references to Appendices
LINDENHOEK Thursday 8th April	Blustery and showery day. Busy arranging about move of Brigade. One section of each Battery marched off to YPRES at 8 p.m.	Sections are under orders of O.C. 31st Bde RFA
Friday 9th April	Cloudy uncertain looking day. Nothing of interest occurred. 28th Bde Hqrs hands over command of LINDENHOEK front Batteries march and marches for YPRES at 6 p.m. and are in action ready to fire by 12.30 a.m. O.C. 28th Bde takes over command of "Left Group" at that hour. (from DRANOUTRE at 6 p.m.)	
YPRES Saturday 10th April	Fine day. No shooting done except registering. Positions of Batteries as per margin. Left Group consists of 26th Bde RFA, 15th Bde RFA (62nd + 150th Bty) and 130 How. Battery RFA	Bde Hqrs – I.6.3 3.1. 122 Bty – I.9.a. 1.1 123 Bty – I.9.c. 2.5 124 Bty – I.8.d. 7.6 Wagon lines 1 Bde Am Col Wissen & 1 mile South of PLUMERTHOUSE. Capt G Gillman left sick to be attached to the 2nd North Midland Bde at DRAN- OUTRE.
Sunday 11th April	Very good day. Aeroplanes of 15th sides very active. 15th Inf Bde now holding our front, having taken over from 13th Inf Bde last night.	2nd Lieut A. ELLISON RFC joins the Bde. Gr Kenshaw 122 Bty severely wounded while with "R" Clay at night.

(73989) W4141—463. 400,000. 9/14. H.&J.Ltd. Forms/C. 2118/10.

Army Form C. 2118.

WAR DIARY
or
INTELLIGENCE SUMMARY.
(Erase heading not required.)

Instructions regarding War Diaries and Intelligence Summaries are contained in F.S. Regs., Part II and the Staff Manual respectively. Title pages will be prepared in manuscript.

Hour, Date, Place	Summary of Events and Information	Remarks and references to Appendices
YPRES Monday April 12th	Fine, good day. Nothing of interest to relate. "Zeppelin" flew over Ypres about 10.30 pm, and drops bombs from VLAMERTINGHE to OUDERDOM, each if road between those two places. Trying to hit wagonlines & Infantry huts along two line.	
TUESDAY April 13th	Good day, but cold in the morning. Quiet on our front.	2/Lt Tyler 122 Bty relieved from sick leave in the morning. On 15th No 71872 "Cpt" J. Ormond 123 MGK wounded. Capt Lord Alfred Browne left to join Canadian Division. Lt E.C. Baldwin R.A.M.C. left to join 15th Field Ambulance. Lt Lt Gordon R.A.M.C. joined. On 16th No 45794 2/cRaw 122 RFA wounded.
WEDNESDAY April 14th THURSDAY April 15th	Fine stormy day brighter sunshine. Quiet on our front. Fine days, nothing doing on our front. Infantry on our front thought they were going to be attacked. Cold day & rainy. Bee-Wer in our front Batterys registered.	
FRIDAY April 16th	Pleasant warm day. Quiet on our front. Batteries registered for an attack on Hill 60. Cr There was humco reported with excellent results & range. Flown overhead. Cyclists found heavy fire but short of line with Hors (shells to etch heliographs.)	
SATURDAY April 17th	Coming up River Kents attacked a topp trees without any difficulty & commenced diggin at once. Getting kept up a rapid rate of fire on trenches to prevent the enemy from working our subway. Rapid rate of fire continued till 7.50 pm when a close rate was opened. Batteries continued a slow rate of fire all night with occasional bursts of rapid fire on the demands [?] of the Infantry.	Lt T.C. Tyler killed in the early hours of the 18th on top of Hill 60.

WAR DIARY
or
INTELLIGENCE SUMMARY.

(Erase heading not required.)

Army Form C. 2118.

YPRES

Hour, Date, Place	Summary of Events and Information	Remarks and references to Appendices
SUNDAY APRIL 18th	At 5 am the enemy counter-attacked & drove the K.O.S.B. back to western edge of hill, the enemy being 300 yards. K.O.S.B.'s hung on to new position. The Artillery supported them very fiercely. The enemy pressed the further gunette all morning being touched to reply by being shelled on further trenches & cutting. Our artillery replied on German trenches & cutting at 1 pm the K.O.S.B.'s were relieved by the Duke of Wellington's at 6 pm a bayonet charge was carried out by the Duke & K.O.Y.L.I. who retook the hill, artillery cooperating by firing on enemy but the Duke was relieved & in rear of the hill after the charge when we obtained off a first investigation two KOYLI's were left on Hill 60 night. Both wings of the infantry were in reserve in the neighbouring trenches & in railway cutting were introduced by shelter emitting a gas with a "blinding" effect, weather fine throughout	No. 82 85 Pte Davis J 12th Bty wounded

Army Form C. 2118.

WAR DIARY
or
INTELLIGENCE SUMMARY.
(Erase heading not required.)

Instructions regarding War Diaries and Intelligence Summaries are contained in F.S. Regs., Part II. and the Staff Manual respectively. Title pages will be prepared in manuscript.

Hour, Date, Place	Summary of Events and Information	Remarks and references to Appendices
YPRES		
MONDAY APRIL 19th	K.O.Y.L.I. were relieved by the East Surreys on Hill 60 & the day passed off quite quietly. Enemy spent it in trying as usual to impede our motion. At 9.30 a.m. Germans started a 5.7" bombardment which lasted about ½ hour. The Batteries fired on their zones in Infantry until 4.45 p.m. when they ceased fire having been at it since 6 p.m. the evening before. At 5.55 p.m. Germans bombarded the area eastward from the trenches to Ypres. S.O.S. sent up by a Battery there with Signal aeroplane flying also. Batteries fired on German Kaper front & their positions. The enemy shells were known to reach up to Hill 60 which was several times, all the time the weight of their commun: trenches was enough to quickly ease this on the enemy the right part of ancients. Weather good & warm. A lot of trouble all day with our Batteries firing short & into our own trenches the Bedfords & 38th Feuillers during the night were wounded whe relieved the East Surreys on Hill 60 & by this time by the enemy, two batteries were got to leave & it was tried down to the 4.7"	Killed in action No 64807 Dr Collier G.H. 122736 33059 Coy Sn Major F.E. 12893 55632 Btr Trueman Wounded No 46717 Sgt Haselwell 122646 20114 A.P.M. Hutchinson R 12258
TUESDAY 20th	relieved the East Surreys on Hill 60 & The Army passed the night the 3.15 p.m.	

WAR DIARY
or
INTELLIGENCE SUMMARY.

(*Erase heading not required.*)

Army Form C. 2118.

Instructions regarding War Diaries and Intelligence Summaries are contained in F.S. Regs., Part II. and the Staff Manual respectively. Title pages will be prepared in manuscript.

Hour, Date, Place	Summary of Events and Information	Remarks and references to Appendices
YPRES TUESDAY APRIL 20th (Cont)	When the enemy commenced shelling Hill 60 & the batteries heavily & the countryside up to & into Ypres. At 6 pm the Germans made another attack on the railway but were repulsed, the attacks were kept up a heavy fire repeated with vigor till 8.25 pm when the fire was reduced to 100 rounds per hour for 4 hours. The was continuous fire more or less between when we resumed to cease firing. Weather fine	ff
WEDNESDAY APRIL 21st	Commenced firing again at 6 am to support infantry who were being harassed at 6.30 am. The Germans shelled our gun position for 40 minutes making life very unpleasant. Billets were shelled. 8.45 am & 9.45 am two casualties resulted. The rest of the day passed off quietly. Batteries firing occasionally answering to the infantry. Fine day after	Killed in action No 57124 Gr Safford H. 122nd Bt Wounded 40777 Gr McClusker 125th Bn JE
THURSDAY APRIL 22nd	a quiet day ate day tea 5.15 am began up work & Ypres began to be shelled with 4.2 cm. Very heavy fighting up north & we got news that a rear trench asphyxiates a gas being driven back	Wounded in action No 54200 Cpl Berry S.R. HQ 25869 Pr Squires A 124 By 9720 Pr Pitcon E.J. 124 By

WAR DIARY or INTELLIGENCE SUMMARY

Army Form C. 2118.

Hour, Date, Place	Summary of Events and Information	Remarks and references to Appendices
YPRES THURSDAY APRIL 22nd (Cont)	After the Canadian Bde & 2 Bft of 28th Division had been driven back as well. We fell back as far as WEILTJE but the Canadian Division, whole went on to its way up to relieve the 29th, was sent into counter attack & held up the German advance. At 11 pm Teurions were ordered up to an advanced position just behind Ypres. in case we were forced to retire. They arrived at 2.15 a.m. & took by. The Pont de Drowsde was the first objective of the 42 guns after one or two horse ones into the Town & then they turned on the Pont de Guilain to try & cut off all reinforcements. After dark the larger guns ceased firing on Ypres but a gun was trained on the Plenin Gate & fired down the road all night at intervals of 3-5 minutes but did very little damage. Our Batteries fired on & off during the night.	HR
FRIDAY APRIL 23rd	At 10 am Bde HdQrs moved into the carpenter's in the ramparts, our front was fairly quiet all the morning being fighting going on north & Ypres was shelled unremittingly from south, East & from Klein Wytschaete Batteries did no tire during the morning. Germans kept up a constant shelling of Ypres & the roads from & to, and they shelled round H.Q. breaking the wires constantly. 124 Bty was shelled for about ½ hour & 122 & 123 Btys got shells	HR

Army Form C. 2118.

WAR DIARY
or
INTELLIGENCE SUMMARY.
(Erase heading not required.)

Instructions regarding War Diaries and Intelligence Summaries are contained in F.S. Regs., Part II and the Staff Manual respectively. Title pages will be prepared in manuscript.

Hour, Date, Place	Summary of Events and Information	Remarks and references to Appendices
YPRES		
~~SAT~~ FRIDAY APRIL 23rd (con't)	into their positions and off all day. All Btys fired throughout the afternoon in our front.	122 R.F.A. completed new position West of Railway 1130.
SATURDAY APRIL 24th	About 7 ay- 2 German aeroplanes flew very low over Ypres & our Bde H.Q. a most daring act. H.Q. was moved to round the Church of St JACQUES first into the door of the Convent, because at 8.30 am a 17" shell hit the Church & crashed in the South Aisle completely setting fire to two R.E. Ammt carts filled with cordite & S.A.A. About 20 minutes later a second shell fell about the same place killing R.S.M. Fox & Bgr Appleton who was that stated out along the wires. The enemy also got a direct hit on the pontoon bridge across which was made from Wytschaete Batteries continued firing on our front throughout all day an intermittent fire. 124 Bty gun detached by gun shells by 5.9" Hows. during the morning & the other batteries had a nasty time too but no casualties. A quiet day as far as the Batteries were concerned.	Killed in action No 94423 R.S.M. Fox. A. 74239 Bgr Appleton F.M. H.Q. H.E. 124th Bty Bty would not take up position on march round west 1/14 a.s.c. Night of 24th/25th. JFC
SUNDAY APRIL 25th	Infantry quite happy in our front & did not much support. Ypres was shelled continuously from other ranges. Btys continued to work with week as they from a dug out by the side of the road. About 6 pm communication was also established from a home near the Dunderback Gate & Bde H.Q. were established here. a German he officer wounded towards a found way to our position	

Army Form C. 2118.

WAR DIARY
or
INTELLIGENCE SUMMARY.
(Erase heading not required.)

Instructions regarding War Diaries and Intelligence Summaries are contained in F.S. Regs., Part II. and the Staff Manual respectively. Title pages will be prepared in manuscript.

Hour, Date, Place	Summary of Events and Information	Remarks and references to Appendices
YPRES MONDAY APRIL 26th	Battle fires on & off all day along our front. Ypres was shelled all day as once before. Situation to the north urgent (sic). Yesterday counter attack against St Julien was unsuccessful but heavy reinforcements went up today & a further attack is to be made on our two afternoon East & West front of St Julien. Canadian division lost very heavily during the enemy attacks this pm. Germans captured a great many low-flying	
TUESDAY APRIL 27th	Our front fairly quiet all day. Batteries short a CWEB. 122 Bty position searched with 4.2" How and 124 Bty worked considerably along the Lahore Division counterattacked during the afternoon & made a certain amount of progress N.E. of St Julien R.O. failing to take the village Bde HQ moved forward to alongside 15th Cav Bde HQ near ZILLEBEKE TANK.	Killed in action 32609 Lt Capton w 12/4/15 61112 Gunr Williams " " " 90172 Dr Saunters C 12/3/15
WEDNESDAY APRIL 28th	Hot sunny day. Our front quiet but 122 Bty position got a lot of shelling from 4.2" Hows. Between 10am & 11am neighbourhood of Hill 60 cleared. Germans aeroplanes again very low	Lt H.W.H. ARMYTAGE H.Q. to hospital. Gunner Parlor H.Q. Lt B.G. von B MELLE wounded E.M.H.Q. from 124 R Bty Wounded 65432 Gr HILL T. 122/2/15

Army Form C. 2118.

WAR DIARY
or
INTELLIGENCE SUMMARY.
(Erase heading not required.)

Instructions regarding War Diaries and Intelligence Summaries are contained in F. S. Regs., Part II. and the Staff Manual respectively. Title pages will be prepared in manuscript.

Hour, Date, Place	Summary of Events and Information	Remarks and references to Appendices
YPRES		
THURSDAY APRIL 29TH	Very hot sunny day. A fourth section of 128th Bty registered German trenches in front of 36 trench. A party in reserve in dugouts in the Bund W. of ZILLEBEKE Tank shelled during afternoon. 123rd Bty moved during the night with remainder of guns to 1200 B.3. 124th Bty attached to 27th Bde R.F.A. a move to H.24.b.3.1. hereinwafters & Trench mortars fired at dummy trench.	Wounded 73387 Dr. EDWARDS T. Bty A.A. 127687 [?] HQ
FRIDAY APRIL 30TH	Very hot day again. Trench mortars opened fire in the morning & fired at A.11. 60. a neighbouring trenches shelled during the afternoon as we retaliated. Our German trenches cutting to ZWARTELEN Wood. Large German working parties seen in wood three hours were busy in at a tunnel out to ie Today trench counter attacks N. of Ypres & gained a little ground.	Wounded 46131 Gnr DEWEAR C.E. 12212 [?] 59706 Gr STEAD R. 65621 Dr. VALE P.H. 69533 Sgt EDMONDS E.W. Dr.[?] Dr.[?] W.[?] 63540 Gnr REDMOND C. 61981 ff WILES R.D. 53542 Bt MAYES A. Killed in action 66305 Gnr KENNY P.

H. Broughton
Lt R.F.A.

Wardif R.F.A.

121/5543

5th Division

28th Bde: R.F.A.

Vol X — 31.5.15

Army Form C. 2118.

WAR DIARY
or
INTELLIGENCE SUMMARY.
(Erase heading not required.)

Instructions regarding War Diaries and Intelligence Summaries are contained in F.S. Regs., Part II. and the Staff Manual respectively. Title pages will be prepared in manuscript.

Hour, Date, Place	Summary of Events and Information	Remarks and references to Appendices
CONFIDENTIAL	WAR DIARY. 28th Brigade R.F.A. 5th Division. From 1st to 31st May 1915. Vol. IX	

WAR DIARY
or
INTELLIGENCE SUMMARY
(Erase heading not required.)

Army Form C. 2118.

Hour, Date, Place	Summary of Events and Information	Remarks and References to Appendices
YPRES		
Saturday May 1st	Brigade not called on to shoot during the night. Hot sunny day, but a change in the weather. 122 & 123 Batteries fire at various times during the day to reply to German Artillery fire.	Bde. Am. Col. move their billets to H.2d.C.11. Remaining Section 122 Bty moves to new Bty position after dark.
About 7.30 pm	Bde. Am. Col. shelled in the morning in their billet. German shell trenches - own front with "Chlorine" shells and rapid bursts of fire are opened by us until 10.45 pm. No German attack made.	
Sunday May 2nd	Cloudy and rather cold day. Nothing of special interest occurs till 5.15 pm when heavy German bombardment and attack begins to the N.E. of Ypres. Attack continues till 7.30 p.m., and the neighbourhood of Batteries and our Batteries is shelled. Attack begins again at 9.15pm dies down by about 10pm. Batteries fire during the time.	
Monday May 3rd	Cold, but bright sunny day. 123 Bty fires with one gun on cross-roads behind German lines at 2.30 a.m. Heavy firing to our left. Guns asked to fire at 4.10	Lt. B.G. von Melle 2/Lt. J.C.A. Bell 2/Lt D.L. Tailyour [attached to Bde since 14th April
3.45 am	am but are stopped after three minutes. Over quiet day.	60538 Sgt EDMONDS E.W. 122 v. Bty. died of wounds received April 30th at BAILLEUL

WAR DIARY or INTELLIGENCE SUMMARY

Army Form C. 2118.

(Erase heading not required.)

Hour, Date, Place	Summary of Events and Information	Remarks and References to Appendices
YPRES Tuesday May 4th	Rain in the night. Cloudy morning + sunny afternoon. Batteries do not fire during the night, except 1 gun of 123 Bty. shelling everywhere. This being chiefly due to the Infantry line to the north of the 5th Division being withdrawn during the night to a shorter and straighter front. Enemy's artillery fire a certain amount on our front, to which we always replied.	HOLLEBEKE X road.
Wednesday May 5th	A quiet night. At 8.40 a.m. all batteries open a rapid fire on the front round Hill 60, as Germans have attacked and are using "gas".	
9 am	Learn that Germans have captured "60". Turn guns on the crest of the hill. Fire continued, gradually slackening, till 12.7pm when it is intensified again in response to call for assistance from O.C. Cheshires. Fire continues steadily again.	
2.45 pm	By this time 39, 42, 43, 45 & 46 trenches are all in German hands, but 39,42 are recaptured later.	
	Fire dies down afterwards about 6 p.m.	
8.50 pm	Rapid 10 minutes burst of fire - 36, 39, 40 trenches & gas Bombardment of 60 + trenches each side till 10 pm.	

Army Form C. 2118.

WAR DIARY
or
INTELLIGENCE SUMMARY.
(Erase heading not required.)

Instructions regarding War Diaries and Intelligence Summaries are contained in F.S. Regs., Part II and the Staff Manual respectively. Title pages will be prepared in manuscript.

Hour, Date, Place		Summary of Events and Information	Remarks and references to Appendices
YPRES			
May 5th (continued)	10 pm	Range of guns on 60 lengthened. Infantry attack	Gen. Wanliss O'Gowan, 13th A/13 Bde & O.C. attack.
	10.42	Fire slackened	
	11 pm	Rate of fire gradually reduced. Hear attack has failed, seems to concentrated German fire from all directions.	
THURSDAY MAY 6th – 10 am		Guns turned on to Hill 60. Fire gradually reduced till at 4 am batteries only fire occasional bursts.	
	9 am	Batteries left to fire slowly and steadily all day, to prevent the Germans doing much work consolidating their position. German artillery active during the morning, but quieter afternoon. Some rain during the middle of the day; very warm and close. Nothing special occurs in afternoon & evening. Showery weather.	13th Inf. Bde. is relieved by 13th Inf.Bde. afterdark.
FRIDAY MAY 7th – 2.30 am		Infantry attack "The Salient" (i.e. 43 as in trenches) at 2.30 am but no guns open till 2.45 am, when a fair rate of fire is kept up for a while, slackening till a disintegration when situation is more or less decided as war goes on & other. 1st Coy for Hill at 7 am – batteries fire to halt on how or so. Situation for a long while uncertain, but it soon appears that the attack on the salient have miscarried & failed. Salient shelled during the day – also Hill 60. Huggs, but quiet day. German artillery fairly active during evening.	

Army Form C. 2118.

WAR DIARY
or
INTELLIGENCE SUMMARY.
(Erase heading not required.)

Instructions regarding War Diaries and Intelligence Summaries are contained in F.S. Regs., Part II. and the Staff Manual respectively. Title pages will be prepared in manuscript.

Hour, Date, Place	Summary of Events and Information	Remarks and references to Appendices
YPRES		
SATURDAY MAY 8th	No further attack by us during the night, but 5 minute bursts of fire at 3, 3.30 & 3.40 am. Very heavy bombardment begins at 7am & continues all day; German attack on 27th & 28th Div. Cost just North of us. We fire a fair amount all day on our front. Quiet night.	
SUNDAY MAY 9th	Fine day with cold wind. Situation on 27th + 28th Divisions front doubtful, so our guns wagon teams are moved up to an advanced position for the day; situation is much easier by evening owing to lng British & French attack being launched south of LA BASSÉE in the morning. We fire a little on our front during the day.	Lieut J.W.H ARMYTAGE returns from sick leave. 57706 Cpl. R STEAD 123385 died at BAILLEUL of wounds recd 30/4/15 H.B Wounded No 34643 Pte Knight Q.T. 123324 H.B.
MONDAY MAY 10th	Fine day; warm. 27th Division again attacked during the day & trenches heavily shelled but they do not intend to fall back. Our own front was very quiet. Large fire in Ypres set on fire by incendiary shell.	
TUESDAY MAY 11th	Another fine warm day. 27th Division again attacked this morning but held their ground successfully. Our own front quiet. Our own Battery did not fire. Ypres is still burning fiercely.	

Army Form C. 2118.

WAR DIARY
or
INTELLIGENCE SUMMARY.
(Erase heading not required.)

Instructions regarding War Diaries and Intelligence Summaries are contained in F.S. Regs., Part II. and the Staff Manual respectively. Title pages will be prepared in manuscript.

Hour, Date, Place	Summary of Events and Information	Remarks and references to Appendices
YPRES		
WEDNESDAY MAY 12th	Present on our front each of French attack between LENS & ARRAS which is progressing satisfactorily. Our Batteries do a little shooting in neighbourhood of HILL 60 & 123rd Bty teams up a mountain gun on the hill, at 6.15 & 6.35 p.m. all Batteries made a demonstration for five minutes in front of 3rd Bde to worry the enemy. Ypres is still burning	Severely wounded 2Lt F.H.B. BOND 122nd Bty wounded returning from trench was killed — circumstances unknown. HC
THURSDAY MAY 13th	Rain on & off all day. Very quiet on our own front. Got news from the Seventh Division South, who had advanced considerably & have taken many prisoners & guns etc. Ypres & outlet burning in spite of rain all day.	Died of wounds 2Lt F.H.B. BOND 122nd Bty HC
FRIDAY MAY 14th	Fine day & very quiet on our own front. French made further progress.	HC
SATURDAY MAY 15th	Rained during the night & the day was mostly dull. Ypres fires had died down slightly. observation stations acted on own initiative to fall back to ZILLEBEKE Switch Line.	HC
SUNDAY MAY 16th	Our own front very quiet. Fine day again. Enemy were on the move. Very little to report on our own front which was Quiet. Ypres is completely gutted by fires.	HC
MONDAY MAY 17th	Rained on & off all day & during the night 122nd, 123rd Bties did a little registration. Our front quiet.	
TUESDAY MAY 18th	Country very wet again, rain on & off all day. 123rd Bty found action but goodwin knowing enemy position. 124th Bty registered.	2Lt T.R.O. Winwood from 22nd W.H. R. Rangers Div. Arty attached for instruction 13/6/15. HC

Army Form C. 2118.

WAR DIARY
or
INTELLIGENCE SUMMARY.
(Erase heading not required.)

Instructions regarding War Diaries and Intelligence Summaries are contained in F.S. Regs., Part II. and the Staff Manual respectively. Title pages will be prepared in manuscript.

Hour, Date, Place		Summary of Events and Information	Remarks and references to Appendices
YPRES			
WEDNESDAY MAY	19th	Weather a little better but still damp. 123rd Bty forward section again knocked about by enemy snipers on Hill 60 during the day. Bde HQrs shelled. 122 & 123 registered for a short time about 3 p.m.	Rewarded 57129 G:R HENRY S. Bde H.Q.
THURSDAY MAY	20th	Fine hot day. Very quiet day on our front.	HR
FRIDAY	21st	Very hot sticky day. Our own front quiet. About 5 p.m. the enemy commenced shelling one of the two remaining church towers in Ypres with a 5.9" gun which soon closed one up, made very good shooting.	HR
SATURDAY	22nd	A very hot day. Quiet on our front. This 60 was went in the morning. 123 Bty forward action knocked a lot out of the parapet about on Hill 60 also shelled the Barriques. In the evening 123 Bty took on the trenches in front of 35 trench. About 11 p.m. very heavy firing broke out north of Ypres & extended 20 minutes. There was also a bombardment at this hour.	HR
SUNDAY	23rd	A fine warm day with pleasant breeze. Our four very quiet all day. The Batteries did not fire till at 9 p.m. 123 Bty was turned on to attack hostile opposite 35 trench & fired four rounds which silenced the morning.	HR

(73989) W4141—463. 400,000. 9/14. H.&J.Ltd. Forms/C. 2118/10.

Army Form C. 2118.

WAR DIARY
or
INTELLIGENCE SUMMARY.
(Erase heading not required.)

Hour, Date, Place	Summary of Events and Information	Remarks and references to Appendices
YPRES MONDAY MAY 24th	At 2.45 am very heavy rifle fire broke out from North of Ypres as far as BELLEVARDE Pond & South of HOOGE. The Germans made a gas attack over a front of 4½ miles. Very heavy fighting continued west of the dam. The enemy advanced & retained the ground gained in two places. The 4th Division were driven back from in front of WIELTJE & they now held a line some fifteen hundred yards in rear of their former position passing just west of WIELTJE village. The Cavalry were driven back from their line west of BELLEVARDE Pond & North of the MENIN road a distance of 1000 yards. The 11th Hussars hung on to houses in HOOGE South of the road & were not dislodged. Two counter attacks one in the evening & the other during the night of the 24/25th failed to dislodge the enemy from positions gained. Our own front was very quiet & the Brigade only fired 16 rounds. The weather was very fine & hot. Wind steady from N.E.	H.A.

Army Form C. 2118.

WAR DIARY
or
INTELLIGENCE SUMMARY.
(Erase heading not required.)

Instructions regarding War Diaries and Intelligence Summaries are contained in F.S. Regs., Part II. and the Staff Manual respectively. Title pages will be prepared in manuscript.

Hour, Date, Place	Summary of Events and Information	Remarks and references to Appendices
YPRES TUESDAY MAY 25th	Wind still from N.E., enemy did not renew the attack during the night, there is apparently a gap in our line South of the Menin road about 600 yards in length. Situation easier North of & our front quite quiet.	124 Bty [Battery] however was shelled during the afternoon & with the following casualties. Killed in action. Lt C. Muirhead (attached)
WEDNESDAY 26th	Weather again fine & warm. A quiet night. Wind still blowing from the N.E. This warm day in the afternoon 123 Bty shelled & a the Caterpillar the Hanov shelling 60	34.97 Far Sgt RILEY F. 66299 Gr SAWYER W.P. 77072 Gr DEVLIN T. 27436 Gr SAUNDERS S. 41340 Gr BRUCE C. 56245 Dr LINDSAY T. 55725 Dr SHATTELL T. 54872 Gr DUKE P. Jr. 34123 Gr me. WOUNDED 54872 Br DUKE P. 34123 Gr WEBBERLEY A. 56794 Gr NIXON W. 70577 Gr McLAUGHLIN P. 2892 G.C WALL T. (Sp Rs.) 54484 Dr HOPWOOD W.H. 70302 Dr HARRIS R. 60221 Dr NORRIS T. 24343 Dr BRETT W. Captn F.L. CONGREVE joined from 27th Bde. to take over command of 124 Bty when Major KINSMAN leaves.

Army Form C. 2118.

WAR DIARY
or
INTELLIGENCE SUMMARY.
(Erase heading not required.)

Instructions regarding War Diaries and Intelligence Summaries are contained in F.S. Regs., Part II. and the Staff Manual respectively. Title pages will be prepared in manuscript.

Hour, Date, Place	Summary of Events and Information	Remarks and references to Appendices
YPRES		
THURSDAY 27 MAY.	Much colder but fine. Situation quite quiet and nothing of interest occurs. Our batteries are rather more than usual. Enemy & Germans on our front. A quiet night	2 Lieut W.T.O. Chng. 173 Bty to hospital — German measles. Apps
FRIDAY 28 MAY.	Very good day, and very quiet. R.F.C. put up wireless for us close to our Hqrs. Batteries fire a little.	Went H.Q. 4 Armytage, R&e Major. Leaves & join 1/- North Mid. R.A. on appointment as Adj. RHS
SATURDAY 29 MAY.	Rather cool but a grand day. Our batteries fair hour annoying the Germans off on during the day. Shot bombardment to the North of Ypres at about 7 p.m. which is apparently a small French attack. A quiet night.	2/. J. Woods joins the Bde ex being from D.A.C. & temporal attached to the Bde Hqrs. RHS
SUNDAY 30 MAY.	Rather breezy. A quiet day on our front. German artillery shell Ypres a certain amount.	124 HRS Bty wagon lines move Erquilles Bge
MONDAY 31 MAY.	Good day. Our batteries end fire a little. Enemy shell the counterpoise the and on during the day with heavy shell.	122 Bty wagonline moves to Bde 2/. T.R.O. Smeerood RFA & leaves in W.H.R. Pagan set & to England after to days attachment. Ret.

W. Andy Gwell Rta.

a2
a/6

18/6.015

5th Division

28th Bde R.F.A.

Vol XL 1-30.6.15

Army Form C. 2118

WAR DIARY
or
INTELLIGENCE SUMMARY.
(Erase heading not required.)

WAR DIARY
28th Brigade R.F.A.
from
June 1st to 30th 1915

Vol II

Army Form C. 2118

WAR DIARY
or
INTELLIGENCE SUMMARY.
(Erase heading not required.)

Instructions regarding War Diaries and Intelligence Summaries are contained in F.S. Regs., Part II and the Staff Manual respectively. Title pages will be prepared in manuscript.

Hour, Date, Place	Summary of Events and Information	Remarks and references to Appendices
YPRES		
JUNE 1. Tuesday	Fine day. Intermittent hostile gun fire during the day. Nothing of interest occurs. A quiet night.	RMS
JUNE 2. Wednesday	Very hot day. German bombardment starts at about 9 am on HOOGE – MENIN road front and continues all day. Ypres heavily shelled in the afternoon particularly on prominent church etc.	RMS
JUNE 3. Thursday	Very hot day. Enemy very quiet. Our guns fire a little during the day. A quiet night.	RMS
JUNE 4. Friday	Dull cloudy morning, turning into sunny hot afternoon. An exceptionally quiet day.	RMS 2/Lt H.L. STOCKEY joins the Bde on attachment, reports from Cdn Cdt. RMS
JUNE 5. Saturday	Grand day. Our guns fire a little and so do the Germans. Otherwise quiet.	RMS
JUNE 6. Sunday	Cloudy – hence very hot. Nothing of particular interest to relate. The usual few rounds fired.	4/Lt M.G. CLERY joins Bde as orderly officer. 2/Lt J. WOODS posted to the Cdr. RMS
JUNE 7. Monday	Frightfully hot. Nothing of interest happens. A quiet day.	2/Lt P.M. CHARLTON musters leave. Transfer from trench mortar school ALBERTHUY. RMS Maj. M. CREHAN Staff Captain 4/Lt C.W BUNTON England (sharp) 4/Lt C.J. BUTLER RMS

(73989) W4141–463. 400,000. 9/14. H.&J. Ltd. Forms/C. 2118/10.

WAR DIARY
or
INTELLIGENCE SUMMARY.
(Erase heading not required.)

Army Form C. 2118

Instructions regarding War Diaries and Intelligence Summaries are contained in F.S. Regs., Part II and the Staff Manual respectively. Title pages will be prepared in manuscript.

Hour, Date, Place	Summary of Events and Information	Remarks and references to Appendices
June 8th Tuesday	A quiet day and exceptionally quiet night. Very hot, thunder and rain. Both our own and German patrols made a note.	MAJOR CROFTON } leave to England 2/Lt BUXTON } (4 days) 2/Lt CURTEIS M.C.C.
June 9th Wednesday	Another quiet day and night with some weather as yesterday. 123 fired in co-operation with M Guns on Germans working on a sandbag emplacement in newer corner diamond-shaped wood. M.1.55.C.2.6. (28 N.W. Sheet 3)	2/Lt R. H. Saunders (?C.B?) joined 12th 2/Lt Ellison (R.V.C.) do do Highland M.C.C. M.C.C.
June 10th Thursday	Very heavy rain in the morning. Our batteries did not fire.	M.C.C.
June 11th Friday	Last night (10/11) a little rain but a nice day (fine). Our batteries registered in the morning and again in the afternoon to stop the enemy rifle-grenading on the trenches.	
June 12th Saturday	Another lovely day. Batteries fired a little.	
Sunday June 13th Morning	Batteries registered again in early morning.	MAJOR SEDGWICK } start a 5 day leave England 12th 2/Lt FELLOWES } M.C.C. CLAYTON
Monday June 14th Tuesday	123 fired on Hill 60 and Caterpillar a little. 124 fired on German communications.	M.C.C.
Tuesday June 15th Wednesday	123 and 124 registered very carefully on German wire.	Lt Col STRONG took over to (from) N.C.C. (13th Bde.)
Wednesday June 16th Thursday	Weather continues to be very fine. V Corps attacked on line HOOGE - BELLEWAARDE FARM beginning at 3 a.m. Bombardment lasted all day. We co-operated with our fire.	Lt Col SANDYS left on Brigade to England M.C.C.
Thursday June 17th Friday	A fine day. Brigade only fired 4 rounds	
Friday June 18th Saturday	An uneventful day, none of the batteries fired	18th Lt Col SANDYS, C.M.G. was invested by H.M. the King with the C.M.G. 2/Lt Shier do in England 2/Lt R.H. Masefield joined Brigade 17/6/15 Capt to Gollman Brigade Capt J.C. Thorburn } left for leave to England on the 17th M.C.C.
Sunday June 19th Sunday	Guns did not fire again	

Army Form C. 2118

WAR DIARY
or
INTELLIGENCE SUMMARY.
(Erase heading not required.)

Instructions regarding War Diaries and Intelligence Summaries are contained in F.S. Regs., Part II. and the Staff Manual respectively. Title pages will be prepared in manuscript.

Hour, Date, Place	Summary of Events and Information	Remarks and references to Appendices
Sunday June 20th Monday.	123 fired a few rounds re-registering	N.C.C.
Monday June 21st Tuesday	Nothing to report	Capt Cohen left to leave to Ireland. 21.6.15.
Tuesday June 22nd Wednesday	122 fired on a German working party in the morning. In the afternoon replied to Germans shelling NORFOLKS Headquarters with a few rounds. At 8 o'clock the Brigade cooperated with the III Div in an attempt to straighten the line at HOOGE by firing on "Hill 60" and the "Caterpillar". Our Forward Observing Officer reported fire was very effective — the German trench parapet was knocked down in several places and a machine gun silenced.	Cpl SANDYS returned from leave and resumed command of left group. 21.6.15. N.C.C.
Wed. June 23rd Thursday	Nothing to report.	The foll: Officers, N.C.O's and N.C.C. men were mentioned in despatches today. (24.6.15)
Thursday June 24th Friday	A little rain; we did not fire.	2d Woods & Ambrose gazetted in advance.
		Major. G.R.V. Kingman
		" R.H. Skeddon
		Lieut. H.W.H. Armytage
		" R.H. Ambrose
		2 Lieut. " Carey.
		" N.C. Hunter.
		B.S.M. J. Wilson.
		B.S.M. H. Poyner
		Battery Q.MSE.J T.R. Page.
		Cpl. T.R. Dixon.
		Bx J. Connor.
		" Bx T. Phyall.
		Gr W. Tullett (decd)
		Bx W.J. Tullett (decd) N.C.C.

Army Form C. 2118

WAR DIARY
or
INTELLIGENCE SUMMARY.
(Erase heading not required.)

Instructions regarding War Diaries and Intelligence Summaries are contained in F.S. Regs., Part II. and the Staff Manual respectively. Title pages will be prepared in manuscript.

Hour, Date, Place	Summary of Events and Information	Remarks and references to Appendices
YPRES		
F. Saturday June 25.	We don't fire a single round. Cloudy, close day, with very heavy thunderstorm of rain in the afternoon.	12th Bty hand over. In lieu of honours received today Major C.R.V. Kinnersley D.S.O. awarded M.C. Sgt A Sage 123 Bty wounded. RHS
Saturday Sunday June 26.	Sunny day, and ground dries up quickly. All Batteries get a 'Wireless' call to shoot at Naval Gun known as "Percy". Even Battery fires 8 rounds. Hostile artillery more active than usual. Our B/Ops register to myolight the enemy.	12.3 goes into reserve after dark comes back into action 12.2 definitely occupies new position in I.26.B.3.1 RHS
S. Monday June 27	Very close day. Registering continued. Slight rain in the afternoon.	Capt Cosgrove goes on leave in the afternoon. RHS
Monday June 28.	A very quiet day. Cloudy with a light rain occasionally. Registering carried out.	Sgt Turner DCL. takes over Command of 2nd Siege Bty. 2/Lt Sheer Hall Ffroutt goes on leave in the afternoon. RHS
Tuesday June 29.	Dull weather. Nothing except registering to report.	Gun traps gd Shelled to ... in the morning. 2/Lt McCrae goes on leave on the afternoon. RHS
Wednesday June 30.	Weather fine. Fires registers a "whiz-bang" battery by aeroplane. A quiet day.	RHS

Wardrof Trevor Rita
Com^g 28th Bde RFA.

5th Division

121/6427

28th Bde. R.F.A.

Vol XII

From 1st to 31st July 1915

Army Form C. 2118.

WAR DIARY
or
INTELLIGENCE SUMMARY.

(Erase heading not required.)

Instructions regarding War Diaries and Intelligence Summaries are contained in F.S. Regs., Part II and the Staff Manual respectively. Title pages will be prepared in manuscript.

Hour, Date, Place	Summary of Events and Information	Remarks and references to Appendices
	War Diary 28th Brigade R.F.A. 5th Division July 1 — 31. 1915 Vol. 12.	

Army Form C. 2118.

WAR DIARY
or
INTELLIGENCE SUMMARY.
(Erase heading not required.)

Instructions regarding War Diaries and Intelligence Summaries are contained in F. S. Regs., Part II. and the Staff Manual respectively. Title pages will be prepared in manuscript.

Hour, Date, Place	Summary of Events and Information	Remarks and references to Appendices
Thursday July 1st	Batteries registered.	
Friday July 2nd	More registration carried out.	
Saturday July 3rd	122 Battery fired on Caterpillar	
Sunday July 4th	Weather is a little cold – forward section 123 fired on communication trenches behind Hill 60	
Monday July 5th	German minenwerfer started firing at 3.20 p.m. 38 and 42 ? trenches worrying them considerably. 123 battery co-operated with our heavy guns in retaliation	
Tuesday July 6th	123 forward section fired on back of Hill 60 in the evening. 124 retaliated on German Eisbang?	
Wednesday July 7th	123 forward section on back of Hill 60 again	
Thursday July 8th	The forward section again opened the "dose" on Hill 60.	
Friday July 9th	At 10.44 the minenwerfer started again but soon stopped of bombing – 123 co-operated. Between 6.30 and 7 p.m. we joined in a general bombardment of enemy trenches in the neighbourhood by shooting (ricochet) of 123. The weather was continuously poor, a little drizzling rain in the evening. German guns much more active, putting some large shrapnel near the headquarters.	

(73989) W4141—463. 400,000. 9/14. H.&J.Ltd. Forms/C. 2118/10.

Army Form C. 2118.

WAR DIARY
or
INTELLIGENCE SUMMARY.
(Erase heading not required.)

Instructions regarding War Diaries and Intelligence
Summaries are contained in F. S. Regs., Part II
and the Staff Manual respectively. Title pages
will be prepared in manuscript.

Hour, Date, Place	Summary of Events and Information	Remarks and references to Appendices
Saturday July 10th	Nothing to report	
Sunday July 11th	122 Battery replied to German guns firing in early morning. 123 also fired at back of Hill 60 and on the Observation Stations there in the afternoon. Germans shelled a good deal during the day. They fired at Headquarters to about 20 runs with 4.2 shells. Two shells hit the house - no harm done	Lieut L. G. Bonner attached 28th Bde Hqrs
Monday July 12th	A German mine opposite 58 were exploded & did considerable damage. Another German mine shortly after, blew up probably to the German parapet down. 123 fired a lot during the night in reply to the Germans. One section of each battery relieved by STAFFORDSHIRE Brigade R.F.A.	From Gazette July 10th The following were promoted to 2nd Lieut R. H Anfrobus W. C. Glenn " C. J. Cruise " R. W. L. Fellows " B. F. Shaw " J. Woods
Tuesday July 13th	Nothing to report	
Wednesday July 14th	Germans again shelled Headquarters in the evening. Remaining sections of batteries relieved & returned to wagon line to rest.	2/Lt Hutching & 2/Lt Aspinall returned 2/Lt Todd during the latter's absence on leave.
Thursday July 15th	Batteries and Brigade Headquarters looking at wagon line. Bde completely at B action first line since ten began. Batteries sent first sections into action near DICKEBUSCH.	
Friday July 16th	A little registering done. Batteries sent up remaining Sections and were completely in action. Col SANDY'S took over "Right Group" at midday & headquarters moved into MAIRIE DICKEBUSCH.	
Saturday July 17th		
Sunday July 18th	"Registering" - The Burgomaster (N.G.C. Y2) was shelled about 2 p.m today by Germans with 5.9" Howitzers. The Germans also put a couple of those shells into houses near DICKEBUSCH CHURCH. 8 Bde No 22	
Monday July 19th	Registering continued. Factory & Hangars hit were heavily shelled about 8.30 pm when Germans were shelling Westoutre.	

WAR DIARY or INTELLIGENCE SUMMARY.

(Erase heading not required.)

Army Form C. 2118.

Instructions regarding War Diaries and Intelligence Summaries are contained in F.S. Regs., Part II. and the Staff Manual respectively. Title pages will be prepared in manuscript.

Hour, Date, Place	Summary of Events and Information	Remarks and references to Appendices
July 20th Tuesday	"Registration continued" - "1 German also continued" at the Town - another three slightly wounded.	
July 21st Wednesday	Registration completed - officers of 72 Bde approved preparation is taking over - We shot a little to demonstrate lines & zones.	
July 22nd Thursday	Nothing much done except further "demonstration" to officers of 78 Bde.	
July 23rd Friday	Continued shoot of morning on trenches on "Picadilly Farm". Several direct hits & apparently effective shooting. At 5 p.m. 1/4 15" fired on a spot where a German Field Gun, placed behind was supposed t.b. 4 Flash had been spotted on a standing we saw smoke. The forward observing officer reported shooting appeared effective. That section silenced. Practice march along by 78 Bde R.F.A tonight.	
July 24th Saturday	All quiet - pulled of finally on night of 25th	
July 25th Sunday	Marched from Neger 25/26 & attached next to rest in vicinity of HONDEGHEM. Rest during day.	
July 27th Tuesday	Afternoon - Brigade parade & moment for inspection by C.R.A Parade State - Col SANDYS - 21 Officers - 635 men. Complimentary Speech.	
July 28th Wednesday	At Rest - Brigade parade for inspection by G.O.C 2nd Army Gen Sir Herbert Plumer K.C.B. Most complimentary speech at work throughout war and appearance on parade. Col SANDYS, 21 Officers and 648 men present.	

(73989) W14141-463. 400,000. 9/14. H.&J.Ltd. Forms/C. 2118/10.

Army Form C. 2118.

WAR DIARY
or
INTELLIGENCE SUMMARY.
(Erase heading not required.)

Instructions regarding War Diaries and Intelligence Summaries are contained in F. S. Regs., Part II and the Staff Manual respectively. Title pages will be prepared in manuscript.

Hour, Date, Place	Summary of Events and Information	Remarks and references to Appendices
July 29th	At rest, billeting party left for unknown.	Lt Todd returned from leave. 2nd Lt SPROTT RFA left under orders for England. Lt Hitchings left.
July 30th	Batteries marched to and entrained at CASSEL.	
July 31st	Batteries detrained at Monsieur L'Abbé and marched to BONNAY where they were billeted.	

Maudly Lrourta
Com'g 28th Bde RFA

121/6857

5th Division

28th Bde R of N.

Vol XLII

August 15.

ar
a/6

Army Form C. 2118.

WAR DIARY
or
INTELLIGENCE SUMMARY.
(*Erase heading not required.*)

Instructions regarding War Diaries and Intelligence Summaries are contained in F.S. Regs., Part II. and the Staff Manual respectively. Title pages will be prepared in manuscript.

Hour, Date, Place	Summary of Events and Information	Remarks and references to Appendices

WAR DIARY

26th Brigade RFA.
5th Division

August 1915

Volume 13.

Army Form C. 2118.

WAR DIARY
or
INTELLIGENCE SUMMARY.
(Erase heading not required.)

Instructions regarding War Diaries and Intelligence Summaries are contained in F.S. Regs., Part II. and the Staff Manual respectively. Title pages will be prepared in manuscript.

Hour, Date, Place	Summary of Events and Information	Remarks and references to Appendices
Sunday Aug 1st	Batteries noting at Bonnay.	n.c.c
Monday Aug 2nd	Batteries continued at rest. Ammunition Column rejoined Brigade	n.c.c
Tuesday Aug 3rd	Brigade marched to TREUX and bivouaced in valley there	n.c.c
Wednesday Aug 4th	Battery Commanders ordered to send half-batteries into action during night 3/4th. Today Batteries commenced registering.	n.c.c Capt. A.G. Gillman takes over command of 123. R.F.A. vice Major F.R. Sedgwick who leaves for ENGLAND (Aug 4th)
Thursday Aug 5th	During night 4/5th, remaining halves of batteries came into action. Col SANDES takes over command of left Group from French	n.c.c 2Lt A.G. Duggens reported from RHA to act as Captain to 123. R.F.A. (Aug 5th) under date Aug 6th
Friday Aug 6th	Registering	n.c.c 2Lt L. Bonner posted to 123 Bry
Saturday Aug 7th	Registering	n.c.c " R.F. Mason " " 123 Bry
Sunday Aug 8th	Germans fired a few 6" shells into sector 5 from north – Continued registering	n.c.c " N.F. Hall " " 5 D.A.C wh
Monday Aug 9th	Registration continued. 124 scored a few direct hits on houses in FRICOURT	n.c.c he joined on 7th August.
Tuesday Aug 10th	Registration continued	n.c.c
Wednesday Aug 11th	a few more registration rounds	n.c.c
Thursday Aug 12th	Nothing except registering.	n.c.c
Friday Aug 13	Still registering	n.c.c
Saturday Aug 14th	122 fired at sap in aeroplane hatch. Photo correspondent to visited 124 Batterys Observation Station.	n.c.c
Sunday Aug 15th	Registered on switch 30n0.	h.c.c
Monday Aug 16th	More registration onto switch 30n0	n.c.c.
Tuesday Aug 17th	124 Bry continued in a short with 6" Hows against farm. war centre of L 34 at 4:30 p.m. Several direct hits were scored by Howitzers.	n.c.c
Wednesday Aug 18th	more registering.	n.c.c
Thursday Aug 19th	123 located Machine Gun emplacement in 479 - shot at and hit it.	n.c.c
Friday. Aug 20th	"Registering 123 fired at two supposed "Machine Gun" emplacements – (i) P.3.7.10 (ii) P.3.8.9. Registration continued - at 145. 124 Battery dispersed working party. German movements and work going on round MARTINPUICH, BAZENTIN LE [illegible] PETIT, POZIERES & CONTALMAISON.	n.c.c
Saturday. Aug 21st.		

Army Form C. 2118.

WAR DIARY
or
INTELLIGENCE SUMMARY.
(Erase heading not required.)

Instructions regarding War Diaries and Intelligence Summaries are contained in F.S. Regs., Part II and the Staff Manual respectively. Title pages will be prepared in manuscript.

Hour, Date, Place	Summary of Events and Information	Remarks and references to Appendices
Sunday Aug. 22.	Registration - 124 fired at Machine Gun emplacement M 493 - BEDFORDS reported 3 Machine Guns firing last night (i) FRICOURT SE CORNER (ii) OPPOSITE BOIS FRANCAIS (iii) in main German Trench 70 yds IV of North prong of aeroplane trench.	
Monday Aug 23rd	Registering a little - 122 and C.B.S. fired between 12 noon and 1p.m at Machine Gun & minenwerfer near S.W. Corner of BOIS ALLEMAND. Good shooting done! Germans very annoyed - C/85 silenced the minenwerfer German Howitzer Battery located in small wood. N 31.2.8. h.c.c.	
Thursday Aug 24th	Registering done. 123 fired on machine Gun midway between 482 and 483. During the night sections were withdrawn and replaced by 82 and 84 Bdes. h.c.c	
Wednesday Aug 25	No sections registered - remaining sections of our Brigade withdrawn during the night. During the day, that part of 2nd Bde out of action (less Ammunition Column), marched in dribletts to SAILLY LE SEC and formed "Army Reserve". The sections in action, as soon as they pulled out, marched direct to same village h.c.c.	Aug 26 Russian decorations announced on 26th - following gained rewards:- 63782. Dr. QU G. Canvin 112 RFA 49429 Gr. W.J. Brady 183 RFA Dr. Canvin was awarded Cross of St George 4th Class; Gr. Brady, Medal of St George 3rd Class
Thursday Aug. 26.	Ammn Col. marched in during the morning to SAILLY LE SEC.	

WAR DIARY
or
INTELLIGENCE SUMMARY.

Army Form C. 2118.

(Erase heading not required.)

Hour, Date, Place	Summary of Events and Information	Remarks and references to Appendices
Friday Aug. 27th Saturday Aug. 28th Sunday Aug. 29th Monday Aug. 30th Tuesday Aug. 31st	} Brigade in Army Reserve at SAILLY LE SEC. N.C.C. Wardrop McRitta Comd. 26.P Bde RFA.	27.8.15 Lt. R.E. Inchbald joined from 27 Bde R.F.A. vice Capt. Coke R.F.A. posted to 52 Bty R.F.A 28.8.15 Lt. A.T. Todd R.A.M.C. promoted Captain dated from 5th Aug.

121/7381

5th Division

28th Bde R.F.A.

Vol XIV
Sept '15

Army Form C. 2118.

WAR DIARY
or
INTELLIGENCE SUMMARY.
(Erase heading not required.)

Instructions regarding War Diaries and Intelligence Summaries are contained in F.S. Regs., Part II. and the Staff Manual respectively. Title pages will be prepared in manuscript.

Hour, Date, Place	Summary of Events and Information	Remarks and references to Appendices
	WAR DIARY 28 Bde R.F.A. 5th Division September 1915 Volume 14.	

Army Form C. 2118.

WAR DIARY
or
INTELLIGENCE SUMMARY.
(Erase heading not required.)

Instructions regarding War Diaries and Intelligence Summaries are contained in F.S. Regs., Part II. and the Staff Manual respectively. Title pages will be prepared in manuscript.

Hour, Date, Place	Summary of Events and Information	Remarks and references to Appendices
Wednesday Sept 1st		Lt.Col. W.B.R. Sandys is promoted Brigadier General and appointed to 14th Division. 2Lr. C.E.V. Buxton appointed A.D.C. to G.O.C. R.A. 47th Divn.
Thursday Sept 2nd		2r. Butler posted 124 vice 2Lr. Buxton.
Friday Sept 3rd		
Saturday Sept 4th		2Lr. 12.S. Inchbald posted as Captain to 27 Bde. — 2.K.M. Macrae is given command of Ammunition Column. Major E. Harding Newman moved to take over brigade.
Sunday Sept 5th		
Monday Sept 6th		
Tuesday Sept 7th	Brigade in Army Reserve	2r. Ching rejoins Bde from Horse Artillery
Wednesday Sept 8th	at SAILLY LE SEC	
Thursday Sept 9th		
Friday Sept 10th		
Saturday Sept 11th		
Sunday Sept 12th		

Army Form C. 2118.

WAR DIARY
or
INTELLIGENCE SUMMARY.
(Erase heading not required.)

Instructions regarding War Diaries and Intelligence Summaries are contained in F.S. Regs., Part II. and the Staff Manual respectively. Title pages will be prepared in manuscript.

Hour, Date, Place	Summary of Events and Information	Remarks and references to Appendices
Monday Sept 13th	Brigade still in Army Reserve	
Tuesday Sept 14th	Brigade still in Army Reserve	
Wednesday Sept 15th	4 guns of 122 Battery go into action in valley P.27 vice A.82	
Thursday Sept 16th	Headquarters moved into BRAY + dug-outs in the same valley. Left section of 122 Bty comes up and we take over group of 122 & B.82 from Col. Lambert.	Mr R H Stoddart? appointed Mr L G Lutgens? Temporary Captains
Friday Sept 17th	123 & 124 move into action near Suzanne after dark. They are in Lt Colonel Fitzmaurice's group. 122 registers. Remaining sections of 123 & 124 continue registering. 122 fired 4 rounds opposite trench 311 in retaliation for "sausages"	
Saturday Sept 18th	122 fired little. "Sausage" was again firing	
Sunday Sept 19th	122 did not fire. "Sausages" fired at 9 p.m.	
Monday Sept 20th	Whole of Headquarters in BRAY. The howfolks last night called on 28th Siege Howitzer to retaliate at trench 311. The Howitzer fired 4 rounds at the same time as 122 – the howfolks seemed pleased with result. Germans altogether fired 5 rounds from "Minenwerfer". Germans were much more active	
Tuesday Sept 21st	122 fired about 20 rounds than usual with their guns – They fired about 6 shells from 4.2" gun into valley. A moral victory, the "minenwerfer" did not fire	Capt. J F Knoium posted from 122 to 18 Divisional Art'y

WAR DIARY or INTELLIGENCE SUMMARY.

Army Form C. 2118.

(Erase heading not required.)

Hour, Date, Place	Summary of Events and Information	Remarks and references to Appendices
Wednesday Sept 22nd	122 By fired a few rounds registering and in retaliation. Some sausages were fired last night well to the left of C² Sector of the next door Division. Apparently they have been frightened from the old pos" being 311. M.C.C.	
Thursday Sept 23rd	Nothing to report except "minnenwerfer" again firing on our left. M.C.C.	Capt R.W. Adagh from OC 8th Bde to 122.
Friday Sept 24th	Nothing to report.	
Saturday Sept 25th	O.C. 122 reports he had a successful shoot with High Explosive today. Between 4.45 and 4.50, all batteries fired a few rounds at German trenches. Infantry then cheered. Germans disclosed a Machine Gun at junction of 311 & 513. N.C.C	
Sunday Sept 26th	122 fired at the above machine gun. Germans reached fire 122 with 20 or 30 rds but did not get nearer than 400 yds in French about P.11.55. N.C.C	
Monday Sept 27	Nothing to report. 122 fired gun in "sausages". M.C.C	
Tuesday Sept 28	A blank day	
Wednesday Sept 29	122 fired 2 rounds behind 311 in retaliation for "sausages". German guns fired about 30 rds of HE and Shrapnel near 122 forward gun from direction of MONTAUBAN	
Thursday Sept 30	122 fired 2 rounds in retaliation for 2 German sausages from direction of 315.	

Thursby Thompson Maj
Comg 25th Brigade RHA

Army Form C. 2118.

WAR DIARY
or
INTELLIGENCE SUMMARY.
(Erase heading not required.)

Instructions regarding War Diaries and Intelligence Summaries are contained in F.S. Regs., Part II. and the Staff Manual respectively. Title pages will be prepared in manuscript.

Hour, Date, Place	Summary of Events and Information	Remarks and references to Appendices
	The following has been compiled about 123 & 124 Batterys. R.F.A. not under control of this Brigade since it returning into action in accordance with G.R.O 1187:–	
17. September.	123 battery was ordered to relieve one section of D. of 98 Battery in position ½ a mile north of SUZANNE. Two guns of 124 Battery relieved a section of 98.A. A third gun was brought into action in forward position, shooting at MOULIN de FARGNY. WCC	
18. Sept.	Three more guns of 123. RFA were brought into action in same place as previous section. The remaining guns of 124 brought into action. The day was spent entrenching and reguising. WCC	
19th Sept. 20th Sept. 21st Sept.	Registering. WCC Registering. WCC (124) had position reconnoitred & one gun brought into action in 90th Battery position. WCC nothing to report from 124. In the evening the 6th gun of 123 Battery moved into a position near BRONFAY FARM (Q 20.19). WCC	
22nd Sept.	4 guns shifted to a position west of BRONFAY Farm occupied by 2 guns of 124th RFA. The FOUR GUNS of 123 RFA fired 512 rounds at Germans were attempting to and the single gun registration its new position. In the dark 3 guns returned to previous position and single gun opened fire on the 6th gun near BRONFAY FARM. WCC	
24 Sept to 30 Sept	Both batteries merely fired a few registering rounds, otherwise all quiet. WCC.	

28ième B^(se) R.É.A.

Oct + Nov.

Vol. XV

121/7730

6^(th) Bureau

Army Form C.

WAR DIARY
or
INTELLIGENCE SUMMARY.
(Erase heading not required.)

Instructions regarding War Diaries and Intelligence Summaries are contained in F.S. Regs., Part II. and the Staff Manual respectively. Title pages will be prepared in manuscript.

Hour, Date, Place	Summary of Events and Information	Remarks and references to Appendices
	War Diary 28 Bde R.F.A. 5th Divn October 1915. Volume 15	

WAR DIARY
or
INTELLIGENCE SUMMARY.
(Erase heading not required.)

Army Form C. 21.

Instructions regarding War Diaries and Intelligence Summaries are contained in F.S. Regs., Part II. and the Staff Manual respectively. Title pages will be prepared in manuscript.

Hour, Date, Place	Summary of Events and Information	Remarks and references to Appendices
Friday, October 1st	122 fired at Trench Mortar near Pt 311. Increase in sniping & hostile gunfire most marked during the day. H.C.C	
Saturday October 2nd	122 fired a few rounds in retaliation to "2 sausages" and the rifle-grenading of our trenches. German Arty very quiet. A Section of 125 & 124 were respectively relieved by B & C. 115 Bde. The relieved sections went to BRONFAY FARM. F.29.b.5.9 H.C.C.	2/Lt E.J. Payne communded & posted to Bde Amm" Column
Sunday October 3rd	A quiet day — nothing to report —	
Monday October 4th	Nothing to report except during latter part of night, 122 retaliated on German Trench Mortar (near 311) worrying our infantry. H.C.C.	
Tuesday Oct 5th	122 fired a few rounds at German trenches in C2 Sector M.C.C	
Wednesday Oct 6th	122 again had to retaliate on Trench Mortar (near 311) M.C.C	
Thursday Oct 7th	122 started work on a forward gun emplacement about F.22.A.10.9. M.C.C	
Friday Oct 8th	Nothing to report. H.C.C	
Saturday Oct 9th	Nothing of interest today. H.C.C.	
Sunday Oct 10th	122 fired on front trenches in F.10.d to stop Germans whiz-banging our trenches — the desired effect — 122 also fired at German working parties. H.C.C.	
Monday Oct 11th	There was a considerable amount of promiscuous whiz-bang & rifle-grenade fire during the day.	

Instructions regarding War Diaries and Intelligence Summaries are contained in F.S. Regs., Part II. and the Staff Manual respectively. Title pages will be prepared in manuscript.

WAR DIARY
or
INTELLIGENCE SUMMARY.
(Erase heading not required.)

Army Form C. 21

Hour, Date, Place	Summary of Events and Information	Remarks and references to Appendices
Tuesday Oct. 12th	122 fired 6 rds at German front trenches in F.10.d. The section of 123 at BRONFAY FARM withdrawn.	
Wednesday Oct 13th	German Snipers + guns generally more active today. 122 silenced a rifle grenade battery. MEAULTE had a few rounds fired into it during the night. Section of 124 withdrawn from near BRONFAY. H.C.C.	
Thursday Oct 14th	122 fired a few rounds to quell German Why bang and rifle-fire on our front. Germans again more active. Nothing of interest to report. N.C.C.	
Friday Oct 15th	German - Whizzbang fire more active again. N.C.C.	
Saturday Oct 16th	German fired trench-mortars again – 122 retaliated. Also registered a little. N.C.C.	
Sunday Oct 17th		
Monday Oct 18th	122 fired 2 rds at a trench - mortar. Germans were again firing Trench guns considerably. Germans have occupied a mine blown up last (?) are working on Infantry in front of "D" Ranson. N.C.C.	
Tuesday Oct 19th	German Artillery active again. N.C.C.	
Wednesday Oct 20th	A quiet's generally very mosh day H.C.C.	
Thursday Oct 21st	122 fired a few rounds in retaliation for Why bangs bombs etc. and in conjunction with our grenade fire N.C.C.	

Army Form C. 2118

WAR DIARY
or
INTELLIGENCE SUMMARY.
(Erase heading not required.)

Instructions regarding War Diaries and Intelligence Summaries are contained in F.S. Regs., Part II. and the Staff Manual respectively. Title pages will be prepared in manuscript.

Hour, Date, Place	Summary of Events and Information	Remarks and references to Appendices
Friday Oct 22nd	Germans fired several sausages about trenches, 60, 62 & 72	N.C.C.
Saturday Oct 23rd	122 registered forward gun in new position — German trench mortars active again	N.C.C.
Sunday Oct 24th Monday Oct 25th	German mine exploded, flowing in R & 73 trench. 122 fired at mine craters & earth thrown up by succession of minis opposite 73, wh were occupied by Germans in conjunction with 6" Hows Battery.	
Tuesday Oct 26th	122 fired at German guns in wood X.22.C.5.6 wh were seen firing. Germans fired a little more than usual today.	H.C.C.
Wednesday Oct 27th	A lot of movement of enemy's men & small parties was observed about midday on the road by the VILLA DE CONTALMAISON. At 12.29 p.m. a white flag was seen by G. Turner out of the wall near the VILLA CONTALMAISON, and for the next few or so movements to & from the wall were observed	

Army Form C. 2118.

WAR DIARY
or
INTELLIGENCE SUMMARY.
(Erase heading not required.)

Instructions regarding War Diaries and Intelligence Summaries are contained in F.S. Regs., Part II. and the Staff Manual respectively. Title pages will be prepared in manuscript.

Hour, Date, Place	Summary of Events and Information	Remarks and references to Appendices
Thursday October 28th	122 Bty fired a few rounds opposite C₂ section	2 Clery app'td adj vice Cpt R.A. Sladden
Friday October 29th	122's forward gun in trenches in C₂ was successfully withdrawn and moved to position F.22 @ 9.5.	posted to 122 Bty; 2nd
Saturday October 30th	Six Sausage balloons seen up during the day all far away	Lt Hooper posted to 22th Bde.
Sunday October 31st	Nothing of interest to report.	

Hunting Henderson Lt.Colonel
Comdg 2nd Brigade R.H.A

Army Form C. 2118.

WAR DIARY
or
INTELLIGENCE SUMMARY.
(Erase heading not required.)

War Diary

November 1916

28th Bde. R.F.A.

5th Division

Volume 16

Army Form C. 2118.

WAR DIARY
or
INTELLIGENCE SUMMARY.
(Erase heading not required.)

Instructions regarding War Diaries and Intelligence Summaries are contained in F.S. Regs., Part II. and the Staff Manual respectively. Title pages will be prepared in manuscript.

Hour, Date, Place	Summary of Events and Information	Remarks and references to Appendices
Monday November 1st	122 fired a few rounds at supposed German gun emplacements	
Tuesday Nov 2nd	Nothing to report	
Wednesday Nov 3rd	Nothing of interest today	
Thursday Nov 4th	A very quiet day. Q working party was plainly visible, seen in light & seen in dark grey uniform at X 23 D 18. Also at corner of wood X 23 D 18.	
Friday Nov 5th	Nothing to report.	
Saturday Nov 6th	All batteries registered the trench mortar which has been troubling our infantry. It has not fired since.	
Sunday Nov 7th	122 fired a few rounds in trench defences C.2. Sadin.	2nd Lt Stokes RFA posted to 26 Div'l Artillery
Tuesday Nov 8th	122 fired 4 rounds at Germans working at corner of T3 wood.	

Army Form C. 2118.

WAR DIARY
or
INTELLIGENCE SUMMARY.
(Erase heading not required.)

Instructions regarding War Diaries and Intelligence Summaries are contained in F.S. Regs., Part II. and the Staff Manual respectively. Title pages will be prepared in manuscript.

Hour, Date, Place	Summary of Events and Information	Remarks and references to Appendices
Tuesday Nov. 9th	122 fired a few rounds ages tiring	
Wednesday Nov 10th	Everything very quiet	
Thursday Nov 11th	At least 15% of the German shells fired today were "Blind shells".	
Friday Nov 12th	Practically no guns or rifle fire during the day.	
Saturday Nov. 13th	122 fired a few rounds in retaliation in trenches opposite Cr. Sector to shyshlange.	
Sunday Nov 14th	Nothing to report. Quiet thing trout the day	
Tuesday Nov 15th	122 fired a few rounds in - registering trenches in front of Cr. Sector.	
Tuesday Nov 16th	About 60 Germans was afterward to get out of their trench, he driven in front of them by shell, but when heavily fired upon, doubled back. A quiet day.	

Army Form C. 2118.

WAR DIARY
or
INTELLIGENCE SUMMARY.
(*Erase heading not required.*)

Instructions regarding War Diaries and Intelligence Summaries are contained in F.S. Regs., Part II. and the Staff Manual respectively. Title pages will be prepared in manuscript.

Hour, Date, Place	Summary of Events and Information	Remarks and references to Appendices
Wednesday Nov 7th	Nothing to report.	
Thursday Nov 18th	Very quiet & nothing all day. No shells on Bn H.Q.	2/Lt McGuire attached
Friday Nov 19th	Nothing of interest to report.	
Saturday Nov 20th	12:2 fired 16 few rounds on German trenches about G.6.7.2	
Sunday Nov 21st	Everything quiet on our front.	
Monday Nov 22nd	6" gun at C.2.3 ⊕ took in front position E of Y wood	
Tuesday Nov 23rd	G quiet day. Little shelling on rifle fire — very quiet	
Wednesday Nov 24th	2 guns occupied the position at F.29.B.2 & Tu. found guns & Kr about as from the Battery position. Was moved to this pos.	
Thursday Nov 25th	122 Bty fired 136 rounds at II D.31.9, Cutting wire	Capt Ast R G A posted to 65th How Bty Capt Newcomb R.F.A. posted to 122 Bty

(O 29 6) W 2794 100,000 8/14 H W V Forms/C. 2118/11.

Army Form C. 2118.

WAR DIARY
or
INTELLIGENCE SUMMARY.
(Erase heading not required.)

Instructions regarding War Diaries and Intelligence Summaries are contained in F. S. Regs., Part II. and the Staff Manual respectively. Title pages will be prepared in manuscript.

Hour, Date, Place	Summary of Events and Information	Remarks and references to Appendices
Friday Nov 26th	During the day the new cut Bay yesterday was repaired	2nd Lt Truan RFA attached to 122 By 2nd Lt Oldham RFA attached to 124 By
Saturday Nov 27th	German Sampans & small Torpedoes boat fired in retaliation	1st Lt Butler RGA attacked 8th Army Corps
Sunday Nov 28th	Today 122 By fired a lot. Nothing to report.	
Monday Nov 29th	Very little firing	
Tuesday Nov 30th	A lot of enemy shells fell near the enemy lines	

Wardingurumn Lt Col
Comdg 28 Brigade RFA

Army Form C. 2118.

WAR DIARY
or
INTELLIGENCE SUMMARY.

(Erase heading not required.)

5

Hour, Date, Place	Summary of Events and Information	Remarks and references to Appendices

5th Div

War Diary
December 1916 -

28th Brigade R.F.A.

Vol XVI

Army Form C. 2118.

WAR DIARY
or
INTELLIGENCE SUMMARY.
(Erase heading not required.)

Instructions regarding War Diaries and Intelligence Summaries are contained in F.S. Regs., Part II. and the Staff Manual respectively. Title pages will be prepared in manuscript.

Hour, Date, Place	Summary of Events and Information	Remarks and references to Appendices
Wednesday Dec 1st	124 fired in retaliation — a quiet day	
Thursday Dec 2nd	124 fired a lot at gun positions and in retaliation	
Friday Dec 3rd	Right section of 125 Bty fired on two new Batts of 127 — 122 fired at transport	
Saturday Dec 4th	Centre section of 123 Bty fired on two centres section of 122. 123 guns registered from 122 position	
Sunday Dec 5th	124 registered a machine gun emplacement. 123 fr registered points on C2 section.	
Monday Dec 6th	124 fired a lot in retaliation	
Tuesday Dec 7th	Successful shrapnel against the enemy in combination with the infantry — 123 firing a lot during the night Y-Z 123	
Wednesday Dec 8th	Nothing of interest to report	
Thursday Dec 9th	A misty day and very quiet	

Army Form C. 2118.

WAR DIARY
or
INTELLIGENCE SUMMARY.
(Erase heading not required.)

Instructions regarding War Diaries and Intelligence Summaries are contained in F.S. Regs., Part II. and the Staff Manual respectively. Title pages will be prepared in manuscript.

Hour, Date, Place		Summary of Events and Information	Remarks and references to Appendices
Friday	Dec 11th	Nothing to report	
Saturday	Dec 12th	123 fired a few rounds in retaliation	4.30
Sunday	Dec 13th	125 registered points of day and night lines on C₂ South. Hostile artillery active on C₂ South	4.30
Monday	Dec 14th	123 again registered prominent pts on C₂ South	3.30 / 4.30
Tuesday	Dec 15th	123 fired at two hostile artillery observers	3.30
Wednesday	Dec 16th	124 fired a test on A.2	3.30 / 4.30
Thursday	Dec 17th	Nothing to report	3.30 / 4.30
Friday	Dec 18th	A very quiet day	3.30 / 4.30
Saturday	Dec 19th	Inspection of 123 bty by Brig General Gordon	3.30 / 4.30
Sunday	Dec 20th	123 fired opposite C₂ Redn in retaliation	3.30 / 4.30
Tuesday	Dec 21st	Trenches worked fired a rds on C₂ South	10.30 / 4.30
Wednesday	Dec 22nd	Nothing of interest to report	10.30 / 4.30
Thursday	Dec 23rd	A very quiet day	10.30 / 4.30
	Dec 23rd	German 69 fired on WELLINGTON REDOUBT. 123 retaliated	10.30 / 4.30

Army Form C. 2118.

WAR DIARY
or
INTELLIGENCE SUMMARY.
(Erase heading not required.)

Instructions regarding War Diaries and Intelligence Summaries are contained in F. S. Regs., Part II. and the Staff Manual respectively. Title pages will be prepared in manuscript.

Hour, Date, Place	Summary of Events and Information	Remarks and references to Appendices
Friday Dec 24th	German 4.2 gun fired on B.B.G. slight damage to 173 mgm line	
Saturday Dec 25th	123 retaliated on hostile shelling on our trenches	
Sunday Dec 26th	Enemy shelled C2 twenty 123 fired on C2	
Monday Dec 27th	Enemy's artillery very active	
Tuesday Dec 28th	123 combined with the 60 pdr in shooting on effective retaliation in hostile shelling	
Wednesday Dec 29th	173 fired 6 rd shrapnel C2 sector	
Thursday Dec 30th	Nothing to report	
Friday Dec 31st	123 registered battery about X 16 c 1.2	

E Marlburghurn in F.L.
Comg 28thBrigade R.F.A

28th Bde. R.F.A.
5th Div.

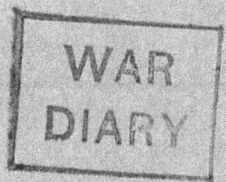

123rd BATTERY, R.F.A.

JANUARY to DECEMBER

1915

War Diary

123rd Battery R.F.A.

January to December 1915

123 Battery R.F.A.

Jan 1st. To position at NEUVE EGLISE.

Jan. 3rd. To Reserve.

On January 6th the 15th Brigade R.F.A was temporarily withdrawn from the V Div. to go to 27th Division.

To fill the gap in the artillery line the 123rd Battery, 28th Bde R.F.A & the 119 Bty R.F.A 27 Bde R.F.A. were formed into a central group under Colonel F.J. Duffus R.F.A

This group was placed in action West of the LINDENHOEK – NEUVE EGLISE road & North of the Windmill near NEUVE EGLISE.

The 123rd Battery took over the position vacated by the 52nd Battery, this position was found to be partly visible to the enemy at MESSINES. & was shelled by a heavy Howitzer Battery, there were no casualties but the B.C. changed the position to a fresh one about 400 yards north of the Windmill.

The Observing Station was close in front of the Battery in the roof of a Barn.

Jan.6: Feb.10. 1915.

The targets registered were various points in the whole length of the MESSINES WYTSCHETE ridge.

The Billets of the Battery was moved to a point about ½ mile west of the LINDENHOEK - NEUVE EGLISE road close to the DOUVE River.

There was very little firing done during the whole period that the battery was in this position.

One section was allowed to remain out of action & Squads of layers & telephonists were trained, the weather was constantly wet & the mud very bad, nevertheless the health of the Battery was good, Bathing & Laundry arrangements were made.

Feby 10th
The 15 Bde R.F.A (less one battery) having returned to the V Division, the 123rd Bty returned to the command of Colonel Sandys.

Feb 10. 1915

The task allotted to the 28 Bde R.F.A. plus 1 Battery Howitzers (the 65 Battery R.F.A.) was to cover the immediate front of the infantry from a conspicuous farm about 700 yards due W. of the old forward observing station on the WULVERGHEM-MESSINES road as far as point 76.

The right hand portion of the line viz from the above mentioned farm known as the farm in N36 (a) or Redoubt Farm as far as the KRUISTRAAT-WULVERGHEM road was assigned to the 123 Battery.

The Battery position was north of the DOUVE River about 400 yards S. of the LINDENHOEK-DRANOUTRE road & 1000 yards W. of the LINDENHOEK-NEUVE EGLISE road. The position was almost identical with the retrenched position prepared by the battery on Nov 11th.

Observing Station on the Southern peak of Mont KEMMEL.

The billet was not changed.

Feb. 10. 1915

The Original Order was for the Battery to go into reserve till the 17th & prepare its position, but an alarm due to prisoners reports took the Battery into action, on the 15th & withdrew to reserve on the 17th again.

On February 10th 2/Lieut H.S. Hall (SR) was attached to the battery

The Battery remained in action in this position Ref Map 1/20000 in square N 32(D) 4 (3) with objective the Enemy's trenches from Farm in N 36(D) to Houses S.W. of KRUISTRAAT in N 36(A) 7 (9) until March 1st. The Observing Station was still on Kemmell Hill about N 26 (C) 6 (27)

The Sector of the defensive line covered was D. HQ Inf Bde at Elbow Farm in N 35 (C) 66

A Subaltern slept every night with the Infantry. a special wire run from the Battery position to this Infantry H Qrs

Mar. 1. 1915

MARCH 1st.

There was talk about an attack on the SPANBROEK MOELEN. The particular objective of the 28 Bde R.F.A. was to cut the wire from SPANBROEK MOELEN southwards to the cutting on the KROISTRATT-SPANBROEK road in N30 (c) 4.7. The southern position of this task was allotted to the 123 Battery.

To be able to carry out this task the Battery position was changed. The Battery was brought up to a point on the LINDEN HOEK NEUVE EGLISE road just by the 9th Kilo. Stone. This was one of the positions occupied by the Battery in Nov. & December.

The position was in a bad state, but good platforms were made & excellent pits & shelters.

The wagon line was moved back to the farm near WATERGAT. in T 1 (a).

Observing Stations
(1) In defensive area in Mount KEMMEL.

II To attack AREA in cottage 250x to right front of Guns.
(b) in Frenchmans farm N 34 (c) 4.8.

(C)   May 1-12. 1915

A further forward observing station was
taken up by orders of 2n Corps & Pne. +a
wire laid by 2n Signal Coy. This was a
farm just west L in L N de KROISTRAAT
CABARET.
          Communication was maintained
with Inf. Bde HQrs at ELBOW FARM.

          From March 3rd to March 10th the
wire was registered every day in various
parts.
          On March 11 + 12 Lieut C I Curtis.
went out to the F.O. Station which was
within 300 yds of the enemy's trenches. he
reported the shooting to be wonderfully
accurate.

          The attack on hill 76 took place
on March 12th.
          It had been timed to take place
at 7 am. but light was bad & it was
put off until 3.30 pm.
          The attack was to be delivered by
the Wilts, + W'cesters of the 85 Bde (3rd Div.) &
supported on right by units of (5 Div)

          The artillery arrangements were
made by 3rd Division.

Mar. 12. 1915

Two Sections 123rd & 1 Section 122 Batteries fired on the wire, the 124 Battery shelled the trenches from SPANBROEK MOELEN northward

The 121 Battery was brought in to fire on the trenches South of the point of attack.

Registering was carried out at 2.30 pm. Fire was opened at 3.0 pm, stopped at 3.10 re opened from 3.30 to 3.35 at a rapid rate.

At 3.35 the range was raised about 300x to fire on 2nd line trenches.

At 3.40. the Infantry attack was launched, but beaten back with very heavy losses. Only two half battalions made the attack & then was no support sent in.

About 40 of the Worcesters on the right got in where the battery had cut the wire & remained until dusk when they withdrew.

The result was very disappointing & seemed to be due to the Staff having unduly tied the hand of the Regimental Officers.

The firing of the Battery was very Satisfactory, & the Brigade received several complimentary messages about its shooting.

March 13th   Mar 13th 1915

Lieut Antrobus went to the F.O.P & the wire was registered again.

Orders were received this day that the 5th Division was to extend to its right to take up a position of the line of the 4th Division this order was cancelled on the 16th

On the 19th the 5 Division was ordered to close to its left as far as PECKHAM, the group of houses in N.30(a) on the KEMMEL WYCHAETE Road.

Accordingly the 83rd Brigade (Bowles) took up the line from the WULVERGHEM – MESSINES road to the WULVERGHEM – KRUSTRAAT road, the 84th Brigade (Royle) thence to the SPANBROEK-MOELEN & the 14th Brigade (Maude) went to the left of the line

H Qrs NEUVE EGLISE

DRANOUTRE

KEMMEL

Div H Qrs St JEAN KAPELLE.

The 2nd Brigade R.F.A. continued to work with the 84th Infantry Brigade.

Mar 13 - Apr. 3. 1915

The Battery position by this time had been made very comfortable & really quite Artistic decorations had been made by the men.

On March 19th Brig Gen John Grover (GOC RA V Div) visited the Battery.

On March 20th Gen Morland visited the Battery both were very pleased with everything.

March 23rd.
2/Lieut H.E. Hall left the Battery on attachment to the School of Trench Mortars at BERCHEN

March 29. Lieut R.B. Miller having been promoted Capt left the Battery on posting to the Meerut Division.

March 31st. 2/Lieut Ching RFA (SR) was posted to the Battery vice Lieut R.B. Miller.

April 3rd. Orders were received that V Div. was to be relieved by the North Midland (Territorial) Division.

The V Division was ordered to take up the line at present held by the 28 Division S.E. of YPRES.

April 3rd – 9th 1915

On Easter Sunday, Major Sedgwick & Lieut. Aubrey visited the new position & the next day Capt Gilman & Lieut Cullen rode over.

April 7th. 2nd Battery, Staffordshire Brigade R.F.A. relieved the Battery, the centre section remaining in action until the night of the 9th-10th.

April 9th at 8.0 p.m. one section per battery of RHA under Major Sedgwick moved to YPRES via OUDERDOM & VLAMERTINGHE.

The 123rd Battery was to occupy the position held by the 69th Battery, the section was in action in the new position by midnight.
The new position was as follows.

The Guns in the Garden of a Chateau immediately N.W. of the Reformatory School East of YPRES.

Observing Station in the Trenches. Telephonic communication was established to the HQrs of the right Battalion in Sector W, just north of the Canal, Wires were run thence up the communication trenches & observation was made from the trenches.

Apr. 10-12 1915

an Officer & Signaller were on permanent duty at B'n HQ.

Average Ranges 4200 yards.

April 10th
Registration was carried out.

Night April 10th-11th the rest of Battery came up.

The Wagon line was placed near Vlamertinghe on the VLAMERTINGHE-OODERDOM road.

April 11th. Registration was carried out at numerous points along the front from the Railway cutting in I.29(c) to the Canal in O.4(a).

The Zone covered by the battery were trenches 31.32.33 extending from I.34 @ 5.5 to I.34 6.33.

Capt A.C. Pulman was attached temporarily to the (N Mid Dur Territorials)

April 12th A Sap head was fired at also a trench Mortar, In the night continued Gun & Rifle & Machine gun fire was brought in to the sap head.

April 7th Temp Lieut Chumley was attached to the Battery.

Apr 8-17. 1915.

April 8th to 16th The Battery fired on most days in Co-operation with the infantry or else for registration

The trenches in this sector of the line (Sector V) could be readily entered by in the daylight.

Particular attention was paid to the Telephone communication which were duplicated & bridged.

April 17th
A mine was sprung on hill 60 just west of the railway cutting in I-29(c) & the hill was rushed by the West Kents (12 Inf Bde) at 7. 0pm.
The role assigned to the Battery was (a) to shell the front line trenches between the road in I 35 a) and the mound called the Caterpillar south of the railway in I 35.(a). To search the woods in rear of this zone with a view to establishing a belt of shrapnel fire through which the enemy's infantry must pass.

The work was carried out satisfactorily & involved the Battery remaining continuously in action for 48 hours without the detachments getting any rest.

Apr 17-19. 1915.

During the night the F.O Officer Lieut Aubrobus and his three signallers had a most difficult task trying to keep the telephone wires working

They were repeatedly broken along the trenches.

In this service Br Davies was wounded he was recommended for special distinction

April 18th
During the 18th the Battery was shelled a little by a 6" Howitzer.

April 19th
The Battery continued firing sometimes on its attack zone, sometimes on its defensive zone by order of the OC Brigade. Corrections of registration were very difficult on account of the interruptions of the telephone wires Lieut Curlew did very good work during the night 18-19 in this regard, The signallers chiefly engaged in this work were.
Br Tillett & Br Pateman.
Br Davies
Dr Cooney   { Br Tillett } Mentioned in
Gr Corran   { " Davis } dispatches June 15.
Gr Brady.   awarded D.C.M. 20-1-16
                 awarded Russian Order St George 2 Class
                 25.6.15.
Lt Aubrobus went sick with Measles.

Apr. 19-22. 1915.

April 19th
During the day some 6" Howitzers were fired at the Battery for some hours and then later on at intervals.

C.S.M Wager R.A Staff Clerk attached to the Battery on probation for a commission & B⁻ Tulled were killed, & 473⁻ McDowell wounded.

These men were buried in the Churchyard at the junction of the Menin-Roulers road to YPRES.

April 20th Things began to wear off a little the Battery fired a little occasionally & was not heavily shelled.

April 21st The Germans bombarded hill 60 & the line of Guns very severely. During the Bombardment Gnr Stafford was killed & Gnr McCluskie wounded. About 4500 rounds were fired in these three days.

April 22
At 10 am one gun was taken forward by Maj. Sedgwick to a position on the line between I 28 (a) & I 29 (c) to fire at close range on the hostile trenches. In the evening the Germans rushed trenches held by French Native Troops N.E. of YPRES & the situation became precarious, the advanced gun was withdrawn to the wagon line, also a gun which required overhauling.

Apr. 23-29. 1915.

April 23 & 24th the situation was dangerous, the battery however fired little, maintaining its double role of covering trenches 31. 32. 33 & also the trenches & woods in its attack zone.

Night April 24·25 Reinforcements arrived.

April 25th to 29th
The Battery continued in the same position firing but little, & experienced a cross fire from three directions, which fortunately never found the Battery position.

April 27th. A Gun was taken to the same position in the line between I 28(a) & I 29(c)

April 29
A new position was reconnoitred for the battery, and a second gun was taken forward. Capt. Cullman rejoined. Night April 30 - May 1st the Battery was moved to a position in I 20 (a) 8·7. The defensive zone of the Battery was now trenches 34 & 35. The Forward Observing Officer lived at B⁰ HQ. (in this case the Norfolks) & also had charge of the forward guns.

Apr. 29. 1915

The communications at this period were elaborate & appeared as below.

TRENCHES.
36.   35.   34.

Bn. H Qrs

All cross wires & junctions
were made connections

H. Forward Cum

1/0.17   Battery

Bn H Q

May 1st 1915

May 1/. Lieut R H Ankrtson resumed the Battery from Hospital
& Lieut Hall was again attached from the Trench
MORTAR School.

The Wagon line was now in G 16 (a) 8.2

The wagons were not with the guns.

The general plan & section of pits were as follows

[sketch: plan view of gun pits with ammunition recesses and shelter]

[sketch: section showing gun emplacement with sandbag traverse, 2'6" and 2'3" dimensions]

Aeroplane cover was carefully planted to conceal
the guns & constantly renewed. The men slept at the
guns in shelters made of sandbags, & roofed with
Iron Boards Doors etc covered with turf.
The Officers, Servants, Orderlies Cooks Signallers etc
lived in Dug outs in the Railway Embankment.

May 2-7. 1915

The position was any under charge of Lieut C.J Curtis at night & the Guns moved in about 1-0 am.

A Bridge over a stream about 300ᵡ S of the Battery was constructed as an alternative "Bolt hole".

May 2ⁿᵈ 3ʳᵈ 4ᵗʰ Passed without special incident the battery firing when called upon, & for registration.

May 5ᵗʰ The Germans [pushed a hill 60] & three trenches west of that point after an emission of poisonous gases.

The battery fired incessantly from about 7 oam on May 5ᵗʰ till well on into May 6ᵗʰ. The counter attack about 2 oam in the night May 5.+6 failed, the Huns tried to prepare the attack, but the constant oscillation of the Infantry when an occasional round fell short into their trenches induced all batteries to increase their range, consequently the fire was ineffective.

Night 6 & 7ᵗʰ May. The Battery was again firing all night; about 2.30 an attack was made & this time the Huns opened fire after the assault in order to create a Zone

May 8-12-1915.

zone of fire, as a protection to the working parties. The attack made by the 2ⁿᵈ Corps KOYLI. failed.

MAY 8-12

On the 5 Div Front - there was comparative quiet, The defence zone of the Battery was trenches 35 & 36.

The Officer on duty with the Infantry was also in charge of the forward Section, and very good work indeed was done by this section, in Bombarding at close ranges the Trenches, both fire & communication in HILL 60.

This section was worked in conjunction with the Machine Guns, and did very good work driving the enemy out of their dug outs in the Railway cutting and elsewhere.

Bursts of fire were made occasionally at various hours, & occasionally the battery was called upon to check the enemy's fire by retaliating on their parapets.

During the 8ᵗʰ 9ᵗʰ & 10ᵗʰ and to some extent on the 11ᵗʰ there was terrific fighting on the left of the Division or the front held by the 5ᵗʰ Corps.

May 12-15 1915

On May 12th as showing the dangers of the method of Observation from the trenches with periscopes, It may be recorded that Major Sedgwick had two periscopes broken within half an hour, the pieces inflicting some slight scalp wounds.

May 3rd to 10th Lieut R H Ambrose acted daily as Orderly Officer to the OC 28th Brigade RFA

May 10th The Battery continued in the same position, the forward guns continued to do good work, on the 9th they Blew up a small magazine (probably French bombs) on the 11th they had another piece of work exploding a big magazine, which in its turn blew in a Mine Gallery which the Germans were constructing

May 15. 444466 G. Wilcocks was wounded in the arm at the forward guns by a chance over from a rifle bullet.

About this time orders were received to economize ammunition in every possible way.

May 11 - June 7. 1915

Throughout May up to June 11th The Battery remained in action in the same position

The Wagon line was moved back to a position in H 26(a) about 1 mile East of OUDERDOM.

The Battery fired very seldom now and only by Order of O.C. 28 Bde R.F.A., or at the request of the O.C. Norfolk Regiment whose front the Battery was covering

May 11th the 122 Battery went out of action for a weeks rest, the Zone covered by the 123 Battery was then made trenches 36 & 37 & the Caterpillar and the Railway cutting the forward section continued to fire on Hill 60, and the trenches on the southern slope of the mound & the communications in rear.

May 28th Lieut Ching went sick and was Invalided home.

June 7th Leave having been reopened Lieut C.I. Curtis went on leave, followed by Major Sergavist

Leave was also opened to 1 NCO

Leave was only granted to Officers & NCOs who were considered to require a rest after the long period

June 8-to 30 1915

Period of duty in action.
No 34270
June 9th 2/Gnr Farrar was wounded at the forward Gun.

Two or three Horses were hit taking Ammunition to the forward section.

Leave continued until all the officers had had a second turn of leave, and the N.C.O.'s began to go in somewhat larger numbers.

There was very little firing, on June 15th & again on June 22nd a little firing was done to help to cover the attack of the 3rd Division, near Hooge.
June 18th 2/Lt R.F. Mason joined from Vth D.A.C. -took over Lt. Section
On June 23rd No 48265 Sgt. Sage was hit by a bullet at the back of the head & invalided wounded.

Honours & Rewards
In the list of mentioned in despatches published in the middle of June,
the names of
Lt. R.H. Antrobus
No 55632 Bnr Tullet (Killed)
" 8235 Bdr Davies (Wounded)
appeared.

July 1–7 1915

On July 1st B.S Sgt. Major Durant who had served his whole service from boy upwards to be Battery Sergeant Major, in the 123rd Battery, received a commission as Lt in the Royal Field Artillery.

__Rest Billet.__

From June the 26th to July 2nd the Battery was in rest billets.

The Guns where left in action in charge of a guard.

The whole Battery went back to "Buuschepe" & spent a pleasant week doing "riding & driving drill" etc.

This was the first time since the Battery went into action at   early in October That it had been with-drawn beyond the ordinary shell fire & beyond the sound of the rifle fire.

During the whole of that time it had been almost continuously in action, such breaks as it had had amounting in all to perhaps 20 to 25 days, having been spent in the wagon line while changing position near Lindenhoek & Neuve Eglise.

July the 7th N° 69113 Br Crossan one of the signallers was wounded in the head by a shell splinter while coming down the communication trench after testing wires.

cont: July 10-14 1915.

July 10th the Battery heard that it was to be relieved by the Staffordshire Bde. R.F.A. 46th (North Midland) Division.

It was this brigade which relieved the 28th Brigade near Lindenhoek about April 9th.

July 12th one section was relieved.

July 14th the forwarded gun & the last gun in the battery position were with-drawn & the battery collected at the wagon line.

The battery had been almost exactly three months in the Ypres Salient.

During practically the whole time it fired over the trenches South of the railway as far as the ravine. That is trenches 34, 35, 36, 37.

During most of this time the Norfolk Regiment was holding this line.

The casualties were four killed & nine wounded.

About 6,500 were fired in that time principally between April 17th & May 5th.

cont.   July 16-17 1915

Lt A.C.A.B. Chumley had left the battery about
June 25th.

Lt Durant was attached to the battery from the date
he received his commission July 1st to July 18th.

July 16th the Battery did not remain in rest long.
On July 16th one Section went into action to relieve
a section of the 69th Battery 35th Brigade R.F.A.
28th Division & the other Section followed on the
17th. Only four guns were put in action.
A. Section of the 124th which relieved the 103rd
in its position was attached to the Battery.

The battery position was at N.4(B) 4·5 observing
Station H.35 (b) 9·2.

Attached Section 124th Battery N 4(d) 5·9
forward in a wood called the 'Bois Confalnas'
through which the communication trenches to
Sectors O. & P. ran.

The trenches in Sector P. & O. 4 were held by
Northumberland Fusiliers & a company
Liverpool Scottish of the 9th Brigade Infantry.

28th Bde. H.Q. were on the Northen End of
Dickebusch Village.

Cont__ July 1915

The wagon line was in M. 5 (d).

As in the previous position there were no billets, officers & men living in dug-outs & bivouac shelters.

At this period the composition of Army Corps was under-going some change.

Notification was received that a tenth Corps was to be formed under:

   Maj. Gen. Sir Thomas Morland.
General Morland's own division the 5th was to form the nucleus of the Corps, & another division of the new Army was to replace the 5th Division in the 2nd Corps.

Meanwhile   2 Bde 5th Division
       1st Do - 3rd - Do -
       2nd Bde R.F.A.
       1st Bde How. (5th Division)
where lent to the 5th Corps to hold the line from the Vierstraat - Wytschaete road part S'elow to the canal.

The right of this area was held by the 9th Bde (Gen Murray Smith) & the 28th R.F.A. plus part of a Field How. By.

Cont   July 20-23. 1915.

While in this position affairs were very quiet
in the front.

July 20th Captain Gillman had a shoot at
"Piccadilly Farm" a German Stronghold in front of
the Bois Confleurs in conjunction with the 65th (How.)
Battery R.F.A..

July 22nd officers of the 71st Bde. 17th Division (New
Army) arrived to see the position which they were
to take over.

July 23rd "D" Battery 71st Bde. R.F.A. commanded
by Major Henderson arrived at the wagon line
of the battery & camped in a field close by.

That night one Section relieved a Section of the
123rd Battery which (under Lt Curtis) marched
direct to the billeting area in which the Divisional
Artillery 5th Division was to collect.

The Section out of action & the First line wagons
marched under Major Sedgwick.
                                    Captain Gillman
remained to hand over to the new-comers.

All moves took place after dark. The
weather was fine with a full moon.

602
Reference Map Hazebrouck 1/100,000   5th A   July 23-31, 1915
                                              Belgium.

The Section marched via Renninghelst – Boeschepe
Godewaerswelde Neuve.

The Brigade were in billets on the Country Road, South
of S' Sylvestre Cappell & around the railway crossing.
The 123rd Battery being in a big farm 800x N. of the
__ as Hondeghem on the second night Sections marched
via Bailleul & the main road.

July 26th the whole brigade was concentrated.

July 28th the Brigade was inspected & complimented in
its work by Brig.-General J. C. Geddes Cdg. Art. 5th Div.

July 29th the Brigade was inspected & addressed by
Lieut. General Sir Herbert Plumer Commanding 2nd Army
on its approaching departure to the 3rd Army.

July 30th & 31st the Brigade en-trained at Cassel
for its new zone.

The 123rd Battery left at 1.30 a.m. on the 31st.

The Battery marched at 8.45 P.m. on the 30th via
Hondeghem & Longue Croix to Bavinchove were
Cassel Stn is & embarked without incident.

Contd.
Aug. 1 - 4. 1915

Reference Map Amiens 1/80,000.

It arrived about 1·30 P.M. on the 31st at MARICOURT Station, N.E. of Amiens & detrained, going into billets with the rest of the brigade at Bonnay.

The billets were bad with very little accommodation for the men, but the change from Flanders to the downs & chalk streams of Artois was very welcome.

Lt. Antrobus & Curtis immediately procured local rods & set to work to try to catch fish.

August 2nd Major Sedgwick being on the sick list with a touch of Flanders fever, Captain Gillman went out to Meaulte to see the positions of the French batteries which the brigade was to relieve.

News was received that Major Sedgwick was to be sent home to the New Army.

3rd Aug. The battery moved up to Ville Sur Ancre & Lt. Curtis' section came into action alongside the 11th Battery 28th Regiment French Artillery. Capt. Benquet commanding.

4th Aug Major Sedgwick left for England. Capt. Gillman took over the battery.

Aug 5 – Sept 7. 1915

5th August. 3 more guns came into action, the French withdrawing. Lt. Lutgens joined.

6th August. The battery moved into a wagon line at Méaulte. The Norfolk Regt. held the trenches in front.

15th August. A camouflet was started off in front of our trenches. We expected shelling but nothing came of it.

17th Aug. Anniversary of the battery starting from Belfast to war.

18th–23rd Aug. A very quiet time. A few rounds fired daily, either registering new points, or at the request of the infantry in retaliation.

24th–25th. Were relieved by A/84 Bty. one section each night. On 25th the battery marched to Sailly le Sec into reserve.

6th Sept. Still in reserve, Col. Sandys appointed Brigadier to 14th Divl. Arty.

7th Sept. Col. Harding Newman joined Brigade.

Sept 7 - 23. 1915.

The battery remained in reserve until the 17th Sept.

17th Sept. One section was ordered into action, a mile north of Suzanne relieving one section of A98 battery. Got into action about 9 pm.

18th. Three more guns came into action at the same place at about 9 pm.

22nd. Lt. J. Inglis joined the battery for a fortnight's experience. In the evening the 6th gun took up a position near Bonfray Farm, about 1½ miles north of Bray under Cpt. Lutgens. Four guns shifted to a position N.E of present position. All five guns had a busy time entrenching during the night & laying telephone wires &c

23rd
The four guns shot 512 rounds at German wire entanglements. The 5th gun registered from its new position. At dark 3 guns returned to its previous position & 1 gun joined Capt Lutgens guns & entrenched.

Sept. 24 – Oct. 30. 1915

24th Sept – 1st Oct. Four guns remained in old position & two in Capt Lutgens position. A few registering shots fired. Otherwise all quiet.

2nd October. Two guns went to near Bronfay Farm (P24,3,8) under Capt. Lutgens. B115 joined us in old position.

3rd–11th Oct. Guns remained in action firing a few rounds only.

12th October. Guns from Capt Lutgens position (P24,3,8) returned to Wagon Line.

13th–21st Oct. Two guns remained in old position, together with a new Battery. The rest remained out of action. The men employed in building stables &c.

22nd–29th Battery remained out of action.

30th Three guns came into action at 8.0 pm. to relieve the new battery making 5 guns in action.

Nov. 1 - Dec. 3. 1915

November.

Nov. 1st - 17th   5 guns in action - fired a few rounds daily registering & retaliating.

Nov 17th   The 6th gun came up into action.

Nov. 17th-24th   6 guns in action - ordinary routine.

Nov. 22nd   At 6 pm. 6th gun taken forward to a position at edge of very small wood 200x N.E. of 37th Bty position to fire at Y wood. A.23.C.

Nov. 24 R.E.Trease. R.F.A.(SR.) joined from Q.Bty. R.H.A.

Nov. 24th   Forward gun registered on wire in front of Y wood. Difficult shooting on account of ground sloping down in front of our trenches.

Nov. 25th   Forward gun fired a few more rounds as demonstration to Divl Arty Commander.

Nov. 26th   Forward gun withdrawn to Bty position.

Nov. 26th to Dec. 2nd   Ordinary routine.

Dec. 3rd   One section under Lt Antrobus

Dec. 4 – 10. 1915

Moved to position of 122 Bty, L 3 A 5.10
after dusk

Dec 4th Second section under Lt Mason moved
to same position. 122 Bty withdrew.
1/3 Glamorgan Battery took over
our late position.

Captain Arnott Lt Jones & 9 men
of 1/1 Cardigan Battery attached for
a few days.

Dec 5th 3rd Section of Battery joined the other
two four guns. Lt Cradock remained
behind to help Glamorgan Battery.

Dec 6th 7th Ordinary routine & Registering
new zone etc.

On Dec 8th attached party left us
& on 9th Capt Melanie Lt Findlay
& 9 men from 1/4 Glamorgan Battery

Dec 7-15. 1915

were attacked

On night of Dec 7th - 8th the Cheshire Regt. carried out a bombing expedition to the German trenches. The battery cooperated & fired 129 shells. The operation was a success & the battery was thanked by the O.C. Cheshires for its cooperation.

Dec 9th, 10th, & 11th ordinary routine.

Dec 12th we removed No 6 gun from its "Elephant House" & put it into forward gun position.

Dec 13th. Registered forward gun on zero line & a few other points. A good deal of shelling & aerial torpedoes from the Germans.

Dec 14th. Ordinary routine.

Dec 15th Took two balloon officers round trenches. Tried Bois Coppet O.S. not good for our zone.

Dec. 16-23. 1915

Dec 16th. Ordinary routine.

Dec 17th. Party from gun detachments started for work on our alternative position to make it habitable for 4th Glamorgan Bty, coming in for instruction.

Dec 18th. Party from wagon line on alternative pos. Inspection by Gen Geddes.

Dec 19th. Continued rigging. The major of the incoming battery was taken to trenches to see zone.

Dec 20th. Glamorgan battery came in action.

Dec 21st. Very wet & misty. Impossible for them to register.

Dec 22nd & 23rd. Ordinary Routine.
    Glamorgans registered on trenches.

Dec 23rd. Eight 4·2 shells, coming from S.E, fell into battery wagon line. No damage done though horses had to be moved out of stables.

Dec. 24-25.1915

Dec 24th. Quite a busy day in wagon line.

    10.15 a.m. Risc 4.2's into & near wagon line. One man wounded, Dr Rowley.

    11 a.m. 20 shell passed over & fell beyond 65 By wagon line, apparently fired at BRAY—ETINEHAM road.

    3 p.m. 8 more shell into wagon line, one into wagon park & three more very near Centre X stables. Total damage, one horse slightly wounded, one tree cut in two & one gun-limber damaged.

    3rd & 4th Flannigans went out of action. Omitted to return case of whiskey we'd lent them.

Dec 25th. Xmas Day.

    Quiet in Bray. Men thoroughly enjoyed their Xmas dinner. A good deal of shelling on our trenches, especially Wellington Redoubt & 70 bty. 3 infantrymen killed & 7 wounded in 70 bty.

Dec 26.1915 – Jan 4.1916

Dec 26th.
    Lt Antrobus left for Anti Aircraft School at BERTRANCOURT.
    More shelling on Wellington Redoubt & 70 bty.

Dec 27th. Ordinary Routine.

Dec 28th. Lecture on battle of Loos at Mericourt.

Dec 29th, 30th, & 31st. Ordinary routine.

5th Division

28th Bde. R.F.A.

January to December
1916

Army Form C. 2118.

WAR DIARY
or
INTELLIGENCE SUMMARY.
(*Erase heading not required.*)

Instructions regarding War Diaries and Intelligence Summaries are contained in F.S. Regs., Part II. and the Staff Manual respectively. Title pages will be prepared in manuscript.

Hour, Date, Place	Summary of Events and Information	Remarks and references to Appendices
	War Diary 2nd Bde R.F.A. January 1916. Vol XVII	

Army Form C. 2118.

WAR DIARY
or
INTELLIGENCE SUMMARY.
(Erase heading not required.)

Instructions regarding War Diaries and Intelligence Summaries are contained in F. S. Regs., Part II. and the Staff Manual respectively. Title pages will be prepared in manuscript.

Hour, Date, Place	Summary of Events and Information	Remarks and references to Appendices

1916

Saturday January 1st

Sunday January 2nd

Monday January 3rd

Tuesday January 4th

Wednesday January 5th

Thursday January 6th

Friday January 7th

Saturday January 8th

Sunday January 9th

Monday January 10th

Tuesday January 11th

Instructions regarding War Diaries and Intelligence
Summaries are contained in F. S. Regs., Part II.
and the Staff Manual respectively.   Title pages
will be prepared in manuscript.

WAR DIARY
or
INTELLIGENCE SUMMARY.
(*Erase heading not required.*)

Hour, Date, Place	Summary of Events and Information	Remarks and references to Appendices
Wednesday January 12th	Nothing to report	
Thursday January 13th		
Friday January 14th		
Saturday January 15th		
Sunday January		
Tuesday January		
Tuesday January		
Wednesday January 9th		
Thursday January 28th		
Friday January		
Saturday		
Sunday January 29		
Tuesday January		

Army Form C. 2118.

WAR DIARY
or
INTELLIGENCE SUMMARY.
(Erase heading not required.)

Instructions regarding War Diaries and Intelligence Summaries are contained in F.S. Regs., Part II. and the Staff Manual respectively. Title pages will be prepared in manuscript.

Hour, Date, Place	Summary of Events and Information	Remarks and references to Appendices
Tuesday January 26		
Wednesday January 27		
Thursday January 28		
Friday January 29		
Saturday January 30		
Sunday January 31		
Monday February 1		

Army Form C. 2118.

WAR DIARY
or
INTELLIGENCE SUMMARY.
(Erase heading not required.)

Instructions regarding War Diaries and Intelligence Summaries are contained in F.S. Regs., Part II. and the Staff Manual respectively. Title pages will be prepared in manuscript.

Hour, Date, Place	Summary of Events and Information	Remarks and references to Appendices
	War Diary 28th Brigade R.F.A. February 1916. Vol XVIII	

Army Form C. 2118.

WAR DIARY
or
INTELLIGENCE SUMMARY.
(Erase heading not required.)

Instructions regarding War Diaries and Intelligence Summaries are contained in F.S. Regs., Part II. and the Staff Manual respectively. Title pages will be prepared in manuscript.

Hour, Date, Place	Summary of Events and Information	Remarks and references to Appendices
Tuesday February 1st		
Wednesday February 2nd		
Thursday February 3rd		
Friday February 4th		
Saturday February 5th	Brigade in rest at St Gratien	
Sunday February 6th		
Monday February 7th		
Tuesday February 8th		
Wednesday February 9th		
Thursday February 10th		
Friday February 11th		
Saturday February 12th	Brigade in rest at St Sauveur	
Sunday February 13th		
Monday February 14th		
Tuesday February 15th		
Wednesday February 16th		

Army Form C. 2118.

WAR DIARY
or
INTELLIGENCE SUMMARY.
(Erase heading not required.)

Instructions regarding War Diaries and Intelligence Summaries are contained in F.S. Regs., Part II. and the Staff Manual respectively. Title pages will be prepared in manuscript.

Hour, Date, Place	Summary of Events and Information	Remarks and references to Appendices
Thursday February 17th		
Friday February 18th		
Saturday February 19th		
Sunday February 20th	Brigade in rest at St Sauveur	
Monday February 21st	(near Amiens)	
Tuesday February 22nd		
Wednesday February 23rd		
Thursday February 24th		
Friday February 25th	Brigade moves to Longuevillette (nr Doullens)	
Saturday February 26th	in Divn Reserve	
Sunday February 27th	rest	
Monday February 28th	Brigade marches to Beauquesne	
Tuesday February 29th	rest	

Cunningham
Lt Col
Comdg 7 th Infantry Bde NZR

Army Form C. 2118.

WAR DIARY
or
INTELLIGENCE SUMMARY. 23 Bde RFA
(Erase heading not required.)

WO 19/21

Hour, Date, Place	Summary of Events and Information	Remarks and references to Appendices
ARRAS 1916 Jan 2	The Brigade came into action. The Command passed from the FRENCH to the ENGLISH and the 1st Group French Artillery, 23rd Regt of Artillery, was replaced by the Right Group consisting of 123 Bty, 124 Bty & 365 Bty (Horse) and 119 Bty RFA under the Command of O.C 28 Bde R.F.A, Col HARDING NEWMAN.	

Army Form C. 2118.

WAR DIARY
or
INTELLIGENCE SUMMARY.
(Erase heading not required.)

28 Bde RFA

Hour, Date, Place	Summary of Events and Information	Remarks and references to Appendices
ARRAS		
March 12.	123 Bty fired 20 rounds in conjunction with 87 French Mortar	
	124 Bty re-registered tested fuzes	
Mar 13	123 Bty registered 124 Bty registered	Mar 19 "B"supy Capt R.H STUDDERT posted to 15 Bde RFA to command 52 Bde RFA
Mar. 15	do	
Mar 17	124 Bty fired at Rolling H1 + B32.	
Mar 18	124 Bty fired 41 rounds at hops G18 A 5/2. 123 Bty also fired	
Mar 21	A quiet day	Lt RETREASE form attached to posted 28 Bde vice Lt RE ANTROBUS to 7 Airmen
Mar 23	124 Bty fired at trenches German Bty 77 mm H19 B57	
Mar 25	123 Bty registered, 124 Bty fired at various points also registered	
Mar 26	123 Bty fired 70 rounds on G12 A 8/3, 9.12 A 7/3. G 6c G.pt	
Mar 27	124 Bty "Notch" night fire officers J1, 123 Bty fired off J2 - Ent.	
Mar 28	123 Bty registered : 124 Bty registered a horwitz on 14 Dec front.	31 Mar 2 Lt R.C STEWART from A Reserve Kbs RFA attached to 28 Bde RFA
Mar 29	124 Bty fired at working parties 123 Bty registered	
Mar 30	123 Bty fired 1S - J sect J2 124 Bty fired J sect J2	

Comdg 28 Bde RFA

Army Form C. 2118.

WAR DIARY
or
INTELLIGENCE SUMMARY.
(Erase heading not required.)

28 Bde RFA

Instructions regarding War Diaries and Intelligence Summaries are contained in F.S. Regs., Part II. and the Staff Manual respectively. Title pages will be prepared in manuscript.

Hour, Date, Place	Summary of Events and Information	Remarks and references to Appendices
ARRAS		
April 1	Batteries did not fire. Some hostile fire	From 30 April 65 Bty & 8 Bde
2	124 Bty retaliated, also fired rounds at reports of infantry. 123 Bty registered	Dnl 206" will be developed by O.C. 28 Bde RFA
6	123 & 124 Batteries both fired	[Roster letter order S.S.O. of 30 Apl 1916]
7	123 Bty fired for protection of attached Officers. 123 Bty fired at slightly	
8	Considerable shelling ARRAS & neighbourhood.	
11	124 Bty fired at SIX ARBRES. Retaliation; also in retaliation at report of infantry	
13	124 Bty registered new gun in Emplacement scheduled G.n.o.9. 2 Guns	
14	123 Bty fired at plenty of miss-lenft disposed. 124 Bty fired at PASSERELLE	
15	124 Bty fired at G.18.C. 123 Bty fired at G.18.A Considerable movement & seen	
17	123 Bty fired at G.12.A 7½/13½, G.12.C 4/3, G.12.C 7½/9, G.12d 9½/6½, G6c 7½/6	
20	123 Bty fired at German trenches opposite 9.8/100 Working party. 124 Bty fired at SIX ARBRES H.79.d.3/8	
21	123 Bty fired at working party. 124 Bty fired at German huts. Some hostile shelling	
24	123 Bty fired at pork & hen H.7d 5/8. 12m Bty fired 3 rounds - practising Barrage. Considerable hostile shelling	
30	123 Bty fired at working parties, checked barrage etc. Bn Bty fired in retaliation for working parties	

[signature]
28 Bde RFA

Army Form C. 2118.

WAR DIARY
or
INTELLIGENCE SUMMARY.   28 Bde RFA
(Erase heading not required.)

Instructions regarding War Diaries and Intelligence Summaries are contained in F.S. Regs., Part II. and the Staff Manual respectively. Title pages will be prepared in manuscript.

Hour, Date, Place		Summary of Events and Information	Remarks and references to Appendices
ARRAS	May 1	123 Bty fired at working party. 124 Bty fired offsets B5 & B6 trenches. Counter battery hostile shelling	2 May 2/Lt H P Jeffers left for base on being transferred from the Ranks
	3	123 Bty retaliated, fired on Germans seen 124 Bty harassed enemy & took part in combined shoot with trench mortars	
	4	123 Bty fired at Railway CUTTING # 124 Bty fired at working party ARRAS shelled	
	5	123 Bty registered point for instructions Jonny Offices also retaliation	
	6	123 Bty checkerboard & day retaliation 124 Bty fired on working party retaliated	
	7	harassed shelling drew over. 123 Bty fired in retaliation also 124 Bty	
	8	124 Bty retaliated on trenches at m.G.180. 123 Bty fired in retaliation o/p 98, trench	
	9	123 Bty fired in G.12.D.7/1 trenches in 9/3.a	
	10	124 Bty fired searching for TM point No Canada roads G.180. 123 Bty retaliated trench mortar trench H.20.4	
	11	124 Bty fired on trench G.18.A.5.5. 123 Bty fired on MOUND G.60 b.h.	
	12	123 Bty fired on trenches. 124 Bty at SIX ARBRES, Houses in St LAURENT BLANGY	
	13	124 Bty fired on trench G.18.A. Knocked obtained, also trench at CROSS ROAD G.24.A	15 May Capt L G Lutyens Command 37 Bty RFA. handed information by ACMY had retained
	14	A quiet day Hindenburg trestle shelling	
	15	Very quiet day	

WAR DIARY or INTELLIGENCE SUMMARY

(Erase heading not required.) 2/8 Bde RFA

Army Form C. 2118.

Hour, Date, Place	Summary of Events and Information	Remarks and references to Appendices
ARRAS May 27	123 Bty fired 8 rounds in retaliation for shelling of SUNDAY AVENUE	
28	12+ Bty fired on 7 M at 6am & 7/k. 9t coasts firing at once	
	65 Bty fired on Trest M between G.6.d.3/9 to G.6.D.3/- in retaliation in response	
29	123 Bty checked line of front proved in retaliation for shelling SUNDAY AVENUE. 124 Bty Bty fired in retaliation but were confined to stop owing to hostile aircraft. more hostile shelling than usual.	
30	124 Bty fired in retaliation for T.M's + 7.2's on FEBRUARY AVENUE 65- Bty fired on ST LAURENT. Considerable hostile fire	
31	123 Bty fired Test K.1 + registered 124 Bty registered 65 Bty retaliated for shelling of F.2.	

J Rupert Majs
(mdg) 2/8 Bde RFA

Army Form C. 2118.

WAR DIARY
or
INTELLIGENCE SUMMARY. 28 Bde RFA
(Erase heading not required.)

Hour, Date, Place	Summary of Events and Information	Remarks and references to Appendices
ARRAS June 1 1916	12" Bty inspected. 128 Bty fired at T.M about 6 to 1 3/4. 65 Bty fired about 9.3-9.5 trenches in support of Infantry considerable hostile aeroplane activity throughout the day	
2	128 Bty registered fresh productions of attached green, retaliated for shelling of J2 All Batteries tried J2 + possibly J4 for TM3. TMs ceased. ARRAS shelled near CATHEDRAL about 4 to 5.95. J1 + J3 shelled during most of the day.	
3	65 Bty FOO observed for 6" College which retaliated for TM's on J2 between 9.0 am + 10.15am. Enemy fired 5.9 into ARRAS near Cathedral from about 1 pm till 5pm J1+3 were much harassed by many TMs. All Batteries retaliated. 65 Bty opened on T.M at G/25/3. French 220 mm also assisted + fire begun. (Considerably more hostile shelling than usual) A great letter of thanks for the assistance given by the Group was received from the 15 Infty Bde	Amongst the list of Births honoured in "the Times" of Saturday, 3 June 1916, was MILITARY CROSS Capt. L. A. J. PASK. R.G.A (Adj. 65 Bty RFA) Distinguished Conduct Medal No. 137604 Bombr. G. PATEMAN 132" Bty RFA

Army Form C. 2118.

WAR DIARY
or
INTELLIGENCE SUMMARY.
(Erase heading not required.)

Hour, Date, Place	Summary of Events and Information	Remarks and references to Appendices
ARRAS 4 June 1916	123 Bty registered two Spanish mortars; retaliated round for round on J2. 144 Bty. registered from new gun pit; retaliated for shelling and trench mortaring on J1 — fired 166 A× 65 Bty. and 149 B× endeavouring to silence TM's firing on J2 and J1; also 48 B× in retaliation shelling J1. 15 Wig. Res Intelligence summary describes shooting of Commanication trenches 15 pto as "magnificent" Considerable hostile shelling ARRAS — neighbourhood	
About 9.0 p.m	"The Germans put up 3 white — No. 1 opposite 97 + 95 FTs, No.2 near concrete listening post AUGUST AVENUE. No.3 on night of 98 F.T. SOS was sent to W2.26.5 Batteries and the Batteries fired the following number of rounds:- 123 Bty — 301 A + 248 A 144 — 122 65 — 6 211 B×	

Army Form C. 2118.

WAR DIARY
or
INTELLIGENCE SUMMARY.
(Erase heading not required.)

Instructions regarding War Diaries and Intelligence Summaries are contained in F.S. Regs., Part II. and the Staff Manual respectively. Title pages will be prepared in manuscript.

Hour, Date, Place	Summary of Events and Information	Remarks and references to Appendices
ARRAS 1916		
June 5	123 Bty registered various points	
	12 in Bty fired NKTM emplacement G.18.a 4.4. Registered	
	6.5 Bty fired 15 rounds in retaliation for shelling # to	
	night at J2	
	A quiet day - some shelling in AREAS & neighbourhood	
June 6	123 Bty checked J2 night line	
	12 in Bty fired 6 rounds in retaliation for shelling G.17.d 3/5	
	and at S.P. AREAS in retaliation for TMs in Pt D.5.i also	
	4.2 rounds which silenced TM Batteries in G.18.c 3/5 & G.18.A	
	6.5 Bty retaliated for TM's	
	A fairly quiet day except for trench mortars	

Army Form C. 2118.

WAR DIARY
or
INTELLIGENCE SUMMARY.
(Erase heading not required.)

28 Bde RFA

Hour, Date, Place		Summary of Events and Information	Remarks and references to Appendices
ARRAS	May 16	124 Bty retaliated for shelling of B 82 & 83, on G.18 c 575	
	17	124 Bty retaliated on Houses in BLANGY ST LAURENT for shelling of ARTILLERIE	
	18	123 Bty registered guns in new sunpit. 124 Bty retaliated	
	19	123 Bty retaliated on 91 c St-8 7/s on retaliation at request of Infantry. J 2. 124 Bty retaliated. Presumably move Hostile gun them used.	21 May & June 6.5 Howr Bty RFA RFA (becoming part of 28 Bde RFA) on dissolution of 8 Bde RFA
	20	124 Bty fired at SAP and P SIX ARBRES - in Q Emplacement G.18 a 3/ very satisfactory. 124 Bty retaliated on G.12 c 6/3 for H.2.S.	Capt F G FOSTER RMA posted to Bde vice Capt TODD RAMC to Northn Yeomanry
	21	123 Bty Shelled some of day. Considerable hostile shelling	2nd Lt F T N BARBER attached to Bde on Munsterius to 5 Bde RFA
	22	123 Bty fired on German front line Trench.	Lt N C CLERY Adjt 28 Bde to b O 5 pic French Mortars
	23	123 Bty fired rounds of error 9 May. 12m Bty retaliated for shelling Houdennie 65 Bty retaliated for TMs. Considerable hostile fire	
	23	123 Bty fired 216 rounds & 124 Bty 36 for rounds 6.5 Fd Bty 196 Rds in support of Infantry	2 May Capt L G LUTYENS to Command 37 Bty RFA
	24	A great day except for some hostile shelling.	
	25	124 Bty & 65 Bty retaliated for shelling of ARRAS which was considerable	2nd Lt W J BANKS 6 Bty to
	26	123 Bty retaliated on French Trench in M.15.a for shelling of ARRAS. AVENUE Normal for 9 round Command J.15 Bty RFA 65 Bty registered Areas Battalion	
		124 Bty retaliated for TMs shelled - two S."	

Forms/C. 2118/11.

WAR DIARY
or
INTELLIGENCE SUMMARY.
(Erase heading not required.)

Army Form C. 2118.

Hour, Date, Place	Summary of Events and Information	Remarks and references to Appendices
ARRAS 1916 June 7	123 Bty fired at present & Infantry. 65 Bty fired at enemy trenches at request of Infantry. Some shelling of ARRAS neighbourhood. A quieter day.	Lieut H G MORRISON to be appointed Adjutant 28th Bgde R F A with effect from 22-5-1916. 2nd Lieut N C CLERY Attached to Superior Trench Mortar Batteries, between Army & Divisions. Authority GOC 6th Corps No A/1267 d.5-6-1916. Lt MORRISON to be Temporary Lieutenant
June 8	123 Bty checked 85 fuze with 80 fuze. 65 Bty fired at trench mortars. Much shelling of ARRAS's neighbourhood.	
9	123 Bty registered night lines. From about 8.30 pm to 9 pm a number hostile aeroplanes were observed flying over ARRAS & neighbourhood. Several bombs dropped from hostile aeroplanes were	
10	123 Bty registered for "Hurricane" retaliation. ARRAS Practically no hostile shelling	

Army Form C. 2118.

WAR DIARY
INTELLIGENCE SUMMARY.
(Erase heading not required.)

Instructions regarding War Diaries and Intelligence Summaries are contained in F.S. Regs., Part II. and the Staff Manual respectively. Title pages will be prepared in manuscript.

Hour, Date, Place	Summary of Events and Information	Remarks and references to Appendices
1916		11 June
ARRAS 11 June	123 Bty checked registration. 1st Bty fired at Hindenbergfarken. Little hostile fire	Col E HARDING NEWMAN DSO proceeded to 55th Div to take over Command of the Artillery Temporarily. Our Bde under the Command of Major F L CONGREVE (O.C. 1st Bde RFA)
12 June	Batteries fired Hurricane fire in retaliation for T.M.'s on J.2 - Shelling on J.2. 123 Bty fired 47 rds - Misty + showery during day - Observation difficult	
13 June	123 & 6.5 Btys fired "Hurricane" fire in retaliation for shelling J.2.	
14 June	123 Bty fired 52 rds in retaliation.	
15 June	123 Bty retaliated for fire on Crater. A quiet day.	

WAR DIARY
or
INTELLIGENCE SUMMARY.
(Erase heading not required.)

Army Form C. 2118.

Hour, Date, Place	Summary of Events and Information	Remarks and references to Appendices
AREAS 1916		
16 June	123 Bty fired 15 rounds to check error of the day & for instruction of Officer attached. A quiet day.	Among those mentioned in Sir DOUGLAS HAIG's despatch published in the Times 16/Jan/1916 were:— Major M CROFTON DSO 122 Bty Lt C J CURTEIS 123 Bty RFA
17 June	65 Bty fired at Bosch - Maxim Gun. This gun did not give away during the day. Considerable hostile shelling.	
18 June (3.15pm)	123 Bty retaliated on front line support trenches opposite J.2 about 12 hostile heavy guns near ARRAS & NICHOLAS trenches active. Strafing 4 to 30 pm	
19 June	123 Bty. 25 Ar. fired for Academic instruction of Lt. TREASE. A quiet day. 2nd Lieut Rose replaced the 15 Inf. Bde in J1 J2 Sectors	
20 June	123 Bty. 15 Ar. fired for instruction of Lt. C.I CURTEIS by the RIGHT GROUP	

Army Form C. 2118.

WAR DIARY
or
INTELLIGENCE SUMMARY.
(Erase heading not required.)

Instructions regarding War Diaries and Intelligence Summaries are contained in F.S. Regs., Part II. and the Staff Manual respectively. Title pages will be prepared in manuscript.

Hour, Date, Place	Summary of Events and Information	Remarks and references to Appendices

ARRAS

1916
June 21 — 123 Bty fired at reported Infantry. 12M Bty 12/rds fired for instruction of Mr STEWART. A quiet day. Considerable movement observed.

22 — 85 Bty fired 23 Rx Celebration of Jerriat including at Johnny Afrea. A fairly quiet day.

23 — 85 Bty fired 25 × ATHIES-FEUCHY in retaliation for shelling of ARRAS

24 — 12 Bty/Retaliated also fast Bty 85 Bty fired at trench mortars. Previnable shelling of J1 + J2

June 24 — 18.10. so far the Command of Right Group passed to Lt Col BRADELL — Lt COLWELL + SLOWELS GROUP + 46

Army Form C. 2118.

WAR DIARY
or
INTELLIGENCE SUMMARY.
(Erase heading not required.)

Instructions regarding War Diaries and Intelligence Summaries are contained in F.S. Regs., Part II. and the Staff Manual respectively. Title pages will be prepared in manuscript.

Hour, Date, Place	Summary of Events and Information	Remarks and references to Appendices
1916		
BEAUMETZ June 24	On the night of June 24/25 1 section of 65 Bty Left Battery Wagon line to action near BEAUMETZ.	
	Major the Honorable A.V.F. Col REYNOLDS D.C. LEFT Group 5.5 hr.	
	Rest Section Staff moved to BEAUMETZ	
June 25	General Bombardment German trenches all along the British front	Strength
	In the night of 25/26th pivoting Section of B,F,125 Bty Rutherens came into action	
June 26	Bombardment continued	
27	do	
28-30	do	

D. Lumsden MS.
County
28 Bde RFA

Army Form C. 2118.

38th Bde. R.F.A
Storm

WAR DIARY
or
INTELLIGENCE SUMMARY.
(Erase heading not required.)

Vol 23

Hour, Date, Place	Summary of Events and Information	Remarks and references to Appendices
1916		
BEAUMETZ July 1	Brigade still under Command of Lt Col REYNOLDS OC LEFT GROUP	
2	5.5 D.G.	
3	Brigade have not 2 others + moved to REBREUVE	4 July Lieut W D MORGAN from 27 Bde 28 Bde RFA
4-5	The Command of Col E HARDING NEWMAN DSO Brigade at rest.	
6	Staff rides conducted by O C Brigade Battery Commanders + their Staff + Brigade Quartering Staff	
7	Batteries Drilling Head Quarters Staff Signalling	
8	Brigade Drill Order	
9	Under the O C Brigade	
10-13	Batteries individually	12 July 2nd Lt C C COPPERTHWAITE from Res Attached 28 Bde RFA to 65 By RFA
14	Brigade moved to OUTREBOIS	
15	Brigade moved to POCHEVILLERS - Bivked through HEM GEZAINCOURT BEAUVAL + VAL de MAISON	
16	Brigade moved to QUERRIEU via RUBEMPRE + S GRATIEN Came under the 15 Corps, 4 Army.	

Army Form C. 2118.

WAR DIARY
or
INTELLIGENCE SUMMARY.
(Erase heading not required.)

Instructions regarding War Diaries and Intelligence Summaries are contained in F.S. Regs., Part II. and the Staff Manual respectively. Title pages will be prepared in manuscript.

Hour, Date, Place	Summary of Events and Information	Remarks and references to Appendices
1916		
July 17	Brigade moved to HEILLY	
18	V Battery (Major LASCELLES) arrived in Camp Attached to the Brigade for administration. All turned.	Dr H KENNINGTON Attached F.R.R.R from 56 D.A.C.
19	Brigade + V.B.R.y R.H.A. moved from HEILLY ~ Camped in Le CARCAILLOT between MEAULTE and BECORDEL BECOURT	
20	Brigade moved into action West of MONTAUBAN South of the CARNOY MONTAUBAN ROAD. Btty Rect Quarters in German Suffolk trench North of Road Role covering the 95 Inf Bde (1 DEVONS, 1 EAST SURREYS 1 DCLI, 12 GLOUCESTERS) Barrage Lines known S11c571 to S11d 0/0 (MAP LONGUEVAL 57c SW3) 3 Bns on right, 5 Bns on left	

Army Form C. 2118

WAR DIARY
or
INTELLIGENCE SUMMARY.
(Erase heading not required.)

Instructions regarding War Diaries and Intelligence
Summaries are contained in F. S. Regs., Part II.
and the Staff Manual respectively. Title pages
will be prepared in manuscript.

Hour, Date, Place	Summary of Events and Information	Remarks and references to Appendices
MONTAUBAN July 21 1916	S.O.S received from 95 Inf Bde about 10 pm Caterpillar Wood and valley heavily shelled during the afternoon	2nd Lt J.L BRAITHWAITE 1/8 Rif Regt Killed 22/6
22	Brigade Head Quarters shelled from 7.30 pm to 1.30 am. A heavy bombardment at LONGUEVAL by the Germans during the evening	1/23 Reg Light Inf Rif mostly wounded also border Regim attached 3 Machine guns k Trench Mortar Battery attached
23	1s Inf Bde attacked at 3.40 am Bde Head Quarters moved to Angle south of CARNOY-MONTAUBAN Road.	Lt J. H. BOOTHBY 1/8 Rif Regt Killed
24	Considerable hostile shelling all day. Aeroplane reported attack at IV D Cen that the Germans were massing troops for an attack. German trench in 5,11 B + third line between FLERS and MORVAL were reported to be packed with troops	2nd Lt W.A.P. COLERIDGE attached to 1/23 Reg from SDAC
9 pm	A fierce bombardment from HIGH WOOD to WATERLOT FARM was noticed. In a Inf Bde who sent SOS LONGUEVAL and a gas alarm. GAS alarm 4th Bde alarm was false	

WAR DIARY
INTELLIGENCE SUMMARY.
(Erase heading not required.)

Army Form C. 2118.

Hour, Date, Place	Summary of Events and Information	Remarks and references to Appendices
1916 July 24 10 pm 11 pm	DEVONS/infantry situation well in hand. No news from GLOUCESTERS. Firing died down	2/Lt R F G CARTER posted from 123 Bde RFA to 1st Div Ammn Coln Artillery on being Comm- wounded from the Ranks 25% Lt C.F. CAMPBELL RFA RMA wounded
July 25	All quiet 6.0am. From 11.0 am to 5 pm the whole area was heavily shelled by the Germans. Some fires hit. 65 Bde RFA heavily shelled	2/Lt P M BOURNE 65 Bde RFA killed Capt I A J PASK Comdg 65 Bde RFA slightly wounded remained on duty
26	15 inch Bde run from 9.5 Sept. Bde. Heavy 60 Shilling Howh batteries from 9.30 p/m	2/Lt N D T OLIVER posted from S D Ack the Brigade — 123 Bde RFA
27	Our Bombardment Commenced 5.0am. NORFOLKS attacked 7.10am followed by CHESHIRES. 2nd objective on the light reached 3rd Objective the Rly. Company (the N folks in line with 2nd Div) - Through Station with the whole of DELVILLE WOOD. E SURREYS centre	2/Lt R F MASON 123 Bde RFA wounded

Army Form C. 2118

WAR DIARY
or
INTELLIGENCE SUMMARY.
(Erase heading not required.)

Hour, Date, Place	Summary of Events and Information	Remarks and references to Appendices
1916 July 28	3.0 am 95 Inf Bde relieved 15 Inf Bde. An attack was arranged by 95 Bde for 5.30 pm on Sqr 97 to Sqr 6 et 95. It was found not to be necessary as the Germans were found to have vacated practically the whole of DELVILLE WOOD	2/Lt R E TREASE 1/2 R/k slightly wounded - duty
9	95 Inf Bde attacked pre strong points at 3.30 pm in S11c. GLOUCESTERS reported to have attained their objective & points ABC ESUREYS attacked from Dr E. DCLI maintained their position. DEVONS were in reserve. Batteries kept up a steady barrage	2Lt M C P VEREKER attached to 12th Bty RFA from
10 pm	SOS LONGUEVAL received from the Division	

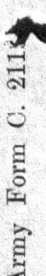

Army Form C. 2118.

WAR DIARY
or
INTELLIGENCE SUMMARY.
(Erase heading not required.)

Instructions regarding War Diaries and Intelligence Summaries are contained in F.S. Regs., Part II. and the Staff Manual respectively. Title pages will be prepared in manuscript.

Hour, Date, Place	Summary of Events and Information	Remarks and references to Appendices
July 30 1916	13 Inf Bde relieved 95 Inf Bde. Att. 4.30 am Patrols were sent out towards German Strong Points. KOSB attacked on night 15 WARWICKS relief at 6.0pm BEDFORDS brought up in Support at 6.30pm. 9pm SOS received.	Lt V D MORGAN posted from 28 Bde RFA to 15 Bde RFA
31	15 Inf Bde relieved 13 Inf Bde. A fairly quiet day. Total Casualties up to date:— 123 Bty R.F.A. 1 Officer wounded-evacuated 1 — wounded-duty 18 O.R. wounded evacuated 3 O.R. Sick do 65 Bty RFA 1 Officer — killed 1 — wounded-duty 8 O.R. do evacuated 2 O.R. Sick do 124 Bty RFA 1 Officer wounded - duty 7 OR do evacuated 9 OR Sick do V Battery RHA 2 Officers killed 1 — wounded-evacuated 2 OR wounded - duty 15 OR killed 1 OR wounded - evacuated do	C Harding Newman Lt Col Comdg 28 Bde RFA

(73989) W4141—463. 400,000. 9/14. H.&J.Ltd. Forms/C. 2118/10.

5th Divisional Artillery.

28th BRIGADE

ROYAL FIELD ARTILLERY

AUGUST 1916

"A" Form.
MESSAGES AND SIGNALS.

Army Form C.2121 (in pads of 100).

TO: 5th Division A

Sender's Number: HAM 1415
Day of Month: Fourth
AAA

Herewith War Diary 28th Brigade R.F.A. for month August.

From / Place: 5th Divisional Artillery

[Stamp: HEADQUARTERS, 5th DIVISIONAL ARTILLERY.]

Army Form C. 2118.

WAR DIARY
or
INTELLIGENCE SUMMARY.
(Erase heading not required.)

2 8 Bde RFA

Vol 24

Hour, Date, Place	Summary of Events and Information	Remarks and references to Appendices
MONTAUBAN Aug 1 1916	52 Sgt Bde/relieved 15 Inf Bde 5 Division at night. 17 Div. On the night of Aug 1/2 the 5 Div Divl Artillery relieved by 17 Division. 5 Div Artillery became Corps Artillery continue to depend 2nd Div (XIII Corps) Front from 7C o/o to S12 a o/o 28 Bde zone S12 a o/o to NORTH STREET 9118 3/2 covering front of 5 2 Inf Bde	Lt. RCA. KINGDOM attached to Bde (123 Bk RFA)
Aug 2	A quiet day	

WAR DIARY or INTELLIGENCE SUMMARY

Army Form C. 2118.

Hour, Date, Place	Summary of Events and Information	Remarks and references to Appendices
1916 Aug 3	U Bty RHA registered points in T13d 5/5 +T7 B A 2/0 starting from ARROWHEAD COPSE. 65 Bty RFA shot at point S11C 6.8 during the day. Rest? fire on normal barrage. very little shelling in the vicinity of the Brigade but hostile Aircraft much more active. Apparently searching for Btys. Reg Bty returned to Wagon line. 124 Bty position 123 Bty fires, the job here took him a long A 'Gas alarm was received but no Gas.	
10 pm Aug 4 3.30-3.45 pm	65 Bty registered points in T13b+d 12B Bty point 18b-9-0. Rest? fire on normal barrage. 5 pm A2d from direction LONGUEVAL across the dry valley on A3b+d + the BRIQUETERIE been shelled until 5.9 and 4.2. very little hostile shelling today with 5.9s. Trying to interrupt Counter-Battery work. Hostile Aircraft very active from 7.0 pm to 8.30 pm and Crew roost near our Trench. Major LASCELLES (under U Bty RHA) appointed to command a Brigade. M field Artillery, 1 Bde.	

Army Form C. 2118.

WAR DIARY
or
INTELLIGENCE SUMMARY.
(Erase heading not required.)

Hour, Date, Place	Summary of Events and Information	Remarks and references to Appendices

1916
Aug 4
9.0 pm
	Zone allotted to the Brigade – TBA 3/7 to S12d 9/5
	(For barrage purposes to S18d 8/a only)
	Brigade finds a F.O.O. with Right Battalion.
	Allotment of Ammunition to the Brigade.
	
	         4·5" How.
	   18 Pounder Day Night
	Day Night
	600 700 300 150
	
	In addition to the above there is no restriction on the Ammunition allowed for firing on harassing points special bombardments etc.
	The above is an extract from Operation Order No 33 by Brig General A H Hussey CB	

WAR DIARY
INTELLIGENCE SUMMARY.

(Erase heading not required.)

Army Form C. 2118.

Hour, Date, Place	Summary of Events and Information	Remarks and references to Appendices
Aug 5 3.0 - 4.30 AM	Our normal barrage. Hostile Batteries checked. A rise to 2 Lt Btys firing in A3 a from direction of HIGH WOOD & 77mm firing on 16 MONTAUBAN from SOUTH WESTERN market shelled. 2 Enemy shell in the vicinity of the Brigade. Observation balloons up during the day. Visual Signalling Communication established between Karon Officer with Rifle Battalion, 51 Inf. Bde & 289th Bde RFA Bde Hd Qrs. Counter Battery by wire with No. 4 KITE BALLOON Section	
Aug 6	All Batteries have registered on T7 d 3-5 by Major CONGREVE From Kite Balloon - results very satisfactory. During the night 11 Bty RHA had one gun hit & destroyed. an battery positions were shelled.	
3.0 - 6.0 pm	Hostile aircraft very active 11 Bty RHA to Wagon Line 12th Bty RFA Came into action from Wagon Line	

WAR DIARY
or
INTELLIGENCE SUMMARY.

Army Form C. 2118.

Hour, Date, Place	Summary of Events and Information	Remarks and references to Appendices
Aug 7 1916 1.30–2.30 p.m.	Batteries fired on normal barrage recorded behind it. All batteries checked their lines. Batteries fired on trenches W. of GINCHY according to programme. OP S 30 b 3/3 New OP DELVILLE WOOD (N. East) TISC WEDGE GINCHY, trenches near GUILLEMONT Station & GUILLEMONT Amn Allotment for night 7/8 doubled	2/Lt B C STEWART (12th Bty RFA) wounded.
Aug 8	All Batteries fired barrage as ordered. Batteries checked lines by Balloon Observation. From 9.0 p.m. 7.8.16 to 4.0 am 8.8.16 the enemy bombarded Area A 3 a+c & A 2 a with 8", 5".9", 4".2", 77mm & incendiary shell — about 4500 rounds being fired. Number of batteries GINCHY. Direct hits on No. 4 gun pit 65 Bty RFA & dugout of OC 123 Bty RFA (blind) & one gun pit 12th Bty.	2/Lt STEWART officially reported wounded

WAR DIARY
or
INTELLIGENCE SUMMARY.
(Erase heading not required.)

Army Form C. 2118.

Hour, Date, Place	Summary of Events and Information	Remarks and references to Appendices
Aug 9 1916	A very quiet night 8/9th. 1&3 Bty to Hazyan line. V Bty RHA Came into action from Hazyan line. Battery fired on normal barrage & allotted task. A few 7mm Shrapnel on A3a 1-. V Bty RHA reported hostile aeroplane over Bty position A3a 5/+.	
10.30 p.m.		
10	65 Bty RFA (A3a 4/+) Shelled intermittently during night of 9th/10th inst with 77 mm Shrapnel & G fired at a very long range. 65 Bty have received gun in place of one disabled. Gun put in a slightly different position to that recouped big gun put out of action all the night of 6th inst. 1st Bty RFA have one gun out of action owing to A tube being completely worn out. All batteries fired on normal barrage. 65 How Bty also fired on hostile battery at W.36.d. 6/1. to 9/1. too much for barrage registration. Not much hostile shelling	2nd Lt J.A.C. STEWART (1st Bty RFA) posted to 25" trench mortar Bty. Lt J.S. SEDDON 25" trench mortar Bty posted to RFA (1st Bty RFA)
11		

Army Form C. 2118.

WAR DIARY
or
INTELLIGENCE SUMMARY.
(Erase heading not required.)

Instructions regarding War Diaries and Intelligence Summaries are contained in F.S. Regs., Part II and the Staff Manual respectively. Title pages will be prepared in manuscript.

Hour, Date, Place	Summary of Events and Information	Remarks and references to Appendices
Aug 12 1916	Batteries checked lines fired on normal barrage. U Bty RHA fired on trench T13a0/5 to T13a2/5 at the request of the Infantry. Very little hostile fire round batteries. F2a Bty to wagon line. 123 Bty came into action from wagon lines.	
13	Batteries registered special points ordered. 65 Bty fired about 30 rounds fired from an 8" How. on right front of Battery. Ammunition was dugout + improved resting gunpits. From 4.0 pm to 9 pm an 8" How firing slowly about A2d + a few rounds near A9a. U Bty RHA new gun-pit completed. Amm. dumps and dugouts strengthened.	Major RICH took command of U Bty RHA
14	Batteries checked lines. Fired on normal barrage. 65 How Bty fired 36 Rx at battery M36d9.3 in FLERS. Fired 10.0 to 11.0 am about 20 5.9s on MONTAUBAN – CARNOY Road just N. of CARNOY. During the night 13/14 – and throughout the day 77mm Bty H.E. fired shrapnel shortly on A3 a, b, c, d & L. No balloons or hostile aeroplanes seen today.	

(73989) W4141—463. 400,000. 9/14. H.&J.Ltd. Forms/C. 2118/10.

Army Form C. 2118.

WAR DIARY
or
INTELLIGENCE SUMMARY.
(Erase heading not required.)

Instructions regarding War Diaries and Intelligence Summaries are contained in F.S. Regs., Part II and the Staff Manual respectively. Title pages will be prepared in manuscript.

Hour, Date, Place 8/16	Summary of Events and Information	Remarks and references to Appendices
Aug 14 (night)	43rd Inf. Bde. 17th Div. relieved 51 Inf. Bde. 17 Div. 43rd Inf Bde consists of :- 6 Bn Somerset L.I., 6 Bn DCLI, 6 Bn KOYLI, 10 Bn Durham L.I, 11th Bn Kings Liverpool Regt. Divnedn	
Aug 15 2.0 pm	About 50 8" on A3d during the day. A hostile aeroplane, without any national markings, flew at a height of about 3000 ft. from the BRIQUETERIE over batteries of the Brigade and then over MONTAUBAN towards LONGUEVAL. 1st Rk RFA were taken over from 123 Bty from 71 Bty RNA. Bde. received two 18 pdrs and two 4.5 Hows - from Drennan 10th equivalents for 5th Divisional Artillery 25.6 wh. Btees who took over South of 7? D.A Some.	Lt. R. B. TREASE, 123 Bty RFA wounded. 2 Lt G. BUTLER (1st Rk RFA) to command No.1 Section 5 DAC
16	Batteries checked lines & fired in normal barrage lines	2 Lt A. J. ATKINS from 5 DAC attached to Bde. (1st Bty RFA)
1.30-3.30 pm	About 40 8" on A3 R+D	
2-2.30 pm	About 4.1 (LHV) on A3a (near Rde Head Quarters)	
	The O.P on TRONES WOOD is being strengthened.	

WAR DIARY or INTELLIGENCE SUMMARY.

Army Form C. 2118.

(Erase heading not required.)

Hour, Date, Place	Summary of Events and Information	Remarks and references to Appendices
1916 Aug 17	Guns repaired & fired according to programme. 2 Gunners of 121st Bty RFA slightly wounded by hostile shelling near Battery position. Hostile aircraft very active. One hostile plane was seen to fall towards POZIERE'S about 10.20 am in flames. Two guns of U Bty RNA occupied advanced position early in the morning.	
18	Batteries fired according to programme. Detached Section of U Bty RNA completed its programme firing 400 rounds. XV Corps attacked enemy trenches E of DELVILLE WOOD, ORCHARD Trench and WOOD Lane. The Corps on right and left attacked at same time.	

Army Form C. 2118.

WAR DIARY
or
INTELLIGENCE SUMMARY.
(Erase heading not required.)

Hour, Date, Place	Summary of Events and Information	Remarks and references to Appendices
1916		
Aug 19	Batteries fired according to programme. 65 How Bty RFA shelled Chicken food at T13 c 6.3. A captured map showed this as a Post. Pt Platoons. 3rd Bay Rde on the new front S18 A 6/4 to T13 A 0/7 relieved by 42nd Inf Rde. Consisting of 5 Bn OXFORD & BUCKS L.I., 5 Bn Kings SHROPSHIRE L.I., 9 Bn K.R.R.C., 9 Bn. RIFLE BRIGADE. 9th Brigade trade & liaison Officer at 42 Rde Head Quarters + at Battn HQ on withdrawing with 15 Rdle RFA.	
Aug 20	Batteries fired on normal barrage. 65 How Bty kept up a steady fire on trenches from T13 d 0/5 to T13 B 6/2 GINCHY and surrounding orchards. Very little hostile shelling. During the withdrawal of 17 Div, 15t from an E+W line through T13 c 0/5 the whole front of 14 Div. 1st from an E+W line through T13 c 0/5 found to the FLERS Road. 28 Rde Zone:- Right boundary E + W line through T13 c 0/5 (but including trenches on W of GINCHY down to T13 d 0/6) SOS line:- 100 yards on enemy side of DELVILLE WOOD from FLERS Road to ALE ALLEY and 100 yds in front of our own trenches from ALE ALLEY Southwards. 7 Div Arty Comm instruction.	

WAR DIARY
or
INTELLIGENCE SUMMARY.
(Erase heading not required.)

Army Form C. 2118.

Hour, Date, Place	Summary of Events and Information	Remarks and references to Appendices
Aug 21 1916	The 14 Div. attacked enemy trenches in DELVILLE WOOD from S.12.b.8/5 to S.12.d.4/0. At the same time XIV Corps attacked trench round GUILLEMONT. The 28 Bde RFA covered the attack made on the 4th Bde. Rde from S.12.c.80/35 to S.12.c.1/6. (18 pdrs) 65 Bty RFA on communication trenches in back areas of barrage. Bdes will keep the left of their line on the FLERS Road during the lifts. A portion of 5 Div. Arty. withdrawn to BUSSY-les-DAOURS. The Artillery covering 14 Div. front have to G.O.C.R.A. 7 Div. The batteries of the Brigade, 71 Bty RHA, 37 Bty RFA (How) & 65th Bty RFA remain in action under the command of Lt. Col. E. HARDING NEWMAN and are known as HARDING NEWMAN'S GROUP. The Brig. General Commanding 5 Div. Arty. received a letter of thanks from Brig. General WOOD CMG Commanding 43 Infty Bde for the way in which the Artillery supported the attack on the 18th inst. & subsequently covered the consolidation of the line.	

Army Form C. 2118.

WAR DIARY
or
INTELLIGENCE SUMMARY.
(Erase heading not required.)

Instructions regarding War Diaries and Intelligence Summaries are contained in F.S. Regs., Part II. and the Staff Manual respectively. Title pages will be prepared in manuscript.

Hour, Date, Place	Summary of Events and Information	Remarks and references to Appendices
1916 Aug 22	All guns checked lines. Fired on normal barrage. 65 How Bty fired 30 Rs at Battery M.35.d.9/4. Some hostile shelling in S.12.R. with 8".	
2.30-3 pm	5.9's dropping round DP in S.16.B.25/55.	
3.0-5.0 pm	Hostile aeroplane very active circling over 37 Btys position. Pras dugout completed by 65 How Bty.	
Aug 23	All guns checked lines. Fired on normal barrage. Guns of 124 Bty firing very irregularly, badly worn overheating. 123 Btys guns also irregular. No Hs fired behind our batteries positions in A.3.a.	
8.0 pm	Hostile aircraft active during the morning. Many aerial combats.	

Army Form C. 2118.

WAR DIARY
or
INTELLIGENCE SUMMARY.
(Erase heading not required.)

Instructions regarding War Diaries and Intelligence Summaries are contained in F.S. Regs., Part II. and the Staff Manual respectively. Title pages will be prepared in manuscript.

Hour, Date, Place	Summary of Events and Information	Remarks and references to Appendices
Aug 24 1916 F 10.30 am 8.0-10 am	Batteries checked lines fired according to programme. A short intense hostile bombardment on the GINCHY - LONGUEVAL Road just North of WATERLOT FARM. 80 Bty position shelled by 4.2's. One gun put out of action & 1 man hit. French Newport Aeroplane brought down this morning close to U Bty position in A3a. U Bty covered the plane with a screen. C/S Bty noticed orderly rendered first aid to pilot. Naval communication established from 700 k Bde & from 37 Bty & 80 Bty to Brigade. In conjunction with Corps operating on our flanks north the French, the 14(light) Division attacked. The front covered the 43rd Inf Bde, whose task was to clear the remainder of DELVILLE WOOD and to establish a line outside DELVILLE WOOD from ALE ALLEY to FLERS - LONGUEVAL Road where offset junction with 33rd Div in TEA TRENCH.	

WAR DIARY
INTELLIGENCE SUMMARY.
(Erase heading not required.)

Army Form C. 2118.

Hour, Date, Place	Summary of Events and Information	Remarks and references to Appendices
1916		
Aug 25	All guns registered on new Zero point & fired on usual barrage. "A" Bty RHA swept the German switch line in S5d for suspected artillery observers. B0 Bty position shelled throughout the day - 2 gun pits, 2 Gun & dumps damaged. The Battery continued to fire throughout.	
9.0 am	Squadrill of 15 pt enemy aeroplanes flew straight over the enemy lines about HIGH WOOD.	
Aug 26		
12.40-1.0 pm	Batteries fired hurricane fire on SOS lines in retaliation at request of Infantry and again from 3.10-3.30 pm. Enemy artillery much more active today from 10.30-11.0 am CATERPILLAR VALLEY was very heavily shelled. B0 Bty position again heavily shelled - 1 gun put out of action.	
5.25 pm	Battery in A3 and A4 shelled with 77 mm shrapnel.	
6.15-7 pm	A3 a was shelled with 8". Batteries worked on new positions during the day.	

Army Form C. 2118.

WAR DIARY
INTELLIGENCE SUMMARY.
(Erase heading not required.)

Hour, Date, Place	Summary of Events and Information	Remarks and references to Appendices
Aug 27 1916	6.40 pm Batteries fired on SOS lines SOS having been received from Right Battalion 43rd Inf Bde. Considerable hostile Artillery activity. BERNAFAY WOOD heavily shelled with 8"	2/Lt M C P VEREKER posted from 12th Bty to X5 "B" Heavy howitzer Bty
5-5.30 pm	3 hostile aeroplanes flew over our lines. Communications complete to all new Battery positions. A small enterprise was carried out between 5 + 6 am in which C Group co-operated with 43rd Infantry Bde., firing on a barrage at a rapid rate. During the night 27/28th U Bty RNA 65th, 80th, 123rd, 124th. 3/ Bty moved Batteries moved to their forward positions. 14 how Bty took over from its forward to its old position. old gd	28 Aug Corps Commander has awarded a MILITARY MEDAL to:- Bdr G H BENTLEY No 64261. 65 How Bty RFA and to No 69683 Gnr TILL X Bty RNA
Aug 28	Batteries reported on new zone. From 5-5.30 pm U Bty RNA 9104 Bty RFA bombarded LAGER LANE at request of 22nd Inf Bde.	
5-7 pm	A, B + D was shelled with 8" (about 50 rounds) One of 123 Bty's gun pits was hit and wrecked – 3 men wounded. German Balloons up during the day	

Army Form C. 2118.

WAR DIARY
or
INTELLIGENCE SUMMARY.
(Erase heading not required.)

Instructions regarding War Diaries and Intelligence Summaries are contained in F.S. Regs., Part II. and the Staff Manual respectively. Title pages will be prepared in manuscript.

Hour, Date, Place	Summary of Events and Information	Remarks and references to Appendices
Aug. 29 1916	All batteries checked lines calibrated guns recorded their zone.	
6.10/pm	12th Bty fired on S O S lines in orders from Bde HeadQrs 60 Bde H Q. Sig Offr was at once called up but no nothing had been heard no other batteries were turned on. The enquiry appears to have been rockets near GUILLEMONT. 65 How Bty shelled intermittently during the day. Direct hit on Officers' Mess — 2 casualties. 5.9's about Bde Head Quarters had A 8 a.m. This meant receive every other day. TRONES WOOD heavily shelled during morning.	
10 – 10.45 am	5 German Balloons were seen up when light was good It was reported that one of our balloons broke away in the storm. Our huts were badly flooded in the rear hastily constructed pits	

Forms/C. 2118/11.

WAR DIARY
or
INTELLIGENCE SUMMARY.

Army Form C. 2118.

Hour, Date, Place	Summary of Events and Information	Remarks and references to Appendices
1916		
Aug 30	All Batteries fired on normal zone. Hostile batteries been on by Howr Bty + 65 Howr Bty. Hostile artillery very active today, searching & sweeping back areas both in trenches & back areas. 71 Bty RHA, 80 Bty, 123 Bty have all been shelled with 8", 5.9" & 77 mm - also the area round the BRIQUETERIE.	
Aug 31	All batteries fired on normal barrage. Batteries fired at rapid rate from 4.0 to 6.0 pm on SOS line owing to reported hostile attack. SOS received 8.40 pm & acted on. Hostile artillery very active indeed today. 71 Bty RHA, 80 Bty, 72nd Bty have been shelled intermittently with gas shell. 65 Howr Bty & 123 Bty have been systematically bombarded with gas shell, shells of all calibres. 65 Bty had 14 casualties & 2 guns put out of action. 123 Bty "23 casualties & 3 guns put out of action. Enemy aeroplanes had the mastery of the air today & a large number were over our lines shelling positions	2Lt RETREASE (123 Bty) awarded MILITARY CROSS Gr S O Donnell (171 Bty) awarded DCM 2t W.T.W. Ching - gas poisoning from gas shell 123 Bty were withdrawn to hagar dive at night

WAR DIARY
or
INTELLIGENCE SUMMARY.
(Erase heading not required.)

Army Form C. 2118.

Hour, Date, Place	Summary of Events and Information	Remarks and references to Appendices
Aug 1916	During the night 31 Aug/1 Sept 1916 122nd Bty suffered from gas shell. The 80 Bty was heavily shelled throughout the night with gas shell - 7 men evacuated to hospital through gas poisoning. Two guns were knocked out and 2 others were hit. The 65 Bty was also heavily shelled throughout the night with gas shell. Capt. I.A.J. PASK was killed & there were 12 other casualties. It is estimated that 5000 rds M.G.A. shell were fired in neighbourhood of 65 Bty. The 65 Bty had a batch of cartridge hit by gas shell. 1/2 hr after the cartridge had been hit 300 rds M.G.A. am? exploded. Casualties in the Brigade during the month of August:- 122nd Bty RFA 1 Officer - gassed 8 O.R. - wounded 6 O.R. - Sick (inc gas) 65 How Bty RFA 1 Officer - Killed 15 O.R. - gassed 10 O.R. - Sick (inc gas) 123 Bty RFA 2 Officers - wounded 2 O.R. - Killed 25 O.R. - wounded 4 O.R. - gassed 18 O.R. - Sick (inc gas) C Harding Newman Comdt. 28 Bde RFA	

5th Divisional Artillery.

28th BRIGADE R. F. A.

SEPTEMBER 1916.

Army Form C.2118
War Diary **Vol 25**

War Diary

Jan. Mary. 28 Dec RFA

Hour Date Place	Summary of Events and Information	Remarks and references to Appendices
14th 1 Bde.	Batteries checked zero lines & fired a burst every hour as ordered. 65 Bty registered guns on zero line from old position to which they had moved by 10:30 am. There has been continual fire on Delville Wood today & heavy shelling in S15c&d.	

WAR DIARY.

Army Form. C.2118

Hour, Date, Place.	Summary of Events and Information.	Remarks and References to Appendices
1916 Sept 2	1/2 Bty returned from 10½pm June to forward position. All Batteries checked lines took part in bombardment on GINCHY and GUILLEMONT which had been postponed. During the night 1/2 Sept. all Batteries were shelled Continuously with gas shell.	2 Lt N NAYLES attached to Bty from 5 DAC
3-5pm	124 Bty shelled with 8" & 123 Bty with 5.9"	
Sept 3	All Batteries fired according to programme. No hostile activity in back areas today.	
Sept 4	All Batteries registered fired according to programme. Hostile activity not so great today. During the day turns to our concentrated artillery fire the Germans declared COCOA LANE as a thoroughfare using Structures T.1.d.3/1 to TEA Trench SUPPORT. Whole hostile aeroplane up over our lines	

Army Form C. 2118

WAR DIARY

HOUR DATE PLACE	SUMMARY OF EVENTS AND INFORMATION	REMARKS AND REFERENCES TO APPENDICES

1916
Sept. 5
	The personnel of the 5 Div Artillery Returns Mead Quarters in the line were relieved this morning as follows :-
	B Ade 28 Bde RFA relieved by 48 15 Bde.
	  80 Bty RFA — 52nd Bty
	  V Bty RNA — 119 Bty
	  123 Bty RFA — 120 Bty
	  124 — 121 —
	  65 — D/15 Bty
	
	The Brigade U Bty RNA, & 80 Bty marched to bivouac lines near ALBERT thence to bivouac lines at LA NEUVILLE. Bde Head Quarters proceeded to Bussy-lez-Daours.
	Brigade at rest.
		The 80 Bty attached to 28 Bde for Administration & discipline from Sept.
		
		8 Sept.
		2/Lt L.G. SYKES attached 123 Bty
		Lt T.G.P. WINMILL attached 124 Bty RFA

WAR DIARY
or
INTELLIGENCE SUMMARY.
(Erase heading not required.)

Army Form C. 2118

Instructions regarding War Diaries and Intelligence Summaries are contained in F.S. Regs., Part II. and the Staff Manual respectively. Title pages will be prepared in manuscript.

Hour, Date, Place	Summary of Events and Information	Remarks and references to Appendices
Bussy-les-Daours Sept 6	Brigade at rest	
10	Permission for Ratting of fire from Brigade Head Quarters preceded to A Beat (Major ADLT.) Batteries practising	
16.	Lt. Col. E. HARDING NEWMAN was in Command of 7 Bde. RHA from 16-23 Sept. Bde under the command of Major CONGREVE	7/8 Sept 2 Lt B F CONLIN attached 65 Rty RFA from Base
19	Lt Captain & Bde Artillery I tried to Young Officers of the Bde & I.K. Brigade subject Ammunition Supply Another lecture was given on "Ammunition Supply" to Young officers	
20	2nd Lt MERCHANT Signal Officer of this Bde. received communications a second lecture was given by ... ... more also from the Signature by the Brigade to all Signallers of the Brigade	
21	H.Q. O.C Brigade returned to Young Officers	
25	H.Q. O.C Brigade had a parade at LA NEUVILLE.	

WAR DIARY
or
INTELLIGENCE SUMMARY.

Army Form C. 2118

Hour, Date, Place	Summary of Events and Information	Remarks and references to Appendices
1916 Sept 29	Personnel of the 5th Div Artillery Batteries Head Quarters in the line were relieved as follows on the 29/30 th. By 27th Bde H.Q relieved 15 Bde H.Q. 90 " Bty 52 Bty RFA 123 " 120 " 124 " 121 " 65 " D15 " — were not relieved D.II " By cause not of fighting but were not relieved Relieving Head Quarters Batteries marched to temporary Wagon Lines near ALBERT so as to arrive there at 2 pm 29 Sept. Batteries which are relieved will on Do not take over Gun Pitts at LA NEVILLE Wood by relieving batteries on arrival there the 119, 120, 121 + 37 Btys will come under the orders Lieut. Col. HARDING NEWMAN	

WAR DIARY or INTELLIGENCE SUMMARY.

(Erase heading not required.)

Army Form C. 2118.

Hour, Date, Place	Summary of Events and Information	Remarks and references to Appendices
1916 Bussy Les Daours September	During the month the undermentioned Honours and Awards have been given to the Brigade	
1 Sept	D.S.O. Lieut Capt A J. Pask, MC, 65 Bty RFA	
2 Sept 18 Sept 22 Sept	MILITARY CROSS 2Lt RETREASE, 123 Bty RFA 2Lt L.C DIESPECKER, 65 (How) Bty RFA 2Lt W.T.W CHING 1st Bty RFA	
2 Sept 18 Sept 22 Sept	D C M No. 71603 Gnr. P. O'CONNELL 1st Bty No. 46819 All W. PATEMAN Head Quarters 28 Bde RFA No. 79654 Sgt T. O'GRADY 123 Bty RFA Signal N. BARNHOUSE	MILITARY MEDAL Sept No. 58411 2Lt J BEASLEY Head Quarters 28 Bde RFA

E Channing Newman
Lt Col
Comd'g 28 Bde RFA

WAR DIARY or INTELLIGENCE SUMMARY. 28 Bde RFA Vol 26

Army Form C. 2118.

Hour, Date, Place	Summary of Events and Information	Remarks and references to Appendices
Oct 1-8	Brigade Head Quarters at Bussy-les-Daours. Batteries in action under the command of Lt. Col. Berkeley, OC 27 Bde RFA. Position N.E. of Delville Wood. About T.7.a. Batteries came out of action & arrived at Bussy.	Major F. L. Cosgrave MC OC 12nd Bty RFA awarded
9	Brigade moved to Beaucourt.	1st Lt. MILITARY MEDAL awarded to No. 110557 Sjt Robert Jaques 65 Bty RFA, 14596 Cpl Jonathan Lord 65 Bty RFA, 60141 Q. Edgar Drake, 70271 Gr James McAldowen — Lt Col RFA
10	Brigade moved to Amplies. Bde Head Quarters at Orville.	
11	Brigade moved to Boubers-sur-Canche.	
12	Bde camped at Heuchin.	108-T/R/F & Bond Runr
13	Bde moved to Locon. Batteries in their permanent wagon lines.	28 Bde RFA
14	Bde. Head Quarters at La Couture. lines near Locon	Newman
	The 5 Brigades Divisional Artillery relieved by 5th Div Artillery during nights 15/16 and 16/17 both. LEFT GROUP under the command of Lt Col E Harding	Bethune Combined Chief to OC
	B/161 - 4 guns - relieved by 12nd Bty - 4 guns F5t +S/25	
	C/B 81st - in Army - 123 Bty - 4 guns - S/d 25/70, M34c 4/3	
	C/188 - 65 Bty - 2 guns - X17A 9/7	
	One section of 12nd Bty in centre group (15 Bde RFA)	8 Octr Col B F Conlin (65 Bty) wounded in action afternoon Medical 38 C.C.S.

WAR DIARY or INTELLIGENCE SUMMARY.

Army Form C. 2118

28 Bde RFA

Hour, Date, Place	Summary of Events and Information	Remarks and references to Appendices
LE TOURET Feb 16 1916	0.161 Rupel Fire own command of Left Group. 65 Bty fired 30 Bx registering zero line adjusted zone 12.3 — " 12.4 — 16A + 2A registering zero line Very little hostile shelling	MILITARY MEDAL 17/16 awarded to No. 34736 Gr. F BROOKS 65 67606 Gr. D GALVIN } Bty RFA 74216 Bdr A A ALLEN } 123 Bty RFA 29366 Bdr W G JEWEEL } 124 Bty RFA
17	Batteries registered. Some hostile shelling	
18	Batteries registered, checked lines. Some hostile shelling. Continued work reported opposite Trench Mortaring Island No. 14 (S27 d 69z)	

WAR DIARY
INTELLIGENCE SUMMARY.
(Erase heading not required.)

Army Form C. 2118

Hour, Date, Place	Summary of Events and Information	Remarks and references to Appendices
LE TOURET Feb 19	65 Bty fired 14 Rds in retaliation at point of supporting + 2 - hurricane fire in consequence with 123 Bty in retaliation for trench mortars. 1st Bty fired in retaliation for trench mortars. BREWERY OP (S20d 4525) was shelled with 30 + 2 "5" trench mortars very active during the day.	Major A G GILLMAN O.C. 123 Bty R.F.A to command of T Bty 1st Cavalry Division 2 Lt R H L GORNHYN joining SDA no attached to the Bde (124 Bty RFA)
20	Batteries registered. A few rounds fired at FACTORY OP (S9187) 65 Bty registered with KITE BALLOON. Registration failed, shots unobserved.	
21	123 Bty registered with KITE BALLOON. Very little hostile fire. Considerable movement today - also considerable traffic on FOURNES - LA BASSÉE ROAD.	

Army Form C. 2118

WAR DIARY
or
INTELLIGENCE SUMMARY.
(Erase heading not required.)

28th Bde RFA

Hour, Date, Place	Summary of Events and Information	Remarks and references to Appendices
LE TOURET Oct 22	65 Bty fired 27 Rds - re-registration & destruction of enemy defences	2Lt SYKES started 123 Bty 15th Army T.M. School
	123 Bty retaliated for TMs. Some movement & work observed.	25 T.M. Battery attached to Bde for discipline
	At 11.15 am & 12.45 pm hostile planes were seen over 124 Bty's position	Capt L.G. LUTYENS posted to Bde from 27 Bde RFA (2 echelon 123 Bty RFA)
23	123 Bty registered. 124 Bty fired a few rounds on Zero line. Some hostile shelling. Considerable French mortar activity in both sides. During the morning & at 2.30 pm enemy fired heavy minenwerfer on to GIVENCHY - about 50 rounds	Capt R BOLSTER posted to the Bde from 15th Bde RFA (TO command 124 Bty RFA)
24	Batteries did not fire. Light bad.	Lt R.W.L. FELLOWES from 124 Bty to 27 Bde RFA

Army Form C. 2118.

WAR DIARY
or
INTELLIGENCE SUMMARY.
(Erase heading not required.)

Instructions regarding War Diaries and Intelligence Summaries are contained in F.S. Regs., Part II. and the Staff Manual respectively. Title pages will be prepared in manuscript.

Hour, Date, Place	Summary of Events and Information	Remarks and references to Appendices
LE TOURET 19/16 Oct. 25	105 Bty fired at Bk at DISTILLERY TANK for instructional purposes & registration of guns. 123 Bty fired in retaliation, also 124 Bty. 104 Bty fired 30 A x at MOUND S82d 05/25 - an instructional shoot. More hostile fire than usual. Less work movement observed.	
26	123 Bty fired 30 A x for instruction, also 15 A x retaliation at enemy's infantry from Wellery of CADBURY STREET. 18 A x retaliation to T.M's	
3.30 pm	Hostile Anti-aircraft guns fired on our planes, 28 rounds sent over the [?] area.	
27	123 Bty fired at Heavy TM S16c15 located. Some enemy trench mortaring. A certain amount of movement along LA BASSÉE - FOURNES Road	
11.50 am	About 100 men seen going along LA BASSÉE - FOURNES Road at T.16.6 towards LA BASSÉE. Considerable amount of smoke observed.	

WAR DIARY
or
INTELLIGENCE SUMMARY.
(Erase heading not required.)

Army Form C. 2118.

Hour, Date, Place	Summary of Events and Information	Remarks and references to Appendices
LE TOURET 1916		
Oct. 28	65 Bty fired 40 Rds at YANKEE DISTILLERY at SP'd 10/8/9. 12th Bty fired 20 A in retaliation for enemy TMs on our front. Enemy fired 43rds 77mm about S22c8/9. Much traffic observed during the morning on LA BASSEE - FOURNES-EN-WEPPES Road.	MILITARY MEDALS Awarded to No 59539 Gr VCD MILES 124 Bty 9168 Gr ARTHUR COX RFA
29	12 & 124 Batteries fired for instruction to find corrector & for registration. Some hostile shelling. Signalling lamp again observed by 12 Bty, about S20C o/7	
30	Considerable movement observed. No hostile shelling.	
31	65 Bty fired for instruction. Registered. 12 Bty registered. 10 rds fired on Right Battn front at 9.10 pm 77mm 16 rds on Left Battn about 10 am morning of 1 Nov	

Army Form C. 2118

WAR DIARY
or
INTELLIGENCE SUMMARY.
(Erase heading not required.)

Place	Hour, Date	Summary of Events and Information	Remarks and references to Appendices
LE TOURET	19/16	Considerable movement observed & traffic along Fournes - La Bassée Road.	
	31 Oct.	On the night of the 31st the 1st Batt. BEDFORDSHIRE Regt (15 Inf Bde) penetrated the enemy trenches at S22 C6/6. Three grenades were captured, 6 killed, + 1 machine gun emplacement destroyed. Our Casualties were 1 killed, 17 wounded + 5 missing. Prisoners belong to 6 BAVARIAN REGT.	

Standing Newman Lt.Col.
Comdg 28 Bde RFA

Army Form C. 2118.

WAR DIARY
or
INTELLIGENCE SUMMARY. 28 Bde RFA

(Erase heading not required.)

Instructions regarding War Diaries and Intelligence Summaries are contained in F.S. Regs., Part II and the Staff Manual respectively. Title pages will be prepared in manuscript.

Hour, Date, Place	Summary of Events and Information	Remarks and references to Appendices
LE TOURET 19/16		
Nov 1	65 Bty RFA fired a few rounds Retaliation. 123 Bty retaliated & fired 20 A+ for registration. 12m Bty registered. Some hostile shelling. Considerable movement observed.	
2	65 Bty retaliated on suspected hostile TM about S.17.a.5/6 and Hurricane fire on ADALBERT ALLEY and other trenches. 123 Bty fired Hurricane fire on trenches in S.16.c – retaliation Registered by Balloon. 12+ Bty registered Road S.23.B.9.2. Considerable movement observed. 3 Balloons + 1 hostile Aeroplane up. Some hostile trench mortaring.	MILITARY MEDAL awarded to:- 61076 B.Q.M.S. S.W. RAWSON 67156 Bn. E. PRICE.

Army Form C. 2118.

WAR DIARY
or
INTELLIGENCE SUMMARY.   28 Bde RFA
(Erase heading not required.)

Instructions regarding War Diaries and Intelligence Summaries are contained in F.S. Regs., Part II. and the Staff Manual respectively. Title pages will be prepared in manuscript.

Hour, Date, Place	Summary of Events and Information	Remarks and references to Appendices
LE TOURET 1916 Nov. 3	65 Bty registered suspected TM emplacement for destruction, registered 124 Bty registered 2 zones on Zero line - FLAT FARM. Some naval burner movement observed. Heavy TM located at S.16 d 05/47 by cross bearings	B.Bty fired
Nov. 4	6.5 Bty fired 36 D Hurricane Zone retaliation for TMs at front of Infantry. 123 + 124 Batteries also retaliated. Some hostile shelling. Considerable movement observed A.77 mm battery rather active about S30c Trench mortars very active during the day.	
Nov. 5	65 Bty registered Battery at S30c 05/40. Registered detached Section 124 Bty fired 43 Ax in retaliation. Considerable movement observed	

Army Form C. 2118.

WAR DIARY
or
INTELLIGENCE SUMMARY.
(Erase heading not required.)

Hour, Date, Place	Summary of Events and Information	Remarks and references to Appendices
Nov 1/9/16 6	65 Bty registered Registered Attacks section Bois Left. 123 Bty registered BEAU PUITS, retaliated fired on Switchm. 124 Bty registered fired Test G.V LEFT Bank. Some hostile shelling + a certain amount of movement observed	Capt L.G. LUTYENS, 123 Bty to be Acting Major. 22/10/16 also Lt R.G. BOLSTER (R70) 124 Bty RFA. LT. C.F. FORESTIER-WALKER to be acting Captain 29/10/16 N.C. RFA 2/Lt R.E. Treves N.C. RFA joined the Brigade.
7	65 Bty retaliated. 123 Bty fired BLAST in retaliation Retaliated. 124 Bty retaliated. Hosty & 1760 & Hostile fire hut same Trenches morteering.	
8	123 Bty fired a shot. 124 Bty fired at Working party & retaliated suspected O.P. Considerable movement observed	
9	65 Bty registered TM at St B 6.5/60 attempted to registered by aeroplane but did not complete owing to bad light. Fired 'BLAST' in retaliation. 123 Bty registered BOARS HEAD etc. Registered with aeroplane. Considerable movement observed and smoke.	Lt M.P. Evans RFA acting Captain wef & comcy A/300 BATTERY attached to the Brigade.

Army Form C. 2118.

WAR DIARY
or
INTELLIGENCE SUMMARY.
(Erase heading not required.)

Instructions regarding War Diaries and Intelligence
Summaries are contained in F. S. Regs., Part II.
and the Staff Manual respectively. Title pages
will be prepared in manuscript.

Hour, Date, Place	Summary of Events and Information	Remarks and references to Appendices
7/9/16 10 Nov.	65 Bty reported hy Kite Balloon aeroplane 123 Bty fired at working party. Registered & retaliated fire. T.M.s at present at infantry.	
11 Nov.	65 fired 4 at Hr retaliation puis, also 123 & 124 Batteries. 65 fired at DISTILLERY TANK for instructional purposes. Registered 124 Bty fired for instruction. M.G. Emplacement. 123 Bty fired for instruction at Enfielded working party & for ammunition.	
12 Nov.	123 Bty fired for instruction 124 Bty fired at small working party. Calculated rounds + instruction. Slow rate of fire & movement. No. 10 Kite Balloon reports that German trenches in BOARS HEAD can be clearly seen to the full of water.	

WAR DIARY or INTELLIGENCE SUMMARY.

(Erase heading not required.)

Army Form C. 2118.

Hour, Date, Place	Summary of Events and Information	Remarks and references to Appendices
13 Nov.	65 Bty fired BLAST, HIT, PUNISH, HARRAS) Retaliation for 123 Bty - BLAST, HIT, PUNISH) friends harassing 1st - - HIT and HARRAS.	
14	65 Bty registered also 123 Hr Batteries. Some hostile fire. Hostile movement observed. 1st Bty report an increase of enemy along the whole front during day	Lt R F Mason rejoined the Brigade.
15	1st Bty fired tr A + at S27d 80/60 Demolition of enemy post + 16 A+ N S27d 90/60 Enemy Position at S.point of Infantry procedure Lane G Sunland Capt L.G. Littyam assuming Command of the Brigade.	Colonel Harding Newman DSO
16	65 Bty registered fused for instruction 123 Bty fired by order of CRA on SO Stores Some hostile shelling 1st Bty retaliated registered	

WAR DIARY
or
INTELLIGENCE SUMMARY.
(Erase heading not required.)

Army Form C. 2118.

Hour, Date, Place	Summary of Events and Information	Remarks and references to Appendices
Nov 17 1916	6/5 Rty retaliated for hostile trench mortars fired BLAST & PUNISH 123 Rty fired PUNISH BLAST & [crossed out] 1m Rty fired 7 Cot Bois Regt. Some hostile fire from direction of LORGIES Considerable movement observed. Hostile trench mortar activity Batteries retaliated at request of infantry	
18	Enemy fired about 15 rds corresponding to our H.T.M.fire	
19	65 Rty fired aeroplane test, 1salvo. 123 — test 1m — in retaliation for trench mortaring 169 Rty active fired on S28 a/b and neighbourhood	

WAR DIARY
or
INTELLIGENCE SUMMARY.
(Erase heading not required.)

Army Form C. 2118

Hour, Date, Place	Summary of Events and Information	Remarks and references to Appendices
1916 Sept 20	65 Bty fired Tr̄st retaliated for Trench Mortars. 123 Bty fired at working party, fired Tr̄st retaliated for TMs. Some hostile shelling. more movement than usual observed	MILITARY MEDAL awarded to :- 51594 Sgt. S. BRAND . 122nd Bty 29558 Bv Pte. WESTNEY 123 " 28767 S/Sgt/Fan W. SANDERS " " 74248 Gr. J. REILLY 124 "
21	65 Bty fired aeroplane Tr̄st, retaliated for hostile TMs firing BLAST and HIT. 123 Bty fired BLAST. 124 Bty fired aeroplane Tr̄st + HIT fired considerable Trench Mortar activity rapid	
22	65 Bty fired Tr̄st retaliated for hostile S.O.s on SHETLAND ROAD for Trench hostiling. 123 Bty fired Tr̄st 124 Bty fired aeroplane Tr̄st + HIT Rapid	

Army Form C. 2118.

WAR DIARY
or
INTELLIGENCE SUMMARY.
(Erase heading not required.)

Hour, Date, Place	Summary of Events and Information	Remarks and references to Appendices
Nov. 23	65th Bty registered 1 retaliation on Trench Mortar	
	123 Bty " " "	
	124 " " "	
24	65 Bty retaliated on PRUNE at regnt of infantry with apparent effect. Fired on Light Railway S.17.d.2.5	
	123 Bty registered but population spt at S.17.d.50.15	
	Some hostile shelling & retaliation on our Stokes guns.	
25.	65 Bty fired at 77 mm gun about S.30.d.60.05 - Ph.1-A8D.L. Red light. 124 Bty fired two rounds on	
	Hd-gears enemy RUE du MARAIS	
	& retaliated for our Trench Mortars on CADBURY STREET	
	Little movement observed.	

Army Form C. 2118.

WAR DIARY
or
INTELLIGENCE SUMMARY.
(Erase heading not required.)

Instructions regarding War Diaries and Intelligence Summaries are contained in F.S. Regs., Part II. and the Staff Manual respectively. Title pages will be prepared in manuscript.

Hour, Date, Place 1916	Summary of Events and Information	Remarks and references to Appendices
Nov. 26.	No shelling by enemy. 123 Bty fired few rounds on S.2.31.24 a. Our Trench Mortars were active. Considerable movement observed. Kite balloon were up at intervals, and an aeroplane came over.	
27.	123 Bty fired few rounds to test fuzes, also on Trench looking party. 124 Bty also fired to test ammunition. 65 Bty also fired to test ammunition. Enemy sent over a few rounds before breakfast relief. Considerable activity seen all day. Kite balloon up for few minutes.	
28.	The Batteries of the Brigade came under the Right Group, commanded by Col. Hawkes R.A.	

E Standing Hemming Plat R.F.A
Comg 23rd Brigade R.F.A.

(73989) W4141—463. 400,000. 9/14. H.&J.Ltd. Forms/C. 2118/10.

Army Form C. 2118.

Vol 28

WAR DIARY
or
INTELLIGENCE SUMMARY 2/8 Bde RFA

(Erase heading not required.)

Hour, Date, Place	Summary of Events and Information	Remarks and references to Appendices
LE TOURET Dec 1-9 1916	Batteries under the Command of Right Group	
Dec 10	Lt Colonel HARDING NEWMAN took command of Lt Col HANKES Left Group consisting of :- 123 Bty RFA 120 Bty RFA X5 TM Bty 119 - 121 - 25 - 65 - 37 - A/300 -	

Army Form C. 2118.

WAR DIARY
INTELLIGENCE SUMMARY.
(Erase heading not required.)

Instructions regarding War Diaries and Intelligence Summaries are contained in F.S. Regs., Part II. and the Staff Manual respectively. Title pages will be prepared in manuscript.

Hour, Date, Place 1916	Summary of Events and Information	Remarks and references to Appendices
Dec. 11.	65 Bty searched for Trench Mortar at S.22.b 65.50 and silenced it. 123 Bty checked ranges and S.O.S. lines. N300" registered and disturbed party humping water out of front line. Enemy guns very active north from vicinity of HALPEGARBE. Large percentage of duds. Balloons up & aeroplanes active.	
12.	123 Bty fired for corrector & test jags. N300" registered. Enemy artillery quiet - little movement observed.	
13.	A lively day. 5.9" battery active from direction PILLES. Then Trench Mortars obnoxious. Group ordered retaliation and 65th, 123rd & N300 fired on trenches etc. Outburst of enemy bangs followed red rockets.	

(73989) W4141—463.   400,000.   9/14.   H.&J.Ltd.   Forms/C. 2118/10.

WAR DIARY
or
INTELLIGENCE SUMMARY.
(Erase heading not required.)

Army Form C. 2118.

Hour, Date, Place 1916	Summary of Events and Information	Remarks and references to Appendices
Dec. 14.	123 Battery & 1/300 registered Batt. Front 123 Battery fired at intervals during the night on communication trenches. 4.2" shelled NEUVE CHAPELLE intermittently.	
15.	123 Battery dispersed working parties 1/300 fired a few rounds on hostile working from trench. Enemy field guns more active than usual. No movement observed	
16.	65k Battery retaliated on Trench Mortar. 123rd also fired on them, and working parties. Our trench mortars fired a few rounds 59 Battery active from Auchy & 111ES Field guns also active	

Army Form C. 2118.

WAR DIARY
or
INTELLIGENCE SUMMARY.
(Erase heading not required.)

Hour, Date, Place	Summary of Events and Information	Remarks and references to Appendices
Dec. 1916 17	65th Battery fired several rounds on active trench mortars. M/300 retaliated and our Trench Mortars eventually damaged the enemy trench mortars. 4·2" shelled CADBURY ST from LORGIES.	LT-COL E. HARDING NEWMAN proceeded to BOULOGNE to attend the ARMY COURSE for Brigade Commander Officers. MAJOR. L.G. LUTYENS OC 123rd Battery assumed command of the LEFT GROUP
18	65th Battery registered new gun. Fired at intervals during the night; also fired at intervals on working parties. Enemy fired a few heavy Trench Mortars	
19.	65th & 723rd Batteries relieved a hostile Trench Mortar M/300 fired a few rounds during the night on road near HALPEGARBE and Communication trenches. Usual Trench Mortar activity on the enemy's side. Rounds falling on NEUVE CHAPPELLE & COCKSPUR STREET.	LT-COL E. HARDING. NEWMAN returned

WAR DIARY
or
INTELLIGENCE SUMMARY.
(Erase heading not required.)

Army Form C. 2118.

Hour, Date, Place	Summary of Events and Information	Remarks and references to Appendices
1916 Dec. 20.	65th, 123, & A/300 retaliated heavily on Trench Mortars and Trenches; 65th also fired 65 rounds on active Battery reported by aeroplane. A/300 were shelled with 5.9"; several rounds fell in RICHEBOURG + RUE DU BOIS district including gun & Exploratory pits. 77 mms + 4.2" were also very active. There were frequent flashes seen over our lines during a part of the bombardment.	
21.	123 + 124 Batteries shot at several parties in communication Trenches. Much movement was seen on the LA BASSEE - Festubert Road.	
22.	At 3 pm, A/300, 123,124, 76, & Batteries, with c/15 became the right group of the 37th Composite Artillery, under the command of MAJOR L.G. LUTYENS, R.F.A., headquarters at LE TOURET, covering the 112th Infantry Brigade, in the FERME DU BOIS sector.	

Army Form C. 2118.

WAR DIARY
or
INTELLIGENCE SUMMARY.
(Erase heading not required.)

Hour, Date, Place 1916	Summary of Events and Information	Remarks and references to Appendices
Dec 22	Thirty shells CANADIAN ORCHARD, RUE DU BOIS, and 123rd Battery. A large amount of Lachrymatory shell was used. Several fell in the 123 position, but no damage was done. 123 + 124 Batteries retaliated, silenced Trench Mortars. Enemy Trench Mortars were very busy in the morning.	LT.COLONEL E. HARDING. NEWMAN. D.S.O. became C.R.A. of the 37th COMPOSITE ARTILLERY. a/g q.m. conferred of Right Group - Major H. Hutgins 124th KRs 652rdhms 123" " 6/15 " A/300 " Left Group - Lt Col Pottinger 120 KRs 37 3rd How 119 " " D/262 " 121 " " 1090 " STA(?)
23.	Trench Mortars were very active. 65,123,124 silenced them and started other fronts. 123 fired during the night on certain trenches + roads. 77mm shelled INDIAN VILLAGE, ROPE+ SHETLAND.	
24.	A slow continuous bombardment was carried out on the front line and other points at the order of the Corps Commander in order to prevent any attempt at fraternisation on the part of the Germans. Trench Mortars both fired during daylight. Enemy replied on FESTUBERT, ROPE ST., + RUE DU BOIS. German aeroplanes came over our lines. Trench mortars 12th Battery position.	

Army Form C. 2118.

WAR DIARY
or
INTELLIGENCE SUMMARY.
(Erase heading not required.)

Instructions regarding War Diaries and Intelligence Summaries are contained in F.S. Regs., Part II. and the Staff Manual respectively. Title pages will be prepared in manuscript.

Hour, Date, Place 1916	Summary of Events and Information	Remarks and references to Appendices
Dec. 25.	Bombardment continued; the enemy did not fire much in reply; gave CADBURY some attention. Until movement on DISTILLERY - LA BASSÉE ROAD.	
26.	Strafe continued - our Trench Mortars did great damage. Germans getting more annoyed. Bombarded CANADIAN ORCHARD, BARNTON RD and COVIER TRENCH.	
27.	Bombardment ended. a 5.9" fired on the RUE DU BOIS at one or two points. A quiet day.	Corps Commander specially commended our T.Ms for firing some 1800 rds. in the three days.
28.	/23 Battery fired on several places during the night. Of our and trifilter came over last night. Our Battery and our French Mortars silenced this.	

Army Form C. 2118.

WAR DIARY
or
INTELLIGENCE SUMMARY.
(Erase heading not required.)

Instructions regarding War Diaries and Intelligence Summaries are contained in F. S. Regs., Part II. and the Staff Manual respectively. Title pages will be prepared in manuscript.

Hour, Date, Place 1914	Summary of Events and Information	Remarks and references to Appendices
Dec. 29.	Guns on both sides very quiet. Many men were seen on the LA BASSEE ROAD, also some motor transport.	
30	123724 Batteries detached several working parties, and groups of men on the DISTILLERY road. About noon two parties of probably fifty men were seen marching on the FOURNES – LA BASSEE ROAD, also engine pulling trucks about all day. At night half the guns of the batteries were relieved by the 37th Division and removed to the wagon lines.	
31.	At night the remaining sections were relieved. Batteries proceeded to temporary wagon lines.	

E Harding Newman Lt Col.
Cmdg 28 Bde RFA

(73989) W4141—463. 400,000. 9/14. H.&J.Ltd. Forms/C. 2118/10.

28th Bde. R.F.A.
5th Div.

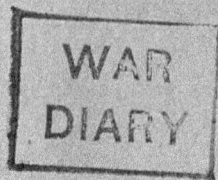

123rd BATTERY, R.F.A.

JANUARY to 13TH MAY

1 9 1 6

War Diary

123rd Battery R.F.A

January To 13th May

1916

13th May (continued)

took place today in retaliation for the German bombardment of J2 & K1 subsectors. During the night the battery shelled their mine heads. ~~[struck through]~~

14th Quiet day, wet.

6

April 28th to May 3rd } Usual routine.

May 4th. The 6th gun put into action about G.16.d.5.2. for the purpose of shooting when hostile aeroplanes are about, so as not to draw hostile fire on the Battery.

May 5th Another gun moved to above position.

May 7th Heavy bombardment of infantry on our front. we fired 370 H.E. on enemy trenches, & all other guns chipped in.

May 8th Lt Canteirs went on leave. Lt Young returned from leave.

— 9th General routine

— 10th A 'strafe' was arranged in retaliation for German shoot on the 9th but was postponed owing to unfavourable weather

— 11th Quiet day ordinary routine. Intermittent fires was kept up during the night on they rendezvous

12th The combined shoot of Siege, Heavy, Field, French & Trench mortar batteries

Apr. 7 — 1916.

7th April. Registered No 1 & 2 guns on the Entonnoir in K. for combined Strafe of next day.

3.30 p.m. Took part in combined Strafe on ﬁg 6" How, 4.5 How, 18 pr & trench mortars.

8th. 11 a.m. Combined Strafe on Entonnoir, right & left of Pope's Nose.
8" How, 6", 4.5", 18 pr & trench mortars.

9th – 13th. Battery Routine.

14th – 18th.   "   "

18th Lt Robley on completion of his tour of instruction, left Battery for England.

23rd Major A. G. Gillman left for Senior Officers Course at .
Lt Stewart left for I^n Div. Art. School at

28th Lt Young on leave.   Major Gillman returned from Senior Officer's Course.

Mar. 19 - Apr. 4. 1916

19th March. Moved one more gun to new position, taken over from 65th Bty. We are taking over four of their gun casements & have two new to build.

21st. Moved fourth gun over.
All Horses in Montenescourt ordered to be picketted in the open. Reason for it — 3 cases of 27th Bde of mange, which could not possibly have been caught in Montenescourt. 28th Bde did not comply at once. — slight trouble —

22nd. 28th Bde horses turned out of stables. Weather turned wet & cold, & next day horses over their fetlocks in slush.

24th. Horses all ordered back in stables by 4 p.m.

30th. Fifth gun moved to new position.

31st. 124 Bty badly shelled. (No 5.9's.) One man wounded only. Lt Wildor of Q Bty killed & Col Barclay & Maj Heather slightly wounded.

April 3d Lt. Stewart sent to be attached to battery. Has been through Gen Botha's campaign, in South West Africa

April 4th. Lt Robley attached to battery for a fortnight from England.

Mar 16-18. 1916.

Gunners Fleatwood, Shedd, & Br Shinfield wounded. Lt Young slightly wounded. Very little material damage done considering, except to mens quarters in Right section, Officers sleeping quarters, & the gas ball. Also, of course, the telephonists dugouts. A German aeroplane was permitted to be hovering over the battery all the time it was being shelled.

The Right section guns, under Lt Curteis left position during the night & took over two gun pits from 65th Battery RFA (Capt Park)

March 17th Gunner Mackin buried in Cemetery at St NICHOLAS. G.16.d.1.6.

March 18th Lt Sutton from Bde. A.C. joined for a fortnight's training with the Battery. Leave reopened.

Mar. 8-16. 1916.

but pits only just concealed from enemy view. Fired 2 or 3 hundred rounds during stay there.

March 8th D sub gun came into No 6 gun position with remainder of battery.

March 10th B sub gun left position to be repaired. D sub gun took over its pit — No. 2.

March 16th Lt. Antrobus, after being with the battery throughout the war, having joined it several months previous to the war at DUNDALK, left to take up a captaincy in a battery of the 7th Division at BRAY. His loss will be greatly felt.

Wagon line moved from WANQUETIN to MONTENESCOURT today.

From 10 am till 11.30 am the battery position was shelled with about 100 4.2 shells. One burst in telephonists' dugout — casualties, Gr Hackin killed,

Feb. 26 - Mar 2. 16

Feb. 26th   Lt Antrobus brought remainder of Battery to LONQUEVILLETTE. Brigade rested there till

"Feb. 28th   Marched via DOULLENS northwards to BOURDRIQUET. Arrived & found VIIth Corps had also selected that village for an Infantry Brigade. Stuffed the men in with Infantry in fair billets — horses in open.

Feb. 29th   Major Gillman & Lt Mason left 8 am for ARRAS, the latter going back later & picking D, E, & F sub guns up at WANQUETIN under Lt Curteis, took them into action in position of the 2me Bir, 23me Bde French Army, in garden in ARRAS. q.21.6.38. Settled in 6 am 2 1st March. D sub gun in public garden separate from other section. q.21.6.66. Good dugouts for men, but whole thing very mixed up & uncomfortable.

March 2nd   A, B, & C sub guns came up, & French battery left ARRAS. Position fair, very good dugouts

Feb. 8 - 24. 1916

no standings had been built. As the horse lines were on the marsh beside the river they were soon in a very bad state of mud.

Feb. 18th Horses moved to better standings near church at ST SAUVEOR — mens billets changed for the better also. Appalling weather, including snow.

Feb 22nd Brigade had surprise turn out, & marched 2 miles or so away, in practise for any suddenly necessary move.

Feb. 23rd Sudden orders, for Division to move & take over from French somewhere in the line.

Feb. 24th Brigade marched at 8·0 p.m. 20 miles through a blizzard via HAVERNAS, CANAPLES, CANDAS to LONGUEVILETTE arriving 12·30 am 25th. Vehemously expressed as being the worst bit of marching any of the Brigade had been through. Battery Cook's & Officers wagon's left behind under Lt. Antrobus. Horses in the open at LONGVEVILLE but men & officers quite comfortable.

Jan. 21 – Feb. 8, 1916

21st Jan. All left X Horses got under cover.
Visit for Brig. Gen. Harry to arrange programme of work.

22nd Capt. Lutyens sent for a fortnight's course to MONTIGNY. Course seems to deal principally with teaching young officers not to wear pink ties & butterfly collars with uniform & to use their knives & forks & not their fingers to eat with. Promises to be most instructive & might be suitable for even very senior officers.

23rd to 7th Feb. Remained at St Gratien training

Feb 3rd Major Gen. Cavanagh presented the D.C.M. ribbons to the Brigade

Feb 6th Capt. Lutyens rejoined the battery.

Feb 8th The Brigade moved back to St. SAUVEUR.
The Officers billets here were comfortable but the mens were not good and the horses were all in the open, and

Jan. 17-20. 1916

another one into our alternative position.
We removed 4 guns to wagon line.

17th. 4 guns + amm. wagons & as many G.S. wagons
as could be begged, borrowed, or stolen marched
to ST. GRATIEN, leaving BRAY 5.20 p.m.
arriving new area 11.30 p.m.

18th. Settling in ST. GRATIEN. Good billets for
officers + men. Both Rt & Centre Section horses
under cover.

20th. Remaining Section marched in, arriving
11.30 p.m.

(Awards gained by the battery
    Lt Antrobus. Mentioned + military Cross.
B.S.M. Belcher. Mentioned
  Sgt Sage   "
Q.M.S. Rowton   "
Bdr Pateman   "
 "   Brown   " + D.C.M.
Gr. Crossen   " + D.C.M.   )

Jan 5-16. 1915

Jan 5th. Shot with single gun to cut wire in front of 65 trench. Ammunition insufficient to be able to guarantee wire cut, but infantry went out in evening. Report two lines cut.

About 9.30 Germans put 30 shell at B S 2. A good many fell in front of our left hand gun.

Jan 7th. Observing station been sufficiently badly shelled, so moved to 75 Trench.

Jan 8th, 9th, 10th. Ordinary routine.

10th. Protheroe took representatives from batteries to see new area at S.t Gratien.

Jan 11th. Long despatch. 10 Antrobus mentioned.

Jan 13th. 30-40 shells in Suzanne. Considerable damage to property & horses.

Jan 14th & 15th ordinary routine.

Jan 16th. Two shells in Bray just over our billet. One Kitchener battery came into our gun position, &

1st Jan. Inspection by Gen. Cavanagh.
 Ugon line again shelled Sgt Jeffery slightly wounded.

3rd Jan. Bray shelled.

4th Jan. Put gun in action in old position at Bronfay farm for a wire shoot in front of 65 Trench.
 Bray again shelled, 7 men killed, 11 men wounded. Ugon line got a few.

WO 95/1532/2

Index		
	SUBJECT.	5TH DIV.
No.	Contents.	Date.

R.A.

Belgian Artillery Reg't

10th Feby – July, 1915

Confidential

War Diary
of
Belgian Artillery Regiment
attd. 28th Div.

from Feb. 10th to March 31st 1915.

Kpt̃.
Capt. C.S.P. Burnell
RHA
attached Belgn A.R. Reg.

Army Form C. 2118.
(1)

WAR DIARY
INTELLIGENCE SUMMARY.
(Erase heading not required.)

Hour, Date, Place	Summary of Events and Information	Remarks and references to Appendices
Feb. 10th 1.30pm	Provisional Regiment of Belgian Artillery arrived at BIXSCHOOTE - Capt Brigg R.H.A. joined as Liaison Officer.	APPENDIX I gives kinds of Battn. of the Regiment
6pm	A section from 3 of the Battns returned a section of 'A' Battery R.H.A. which in 'A' Battery arrived to by itself in at I.16.a.6.4. - The other section at 'A' I.13.c.5.1. 'Q' T.26.6.3. 'U' I.16.c.5.4. - It was desired to give the Battn opposition the kind of an R.H.A. Battery & preferred gun to their Battery before to that position	all References to Belgians (Pres firing) have map Sheet 28 N.W. S.W.
Feb. 11th 2pm	Morning occupied by 3 Belgian sections in rotation in ratch shooting & synchronising communication they & Battery recorded the employment.	See Sketch (1) attached (Appendix II)
3pm	The H.Q. of the Regt (Colonel + 2 officers) Sent to known officers of H.A.C.R. Regt) established at staff at 5 - Rte de MENIN-YPRES. The section in action registered this Zone	
8pm	'A' section Battn RHA handed over their remaining section employment to the Belgian Battns. 2 Belgian Battery resumed its position	See Sketch (2) attached (Appendix III)
Feb. 12th	occupied in Artillery telephonic communications	
Feb. 13th 3pm	'A' Battery (fired) on a captured ———— which had approached to within a yard of the British Trenches.	
7.15pm	'A' Battery fired again on the same.	

WAR DIARY
INTELLIGENCE SUMMARY.
(Erase heading not required.)

Army Form C. 2118.

Hour, Date, Place	Summary of Events and Information	Remarks and references to Appendices
7.6.14 ¥	After continuing an intermittent fire on the observations Supplies	
8.45 p.m.	transport by night, 'A' Battery again fired at it - & then swept the road running along the Ridge of O3a7, at the request of R. of B2.Cr. The fire was continued until 9 p.m. - WB	
8.6.15 4.15 a.m.	The Battery no A Q.R.U. (Base) fired on the trenches in that sector	
6.30 a.m.	'Z' Battery opened fire on the trenches in its sector	
7.30 a.m.	Batteries ceased firing	
5 p.m.	'A' Battery registered on the trench lot the British (0.3672 - 0.36.94) Ot	
6.30 p.m.	Order received from G.O.C.R.A. to open rapid fire a this trench from 8.30 - 8.55 p.m.	
6.40 p.m.	Information received that the trench had clearly been retaken	
6.50 p.m.	A Battery fires for 15 minutes 150 yards beyond the Trench	
	A Battery fired approx 5 mins - Same target & range at the request	
9.15 p.m.	the Inf B.H. Cdr. - There was kept up at intervals until 12.30 a.m. to prevent the enemy from bringing up reinforcements WB	
9.6.15 ¥ 12.30 p.m.	At the request of Inf. B.r. Or 'Z' Battery searched the woods in T 35 -	
	6 +3, where hostile Inf. was reported to be gathering	
8 p.m.	The 2 Trekking Batteries of the Regiment relieved A + 2 Batteries. Arrangements made for the relief by 2 Trekking Batteries to be carried out every 6 days. WB	

Army Form C. 2118.

WAR DIARY
or
INTELLIGENCE SUMMARY.
(Erase heading not required.)

Hour, Date, Place	Summary of Events and Information	Remarks and references to Appendices
2/6/16 9.45pm	All 4 Batteries ordered to establish a 'Barrage Defen' in their sectors.	
9.50pm	Orders received for Batteries to stop firing	
2/6/17 8 am	'H' & 'Z' Batteries established a 'Barrage Defence' in their sectors	
9.30 am	'Z' Battery ordered to sweep ZWARTELEEN village when enemy were collecting ammunition by firing on the cross roads I 29 9 70. The Battery fired for 25 minutes	
10.00 am	'A' Battery ordered to fire a few salvos of high explosive shells at the trenches O.3.6.7.2.	
10.15 am	'Z' Battery again turned on to the village of ZWARTELEEN.	
11.45 am	'A' Battery ordered to register on Trench "O" (O.3.6.7.2 - O.3.6.9.4) on ridge as possible.	
2 pm	'Q' Battery ordered to register. Trench "Mysia" a barrage & fire orders to trenches in B sector.	
2.45 pm	'A' Battery ordered the trench readiness to fire on the sunken road & O.9.7.0.	
10.15 pm	'A' Battery informed that enemy fire might be expected while infantry constructed a new trench in rear of Trench "O"	

Army Form C. 2118.

WAR DIARY
or
INTELLIGENCE SUMMARY.
(Erase heading not required.)

Instructions regarding War Diaries and Intelligence Summaries are contained in F.S. Regs., Part II. and the Staff Manual respectively. Title pages will be prepared in manuscript.

Hour, Date, Place	Summary of Events and Information	Remarks and references to Appendices
25.6.18 1pm	'A' Battery registration from O.3.d.4.2. (HETROFF) - 4th Round target	W
26.6.19 —	—	W
26.6.20 3.15pm	'Q' Battery fired several airbursts at the German Trench in I.34.d.6 prevent the Inf. from moving to the attack	W
26.6.21 —	—	W
26.6.22 7.30pm	Inf. Bd. Or. ord 'd' 'U' Battery to register on the German trenches just to the left of C.16 Sector — Cut the fog winds observation impossible	W
26.6.23 2.30pm	'2' Battery fired at the West edge of the Wood in I.35.a.	W
26.6.24 10am	'A' Battery registered on the German Trench at the foot of hill 58 (O.3.d)	W
	at the request of the Inf. Bd. Or. '2' Battery fired on the N. edge of the Wood in I.35.a.	W
	11am of the Wood in I.29.d. - a the W. edge of the Wood in I.35.a.	W
	2.40pm 'W' Battery searched for a German Battery reported to be b.b RPSE - of 2 WARTELEEN	W

Army Form C. 2118.

WAR DIARY
INTELLIGENCE SUMMARY.
(Erase heading not required.)

Instructions regarding War Diaries and Intelligence Summaries are contained in F.S. Regs., Part II. and the Staff Manual respectively. Title pages will be prepared in manuscript.

Hour, Date, Place	Summary of Events and Information	Remarks and references to Appendices
26.24.II 3pm	'D' Battery opens fire at the N. edge of the Wood Tag D	
3.10pm	'U' Battery fires on German Trench in Tag D.	
26.25.II 9.29am 10-11.13am	'U' Battery fires on German Trenches in its sector	
11.30am	'Q' Battery fired 2 salvos on Trenches in T.35.a	
2.5pm	'A' Battery registered on Trench O.	
4.30pm	'D' Battery fired 25 rounds on Trenches in T.35.a	
26.26.II 1pm	'D' Battery fired on KLEIN ZILLEBEKE — reported fully of Germans	
26.27.II 10am	'D' Battery fired 12 rounds on the Trenches in its sector	
26.28.II 2pm	'Q' Battery Tuesday is practically demolishing two houses T.35.c.88.	
	T.35.a.5. Suspected of being hostile observation stations.	
5.30pm	'D' Battery fires a hostile manifesto in village of ZWARTELEN	
March 1st 10am	'D' Battery again fired a hostile manifesto — continues firing at	
	intervals until 1.15.8pm	
6.10pm	News received that the Division (Artillery) as 6 Corps (Rot) has now	
	come under orders of 2nd Cav. Bde. Belgian + Heavy Artillery remaining in 3rd Corps. 1st/VIII Bde. 3rd to Corps Artillery.	
	Hugh Belgian Artillery still maintain course to ZWARTELEN.	

Army Form C. 2118.

WAR DIARY
INTELLIGENCE SUMMARY.
(Erase heading not required.)

Instructions regarding War Diaries and Intelligence Summaries are contained in F.S. Regs., Part II and the Staff Manual respectively. Title pages will be prepared in manuscript.

Hour, Date, Place	Summary of Events and Information	Remarks and references to Appendices
March 2nd 10 am	"Q" Battery fired high explosive at suspected hostile observation post at I.35.c.9.8.	WS
10.30 am	"D" Battery fired on German Trenches approx 9.0 x 4.3 — & Kerguen	WS for Trenches see Sketch
1.45 pm	"A" Battery fired on reported recently dug German trenches at Chatham O.4.c.3	WS
March 3rd		
4th 10.30 am	"V" Battery fired on "O" Trench & "N" Trench immediately beyond it	OH
11 am	Self reported bomb throwing from the home I.35.a.6.8 — "A" Batt'y fired 5 a tres home at once, from 11–11.45 am	
	Position selected for 2 relay Batteries in case it should be necessary to bring them up. These positions along ridge H.24 & H.30 —	OH
	H.24 & O.3. —	
March 5th 12.10 pm	"A" Battery registered on 16 gunner Trench. Unable to register in front of K2 left of Kn 27 & Pn 3 (O 2 d.)	OH
	During the day supplementary sets for 2 "B" Horse constructed in Approx Tom. ON	
	Sketch on March 5 F.	

(73989) W4141—463. 400,000. 9/14. H.&J.Ltd. Forms/C. 2118/10.

Army Form C. 2118.

WAR DIARY
INTELLIGENCE SUMMARY.
(Erase heading not required.)

Instructions regarding War Diaries and Intelligence Summaries are contained in F.S. Regs., Part II. and the Staff Manual respectively. Title pages will be prepared in manuscript.

Hour, Date, Place	Summary of Events and Information	Remarks and references to Appendices
March 6th 1 p.m.	"A" Battery fired on three trenches – the British trenches in front of the target evacuated for the time. Firing continued until 4.30 pm	
March 7th		
— 8th		
— 9th		
March 10th 11.30 a.m.	"A" Battery fired for 2 an hour at trench "O". Muzzles of the guns being nearly a demonstration.	
— 11th 8.30 a.m.	"A" Battery attempted to destroy batallions eating breakfast in front of Trench "O" by firing no. of Ens Genst shrapnel – result unseen (good)	
March 12th 8.30 am	"Q" Battery fired on 2 horse suppers of thing kettle carmentir stations at T35a8 & T35c9.5. It forestalled an attack directed by 25th Divt.	
— 12.45 pm	"M.2" div. Batteries fired in support portion of German Batteries which 1550 firing on British Trenches –	

Army Form C. 2118.

WAR DIARY
INTELLIGENCE SUMMARY.
(Erase heading not required.)

Instructions regarding War Diaries and Intelligence Summaries are contained in F. S. Regs., Part II. and the Staff Manual respectively. Title pages will be prepared in manuscript.

Hour, Date, Place	Summary of Events and Information	Remarks and references to Appendices
March 3rd 5.30am	'A' Battery fired on chateau O42 near three German Gunners	
	Battery, which was suspected of being an O.O. Stn.	
8.30am	'Q' Battery fired on house T35A87, T35C75 suspected of being German	
	Observation Stations.	
March 14th 9.30am	Cot the request of Inf. Bde. Cor. 'Z' Battery fired on the Trench opposite	
	2 MARTELEEN & thru a Ruin half-self thru three were found	
	Prisoner	
10.15am	'Z' Battery stopped firing.	
5.30pm	'A' Battery fired on German Trenches L.6.c.58 (O.3.0)	
5.40pm	'A' Battery searched the ST ELOI WARNETON ROAD	
6.5pm	'Z' Battery fired on German Trenches opposite 2 MARTELEEN with shrapnel.	
6.30pm	'Z' Battery cease fire	
6.45pm	'A' Battery cease fire	
March 15th 2.15am	'A' Battery fired on the German Trenches opposite L.2.3. with the	
	object of facilitating an attack by the 27th Div. on trenches	
	17-22.	
3.15am	'A' Battery stopped firing	

Army Form C. 2118.

WAR DIARY
INTELLIGENCE SUMMARY.
(Erase heading not required.)

Instructions regarding War Diaries and Intelligence Summaries are contained in F.S. Regs., Part II. and the Staff Manual respectively. Title pages will be prepared in manuscript.

Hour, Date, Place	Summary of Events and Information	Remarks and references to Appendices
March 15th 1.17 pm to 1.50 pm	"Z" Battery fired on the German trenches opposite 2 HARTELEEN	
2.5 pm to 2.40 pm	"Z" Battery fired on German trenches in the rear at Z9 required by B3r Cdr	
2.15 p.m.	"A" Battery fired salvos of shrapnel at irregular intervals on the trenches in h.H 45 S.E of pt E7.01 — Rep.d for By "A" Battery in reverse target which stopped inf enemy at 6.20 p.m in north sector 27th Divl infantry to attack	
6.25-6.35 pm	This attack was not being successful Report received that "A" Battery's fire on E7.201-WARNETON food on trenches to have been very effective in preventing the advance of fresh reserves. This information received from forward —	
2.40 pm	"W" Battery's observer saw the flash of Trench mortar, mentioned on the German Trenches in his sector & "W" Battery fired on this trench for 10 mins	

Army Form C. 2118.

WAR DIARY
or
INTELLIGENCE SUMMARY.
(Erase heading not required.)

Instructions regarding War Diaries and Intelligence Summaries are contained in F.S. Regs., Part II. and the Staff Manual respectively. Title pages will be prepared in manuscript.

Hour, Date, Place	Summary of Events and Information	Remarks and references to Appendices
March 16th 10 a.m.	"U" Battery fired on trenches in B sector to prevent throwing of handgrenades from them.	
11.40 a.m.	"U" Battery Observer reports flashes at I.26.a.5.3 & "U" Battery opens fire on this point. The Gunners cease firing.	
1.15 p.m.	"U" Battery opens fire as at 10 a.m. to stop handgrenades	
12.48 p.m.	"2" Battery fired on trenches opp. 39 to stop handgrenades thrown	
4 p.m.	"D" Battery fired against a sapping reported approach trench 35.—	
9 p.m.	"2" Battery opens fires at trenches opp. 39 to stop handgrenades	WS
March 17th 6 p.m.	"Q" Battery opens fire at trench opposite approach trench 35.	
9 p.m.	"Q" Battery — —	WS
March 18th 1.30 p.m.	"A" Battery fires at a German Battery reported at O.4.6.2.2.	
4.20 p.m.	"A" Battery observes myself German at work digging in to trench O.3.d.8.8 — let fly again fire of German Battery at O.4.c.9.2. from a Branch 2 line trenches — "A" Battery closed fire Battery & the ground for on to be diggers	WS

(73989) W4141—463. 400,000. 9/14. H.&J.Ltd. Forms/C. 2118/10.

Army Form C. 2118.

WAR DIARY
or
INTELLIGENCE SUMMARY.
(Erase heading not required.)

Hour, Date, Place	Summary of Events and Information	Remarks and references to Appendices
March 19th	—	
March 20th 10 a.m.	A Battery shelled by Battery near Chateau 04.D.	
12 noon	"A" Battery was endeavouring to communicate with the German Trenches opposite Trenches 36 & 37 - "A" Battery however arranged to come but owing to the breaking of 2 telephone wires it could not take place. Gun too late.	
1.40 p.m.	2 Battery fired on a German Battery in the bend of the canal at 06.a, who had an aeroplane strafing trenches.	
2.50 p.m.	This German Battery having ceased opening fire, 2 Battery again fired a few salvos at it.	
2.15 p.m.	The Battery near Chateau 04.D. having opened fire, A Battery fired a few salvos in its direction.	
March 21st 10.15 a.m.	A gun (probs.) at 04.D.66 firing a honest/29, Q Battery fired a few salvos at it & stopped it firing.	
2.30 p.m.	This gun began again, & Q Battery (Colonel. ?) fired at it again.	

Army Form C. 2118.

(2)

WAR DIARY
INTELLIGENCE SUMMARY.
(Erase heading not required.)

Instructions regarding War Diaries and Intelligence Summaries are contained in F.S. Regs., Part II. and the Staff Manual respectively. Title pages will be prepared in manuscript.

Hour, Date, Place	Summary of Events and Information	Remarks and references to Appendices
March 22nd 11:30am	Wiltshire Section. "K" Battery registered on German Trenches opposite 36637. After conclusion of registration which was rather delayed by interruptions in Telephone communication.	
3:45pm	"K" Battery fired some high explosive shell at the French - check "Q" Battery fire at the second line trenches.	
2:30pm	The section of "K" Battery not engaged as above fired a few salvoes at the trenches in its sector from which hand grenades are being thrown.	
6pm	"Z" Battery fired upon salvoes at a German Battery reported at O6a22	W
March 23rd	(Wiltshire)	
5pm	"K" Battery reported that hand grenades were being thrown on to the trenches & "K" Battery was ordered to fire a few salvoes in to the German Trenches in its sector.	W
March 24th 4:50pm	at the request of the infantry in the trenches "Z" Battery fired on a German Battery at I36a53.	W
25th	—	
26th — 2pm	"A" Battery registered HOLLEBEKE Church with aeroplane observation	W
March 27th 10am	"Z" Battery registered ECLUSETTE 6 & House at O2.56 with aeroplane observation — left my R.J.	W
March 28th 9.30	"Z" Battery attempted to continue aeroplane registration but the lamps for signalling from the aeroplane would not work & the attempt was a WS	

Army Form C. 2118.

WAR DIARY
or
INTELLIGENCE SUMMARY.
(Erase heading not required.)

Instructions regarding War Diaries and Intelligence Summaries are contained in F. S. Regs., Part II. and the Staff Manual respectively. Title pages will be prepared in manuscript.

Hour, Date, Place	Summary of Events and Information	Remarks and references to Appendices

March 29th 9.30 "Z" Battery again carried out registration on same targets as in march 27th with aeroplane observation, but firing with from the aeroplane × See very few German made was not obtained owing the unsuitable state of the atmosphere at E.9.d.99 × improved up to one round some movement seen 1.15pm "A" Battery fired 3 Salvos at German observers seen a portion of German trenches is not running in the trench O.12.d.18. on lines.

March 30th 9.30am "Z" Battery registered Targets O German guns at O.b.c.56 @ KLEIN DILLEBEKE Crossroads I.3.6.93 @ Trench I.25.T near Pt.

11am Observer moving to far as a measure of reprisal many parties of German O.P. Sta. — "Q" Battery fired a house I.35.a.75 & I.35.a.67.

2pm "Z" Battery registered cross roads O1.c.96 out aeroplane observation —

March 31st 9.30am "U" & "Q" Battery registered targets with aeroplane observation — after ... "U" Battery had registered HOLLEBEKE crossroads on moving to U Batty. "Q" Battery carried on & registered HOLLEBEKE crossroads & FOULSETO 6 - "Q" Batty's but the cart & register carts not be continued —

Appendix. No. I.

Order of Battle of Belgian Artillery Regt.
att'd. 28th Div'n.

Regimental Headquarters.

Lieut. Colonel Dujardin (A.E.M.)ˣ

Captain Reul.

Lieut. Tolinden.

attached Captain C.E.D. Bridge R.H.A.

1st Group (18th Bde)   2nd Group (19th Bde)

HQ/ Captain Van Crombrugge (A.E.M.)ˣ   HQ/ Major Didier
²Captain Bosts (adjutant)   Lieut Nonnon (adj.)
(Paymaster) Lt. Souka   (Paymaster) Lt. Nicolas.
(M. Os.) Dr. Lombard   (M. Os) Dr. Guilinot
         – Maton.   – Coryn
(V. Os) Fostier   (Vet. Os) – Croquet.

(Chaplain) · Herman.   (Chaplain) Van der Cam.

97th Batty   100th Batty
Capt. Verstraete. (A.E.M.)ˣ   Capt van Maldeghem
Lt. Bégault.   Lt Hermans
2/Lt Varlsa.   Lt Nees

98th Batty   101st Batty
Capt. Louvau   Capt. Scheid
Lt. Nicaise   Lt van Sprang
Lt. van Ortroy   Lt Servais

99th Batty   102nd Batty
Capt. Tahon   Capt. Cumont (A.E.M.)ˣ
Lt. Lintz   Lt. Bosts
                                             Lt Timmermans

NB. ˣ A.E.M. = p.s.c.   Continued

Appendix No I (cont.)

Train – Transport Corps.

H.Q. – Capt. Hottlet
(VO) De Nayer.
(MO) Dr. Evely
(Paymaster) ~~Lt. Nayer~~ Lt. François

Ammunition Column. (Horsed)
Lt. Forsont
Lt. Ralet.

M.T. Ammunition Column.
Lt. Van der Hagen

M.T. Ambulance Column.
Dr. Godeau
(Chaplain) Dumont

M.T. Supply Column.
Lt. Daoust.

A. G. The Base

WAR DIARY.
Belgian Artillery Regt
attd. 28th Div.

Appendix III
②

Telephone communication
between A.A. Regt. attd. 28th Div.

- Regtl. Commander
- G.O.C. R.A. 28th Divn
- O.C. 1st Group
- 'A' Batty
  - Obs. Sta.
  - G.O.C. Inf. Bde.
- 'B' Batty
  - Obs. Sta.
  - Trenches
  - G.O.C. Inf. Bde.
- O.C. 2nd Group
- 'W' Batty
  - Obs. Sta.
  - English line available for Inf. of Belgians. — Trenches
- 'Z' Batty
  - Obs. Sta.
  - Trenches

28th Division. no diar.
Apparently attached 5th Division.

Belgian Artillery Regt.

Vol II   1 — 30.4.15.

Army Form C. 2118.

(14)

WAR DIARY
or
INTELLIGENCE SUMMARY.
(Erase heading not required.)

Instructions regarding War Diaries and Intelligence Summaries are contained in F.S. Regs., Part II. and the Staff Manual respectively. Title pages will be prepared in manuscript.

Hour, Date, Place	Summary of Events and Information	Remarks and references to Appendices
April 1st 3pm	"Q" Battery completed Registration with aeroplane & worked on Targets T3n170. Og Bg3, KLEIN ZILLEBEKE Cross roads + T35a 41. "U" Battery registration O5a59. Observation was very difficult owing to bad light. —	C.B.
April 2nd	—	
April 3rd 12/10pm	"Q" Battery observer reports German mine thrown in Sq. I35a + "2" Battery opened fire on those. Air Telephone worked. —	C.B.
April 4th 5pm	"U" Battery completed 16 registration with aeroplane Registration on the following Cross roads T38 b64, Fort Griffe. O5 b23. Salient O6 c12.00 + Salient O12 b28 — Airman was killed [unclear] by a rifle bullet. One man "Q" Battery very wounded on the RITZ de MESSIN by a shell. The German Heavies Howitzer Trenches 34 + 35 about 10½ Somm[unclear]	C.B.
April 5th 5pm	"U" Battery brought sufficient fire to bear on German Trench opposite 36 + 37, at the same time "Q" Battery fired on the German second bar trenches in front of 36 C39.	C.B.
April 6th 12 noon	"U" Battery again brought sufficient fire to bear on Trench opposite 36 + 37 + at the same time "Q" Battery fired on the German Second bar trenches. C.B. Trench mortars reported in house at T35a 57. "A" Battery patterns	C.B.
3.45pm	Destroyed this house. LitH 71 S.	C.B.

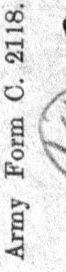

Army Form C. 2118.

(13)

WAR DIARY
or
INTELLIGENCE SUMMARY.
(Erase heading not required.)

Instructions regarding War Diaries and Intelligence Summaries are contained in F.S. Regs., Part II and the Staff Manual respectively. Title pages will be prepared in manuscript.

Hour, Date, Place	Summary of Events and Information	Remarks and references to Appendices
April 7th 3.45 pm	Hostile shrapnel reported in the lodge of the Chateau N 040 - 'A' Battery put a few H.E. through the roof from where observation was being carried out	C.B.
April 8th 7 p.m	'A' Battery again fired at the lodge of the Chateau - fired 2 or 3 rounds through the roof	C.B.
April 9th	—	C.B.
April 10th 1 pm	'2' Battery fired 4 salvos at trench infront reported in I.35.E. On this day the Regt. came under the command of the G.O.C. 2 Div. The Batteries remained in the position occupied - but west of the British Batteries of 28th Div. was replaced by Batteries of 5th Div. -	C.B.
April 11th	—	
April 12th	Nothing received from B.M. R.A. 5th Div. during part of division in our sector. Ref. Appx IV	C.B.
April 13th pm	'2' Battery fired on the trenches in its sector at the request of Inf. - on enemy who throwing hand grenades from them. One other was wounded at POPERINGHE by a bomb from an aero CB place.	

(73989) W4141—463. 400,000. 9/14. H.&J.Ltd. Forms/C. 2118/10.

Army Form C. 2118.

16

WAR DIARY
or
INTELLIGENCE SUMMARY.
(Erase heading not required.)

Instructions regarding War Diaries and Intelligence Summaries are contained in F.S. Regs., Part II. and the Staff Manual respectively. Title pages will be prepared in manuscript.

Hour, Date, Place		Summary of Events and Information	Remarks and references to Appendices
April 14th			
- 15th	2 p.m.	At the request of the Infantry, 'Q' Battery fired on mine throwers at T.35.c.2.9	C.R.
April 16th	11.35 am	'Q' Battery again fired at the mine throwers at T.35.c.2.9	C.R.
	8 pm	O.C. Belgian Artillery issues orders to his Batteries, in accordance with orders received from I.O.C.R.A. 2nd Divn	APPENDIX I. C.R.
April 17th	2 pm	'Q', '2', & 'U' Batteries observed fire, as shewn in APPx I.	
	5 pm	'Q', '2', & 'U' Batteries ceased firing, & remained in Observation as follows:—	
		'Q' Batt. — Cross Roads T.35 d 1.9. '2' Battery on the Railway, trench T.35.c.2.8 Cr. Rd. 'U' Battery on the crossroads T.35.c 9.10 — 'A' Battery on the trenches in its sector. Lt Turcie-Grawau wounded in 'U' Battery Observation Station	
	8.10 pm	'Q' & '2' Batteries observed fire on the eboes line as a counter attack was threatened	
	8.15 pm	'Q' Battery fired a few rounds on the German communic. trench near the Railway w/ just E of the point T.35.c.2.8.	
	10.6 pm	'U' Battery fired on the KLEIN ZILLEBEEK ROAD	
	10.20pm	'U' & '2' Batteries fired on the roads along the canal in O.5.E & O.6.a.	
	10.55pm	'Q','U' & '2' Batteries observed fire on their night lines in 17,21,1/2 to attack German counter attack. These Batteries kept up a slow rate of fire on the same lines till daybreak.	C.R.
April 18th	4.30am	Orders issued to cease firing.	
	5 am.	'2' Battery swept the Railway cutting where hostile infantry were reported to be assembling.	

Army Form C. 2118.

(17)

WAR DIARY
or
INTELLIGENCE SUMMARY.
(Erase heading not required.)

Instructions regarding War Diaries and Intelligence Summaries are contained in F.S. Regs., Part II. and the Staff Manual respectively. Title pages will be prepared in manuscript.

Hour, Date, Place	Summary of Events and Information	Remarks and references to Appendices
April 1/18 5.25 a.m.	"W.U" & "Z" Batteries again opened fire on their lines in reply to enemy counter attack.	
5.50 a.m.	B'tor resumes to reduce rate of fire.	
6.10 a.m.	Batteries order to cease fire.	
8.45 a.m.	'Q' Battery observer reports Germans evacuating in a communication trench at the slope (N.E.) & to machine cutting in T.35.d. & 'Q' Battery fired 3 registering rounds on this trench. But the Beaumont telephone line was then cut.	
8.50 a.m.	2. Battery again fired on the Railway Trench. T.35.b.5.28	
10. a.m.	'2' Battery again opened fired on this trench at a slow rate.	
11.45 a.m.	2. Battery ceased firing.	
4.30 p.m.	Also received that a further attack on the Southern top of Hill 60 was likely to take place at 6 p.m. - O.C. Belgian Artillery issued orders for the cooperation of his Batteries.	APPENDIX VI
6 p.m.	Q.& "U" Batteries opened fire in accordance with these orders.	
6.15 p.m.	Reply fire induced.	
6.30 p.m.	Inf. Bde. O.R. informs "U" Battery that it was ceasefiring in reply to a German counterattack "Q" Battery increased its rate of fire.	
6.40 p.m.	The Battery fired H.E. in the Communication trench N.E. of Palcheon	
	T.35.f. & kept up a slow rate of fire thro' throughout the night	
9. p.m.	'2' Battery ceasefiring under orders recd from Infy. Bde. O.R.	ps.

Army Form C. 2118.

WAR DIARY
or
INTELLIGENCE SUMMARY.
(Erase heading not required.)

Instructions regarding War Diaries and Intelligence Summaries are contained in F.S. Regs., Part II. and the Staff Manual respectively. Title pages will be prepared in manuscript.

Hour, Date, Place	Summary of Events and Information	Remarks and references to Appendices
April 19th 6.30 a.m.	'Q' Battery ceased firing	
12.30 p.m.	'U' Battery opened fire on the ARTILLERY HQRS in response to a communication from the Infantry on hill 60 that they were being much annoyed by hostile enemy howitzer & machine guns from this direction.	C.B.
1.30 p.m.	'U' Battery ceased firing	C.B.
9 p.m.	Congratulatory telegram from C-in-C with reference to attack on hill 60 received through G.O.C. 5th Div. & G.O.C. 2nd Army.	C.B.
April 20th 5.45 p.m.	'Q' Battery opened fire on hostile guns reported on the South edge of the wood in I.35.	C.B. × See April 7th above.
6.15 p.m.	'Q', 'U' & 'B' Batteries (3 guns rapid) fired on this signal night lines × on a known attack from enemy trenches. Gths trenches. Esp. O/Fire, 162 Battalion fired at watermark	C.B.
6.30 p.m.	These three Batteries again fired rapid fire for 3 minutes & then a slow rate.	C.B.
9.15 p.m.	'U' & 'Q' Batteries ordered to stop firing.	
10.15 p.m.	These Batteries again fired rapid fire for 5 minutes.	
11.45 p.m.	Ceas Fire. 1 Telephonist killed at "U" Battery O.P. Sta. — 1 OFFICER wounded & 2 men wounded at "Q" Battery O.P. Sta. Observation Sta.	

Army Form C. 2118.

WAR DIARY
or
INTELLIGENCE SUMMARY.
(Erase heading not required.)

Instructions regarding War Diaries and Intelligence Summaries are contained in F.S. Regs., Part II. and the Staff Manual respectively. Title pages will be prepared in manuscript.

Hour, Date, Place	Summary of Events and Information	Remarks and references to Appendices
April 21st 6.10 a.m.	'Q' Battery fired at the P.B. portion of the Wood in I.35 against a hostile Battery.	
6.20 a.m.	'Q'& 'U' 'Z' Batteries each fired in their sectors at nothing 2th.	
7.45 a.m.	'Q' Battery ordered to fire a R triangular shoot just S. of R. L.R. in I.35.	
8.10.7.	Other hostile wire-cutters dispersed.	
8 a.m.	Inf. report hostile gun situated somewhere near ECLUSE No. 5 - 'Z' Battery ordered to fire 25 rounds to search for this gun.	C.B.
9 a.m.	Batteries ordered to stop firing. —	
April 22nd 1.15 p.m.	Hostile runs Howizers reported somewhere in the S. edge of 2.WARTZEEL Wood or in the Railway cutting. 'U' Battery opened fire on the Wood, 'Z' Battery on the S. edge of the cutting.	
5.15 p.m. 7.30 p.m.	Capt. Bridge R.A. slightly wounded by a Jack Johnson in YPRES.	
8 p.m. 12 midnight	At 8.55 hours 'Z' Battery fired a few salvoes on the ground B.t. the Railway and the S. edge of 2.HARTZEELEN Wood.	
10.30 p.m.	In response to a message to B.M.R.A. 5th Div. — orders received to get the Heavy Wagons for the Batteries in action up close to YPRES. French front at LANGEMARCK reported broken & Germans said to have reached WIELTJE C.2.8.	C.B.

Forms/C. 2118/10

Army Form C. 2118.

WAR DIARY
or
INTELLIGENCE SUMMARY.
(Erase heading not required.)

Instructions regarding War Diaries and Intelligence Summaries are contained in F.S. Regs., Part II. and the Staff Manual respectively. Title pages will be prepared in manuscript.

Hour, Date, Place	Summary of Events and Information	Remarks and references to Appendices
April 23rd 12.15 a.m.	Orders issued for positions to be occupied in case of a withdrawal of troops to the Pilkem.	APPENDIX VII.
1 a.m. 3 a.m.	J/2 Battery again fired a few salvos on the ground between the Railway and the 2 HARTELETT Salient.	
6 a.m.	Q.H. & D Batteries opened rapid fire for 3 minutes as follows:—	
	D on the COURTRAI Railway.	
	'2' on the ground between the Railway & 2 HARTELETT Wood, as far as the cross roads (WAMBEKEN?) 06 c 7.7. —	
	U in the KLEIN ZILLEBEKE Road from crossroads I 35 c 6.7 10.6 the village.	
6.45 a.m.	The 3 Batteries again fired in the above Zones 7 mins rapid fire.	
10 a.m. – 11 a.m.	To regulate an attack on hill 60 the 3 Batteries fired in 3 different occasions bursts of rapid fire in their Zones.	
12.35 p.m.	Airship Aircraft reported enfilading trench 28 from 2 HARTELETT Wood. '2' Battery fired upon it. 1 Telephonist wounded repairing the Battery line.	
	During the night Q Battery fired 3 times in the Railway cutting, between the C.O.s of COURTRAI, against hostile machine guns.	CB.
April 24th 7 p.m.	Road to MENIN being heavily shelled. O.C. Belgian Artillery From Ypres his H.Q to the ECOLE MOYENNE – YPRES – J.8.0.2. —	CB.

Army Form C. 2118.

(21)

WAR DIARY
or
INTELLIGENCE SUMMARY.
(Erase heading not required.)

Instructions regarding War Diaries and Intelligence Summaries are contained in F.S. Regs., Part II. and the Staff Manual respectively. Title pages will be prepared in manuscript.

Hour, Date, Place	Summary of Events and Information	Remarks and references to Appendices
April 24th 3.15 p.m.	Order received from Div. to get horses handy – to all Telephone wires were broken & Belgian artillery sent a motorcyclist to Div. H.Q. to bring order.	C.B.
4 p.m.	Order received to withdraw 'D' & 'C' Batteries at Dir. K. to place them in action in G.H.Q. 2nd line – with the 2 Reating Batteries.	APPENDIX. VIII
VLAMERTINGHE. 7 p.m.	O.C. Belgian Artillery transferred his H.Q. from YPRES to VLAMERTINGHE. H.Q. at 9 a.s.s. The 2 Reating Batteries occupy positions in G.H.Q. 2nd line – 'C' & 'D' Batteries issued in action in original positions. 'U' & 'Z' are to Withdraw. – 'A' & 'B' Batteries left under command of Commandant van Cambridge who reports on arrival to G.O.C. Div. H.Q.	
9 p.m.	The officer of 1 Belgian Battery accepts positions in G.H.Q. 2nd line – 'C' & 'D' Batteries. This officer had been used by G.O.C. 2nd Corps. – 'U' & 'Z' Batteries, which had just arrived after their withdrawal are placed under the order of Major D. Div. – who reported for order at H.Q. 28th Div. =	
11.55 p.m.	Order sent to O.C. Army Batteries to occupy the positions of 'U' + 'Z' Batteries in case of Withdrawal.	C.B.
April 25th 2 a.m.	'U' + 'Z' Batteries with Major D. Div. marches to S.I.14.22 places they went into action under G.O.C. R.A. 28th Div. – During the night R'Batteries fired 30 rounds at the request of the 1 Bel. Commander.	C.B.

Forms/C. 2118/10 (9 20 6) W 4141—463 100,000 9/14 H W V

Army Form C. 2118.

(2)

WAR DIARY
or
INTELLIGENCE SUMMARY.
(Erase heading not required.)

Hour, Date, Place	Summary of Events and Information	Remarks and references to Appendices
April 26th 3 p.m.	"U" "R" Batteries having fired away all the ammunition allowed from 1600 rounds - came out of action, & joined the Regt. at KEMMEL - The OHE went into Billets at BOESCHEPPS.	
10 pm.	Telegram received from Belgian Division stating that 2 Tanks of H.E. & 1 Truck of Shrapnel had arrived at DIKKEBUSCH Station for the Regt. at 7 a.m. 27th April - in all 4456 rounds.	ed.
April 27th	G.O.C. 2nd Corps again offers 2 Belgian Batteries - the two with 250 rounds per gun - to G.O.C. 5th Corps.	
2 pm.	G.O.C. 5th Corps gratefully accepts offer. - Batteries with chs.6890 Kia 2 at present occupying position in J.H.R.2 no line H.16.c. - These Batteries placed under the orders of Commandant Cument for this purpose. - This officer reports for instructions to G.O.C. 28th Divn. to which Div.n the Batteries are to be att.d.	ed.
8 a.m.	Col. Cument's Batteries in action at dawn at 7.1.a.3.2 under orders of G.O.C. R.A. 28th Div. The Resting Batteries from BOESCHEPPS went up yesterday to action in J.H.R. 2 Rd line in H.16.c.	
6 pm	"Q" Battery fired on a hostile Battery in OSB. Col. Cument's Batteries fired on German Trenches to support a French attack to the N.W. of YPRES	ed.

Forms/C. 2118/10

Army Form C. 2118.

(23)

WAR DIARY
or
INTELLIGENCE SUMMARY.
(Erase heading not required.)

Instructions regarding War Diaries and Intelligence Summaries are contained in F.S. Regs., Part II. and the Staff Manual respectively. Title pages will be prepared in manuscript.

Hour, Date, Place	Summary of Events and Information	Remarks and references to Appendices
April 29th	'Q' Battery again fired at a German Battery in O.3.B. 'A' Battery fired at the German trench opposite 27 & her usual round into the trench. One man killed. The cyclist orderly Bdr Cpl Cumont to OP Reptd this	A.B.
April 30th 7:30 am	Cpt Cumont's Battery fired on the German trenches in this sector to support a French attack.	C.B.
7:45 pm	The French attack was delayed & the Battery ceased firing. The French attack took place later & was stopped at hill 29 in C.15.a.	

Appendix. IV

O.C. Belgian Art.

The Sectors of the front of the Divn. have been "relettered". U. V. W & X.

The position of dividing lines between these sectors are :-

Between Sectors U & V - from Southern point of the SPOIL BANK past the eastern end of trenches 27 & 27B.

Between Sectors V & W - N.W & S.E. immediately W. of trench 30b.

Between W & X along the Railway.

sd. A. Bartholomew
Major R.A.
B.M. R.A. 5th D. A.A.

12/4/15

Provisional Belgian Artillery Regt.   APP V

Translation

Extract from an operation order issued to 5th Divisional Artillery for 17th inst.

1) The six mines situated under the hostile trenches under the hill 60 to the E. of the COURTRAI Railway will be blown up on 17th inst. at an hour to be notified later. They will go up in pairs, the first under hill 60, the second to the W. opposite Trench 38 & the third to the East opposite Trench 40.

There will be an interval of 10 seconds between the explosions. The firing centre for the mines will be at the Southern end of the communication trench joining up trenches 39 & 40.

2) Immediately after the mines are blown up 2 Bns of Inf & 2 sections of Engineers under command of Brig. Gen. Wanless O'Gowan will assault hill 60, in order to include it in our lines.

3) The artillery will open fire immediately after the explosion of the first mine. The Belgian Batteries will take part as follows:—

 "Q" Battery will search Wood I 35 a.11 from Écluse No. 6.

 "U" Battery will sweep the KLEIN ZILLEBEKE Road as far as the village & including crossroads I 35 b 7.10, & the footbridge over the canal at O 5 6 23.

 "Z" Battery will sweep the Railway Trench & the communication Trenches to the N. & the footbridge over the Canal at O 5 a 5.7.

 Ammn Expenditure — The following rates of fire will be observed.

  1st 5 mins. 1 round per gun per minute — 60 rounds
  next 10 mins 1 — — — — 120 rounds
  next 30 mins 2 rounds — — — 720 —
  next 15 mins 1 round — — — 180 —
                                   ————
                                  1080 rounds

4) Immediately after the explosion of the mines the infantry & machine guns will open fire along the whole front of the Divn.

5) As soon as the new Trenches are dug on hill 60, "Z" Batty will establish an advanced observation there.

6) If any Batteries are firing short of our trenches, the Infantry will show a red & yellow flag — when the range of Batteries firing in his zone must be at once lengthened.

7) Batteries will deal immediately with counterattacks or hostile machine guns when discovered. 7) bis. XX

8) The most intimate communication will be kept up through out the night between the Inf & Art. & the detachments will remain at their guns.

2   App. V Cont.

~~XX ~~ the ~~group~~
~~commander~~

XX 7 bis.) As soon as the operation ordered in 3) above is finished & unless contrary orders are issued Batteries will lay out night lines as follows - in order to be ready to deal with counter attacks -

'Q' Battery - on the crossroads I 35 d.1.9.
'Z' Battery - on the Railway Track I 35 b.0.8. & on the communication Trenches to the N.E.
'U' Battery - on the crossroads I 35 b 7.1.a & on the KLEIN ZILLEBEKE Road.

'A' Battery will be ready to open fire at a moments notice on the trenches in its sector.

9) Frequent Reports will be sent to me by the group commanders.

For Information
           List of British Batteries taking part
& targets to be engaged by them.

                              16th April 1917
                              Dujardin
                              Lieut
                              Cd

Translation.

Appendix VI

Provisional Regt. of Belgian Artillery

Extract from operation orders of 5th Divisional Artillery

(1) The 15th Inf. Bde will attack at 6 pm today to drive the enemy from the South of hill 60.

(2) 'Q' '2' & 'U' Batteries will cooperate as follows:—

'Q' Battery will fire on both sides of the COURTRAI Railway & will search the ground from the entrance to the communication Trench at I 35 6.2.8 to the Canal.

'2' Battery will sweep the ground between the Railway & the ZWARTELEEN — ZILLEBEKE Road as far as the crossroads 06 C 7.7. —

'U' Battery will sweep the ZILLEBEKE Road from the cross roads I 35 6.7.10 as far as KLEIN ZILLEBEKE.

(3) Note explaining action of English Batteries.

(4) Fire will be opened at 6 pm. — & will be kept up at a rapid rate until 6.15 pm. Batteries will then continue firing as required by the Inf. Bde. C.O.

(5) All arrangements will be made to enable Batteries to open fire on their own objectives at a moment's notice throughout the night.

Sd. Dujardin
Lt Col
C.O.

18/4/15

APPENDIX VII.

Copy

ALL UNITS.

In the event of a retreat being ordered the Batteries will take up following positions:-

British Batteries. — — —

Belgians. 2 Batteries. U & Z. H.16c 7/7 - 9/9, firing S.E.
          2 Batteries Q & A H.16d 7/5 - 7/9, firing. E.

'Q.' 'Z' & 'U' Batteries must withdraw through YPRES or South of it. 'A' Battery by roads to W. & S.W. of YPRES. -

One officer from each Battery must start as soon as possible to reconnoitre roads & positions, which should be reached as soon after daylight as possible.

No retirement will take place except in conjunction with the Infantry with whom close touch must be maintained.

(Signed) A. Bartholomew
Major BM
Res. Ⅰ Div.

12.15. a.m.
23/4/15.

Appendix VIII.

Copy

BM 191.   Date 24.

You are to withdraw U & R Batteries tonight after dark & they are to go into action in the G.H.Q. 2nd line and Your 2 Batteries that are resting should also go into action in the G.H.Q. 2nd line tonight, so that if it is necessary to retire to the 2nd line later, A & Q will be able to go to the rear & not come into action again. AAA. You must withdraw tonight South of YPRES.

A.B.
B.M.jor
5th Div. Art

4. pm.

Confidential

War Diary

Belgian Artillery Regt
attd. 5th Divn

From April 1st 1915
To April 30th 1915

Kept by:—

Capt. C.S.D. Bridge R.A.

121/5506

M03

5th Division.

Belgian Artillery Regiment.

Vol III 1 – 31.5.15.

Army Form C. 2118.

WAR DIARY
or
INTELLIGENCE SUMMARY.
(Erase heading not required.)

Instructions regarding War Diaries and Intelligence Summaries are contained in F.S. Regs., Part II. and the Staff Manual respectively. Title pages will be prepared in manuscript.

Hour, Date, Place	Summary of Events and Information	Remarks and references to Appendices
May 1st 1915 KEMMERTINGHE	Col. Clement's Battery attacked 29th Div. bn. to have registered with aeroplane. All arrangements were made & the aeroplane came over but owing to a fault in the lamp no registration took place.	
	'R' Battery fired at roads in its sector.	
May 2nd		
5 pm.	The Germans attacked the front of R. 28th Div. making use of asphyxiating gas - as soon as the cloud of gas did through was observed all the Batteries (including those of Col. Clement) opened rapid rapid fire on the German trenches. The German attack failed completely.	
	A.O.P. Battery experience heavy shells all afternoon - no casualties Col. Clement's Battery fired on the farm in C.15.a. where the Germans 13.2 said to be massing.	
May 3rd		
10 am		
4 pm.	Col. Clement's Battery again fired in reported assembly of troops in a farm C.15.G.5.2. Further attempt made to register the Battery with aero-plane unsuccessful, as day was too cloudy.	

Forms/C. 2118/10

Army Form C. 2118.

(25)

WAR DIARY
or
INTELLIGENCE SUMMARY.
(Erase heading not required.)

Instructions regarding War Diaries and Intelligence Summaries are contained in F.S. Regs., Part II. and the Staff Manual respectively. Title pages will be prepared in manuscript.

Hour, Date, Place	Summary of Events and Information	Remarks and references to Appendices
May 3rd – 4th	The withdrawal to a line through MOOSE of the troops on the N.E. of the YPRES salient took place during the night. It was without incident. Was successfully carried out with few casualties.	US
May 4th 1 p.m.	Again to wish to register Col. Cuments Battery with our plane observation. The Battery (Cuments) fired at farm C17a44 over Fromens was said to be answering.	US
May 5th Frgaun	The gunners informed of not hydrating gas against kill to. of Trenches 35.36.37 – Trench 37 had to be momentarily evacuated as a part of kill to too hot. Q Battery opened fire at 9 a.m. against the approaches to the kill 60. Rapid fire for 10 minutes then slower rate. Again to wish to register Col. Cuments Battery with aero-plane observation.	US
8.30 pm	Col Cuments Battery replaced by 2 Batteries under Major Didier of the Bns Battery fired at the farm in C18a when German Brig. Genl. R.A. S.E. Div. saw Horses a further 100 yards Buy Sent to the 2 Batteries attd to 6 to E Divn.	US

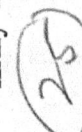

(9 29 6) W 4141—463 100,000 9/14 H W V Forms/C. 2118/10

Army Form C. 2118.

WAR DIARY
or
INTELLIGENCE SUMMARY.
(Erase heading not required.)

Instructions regarding War Diaries and Intelligence Summaries are contained in F.S. Regs., Part II. and the Staff Manual respectively. Title pages will be prepared in manuscript.

Hour, Date, Place	Summary of Events and Information	Remarks and references to Appendices
May 6th. —	"A" Battery changed B.pos of one of its guns & 2nd registered it from the new position.	AS
May 7th. 2am	"D" Battery fired in its sector to support an attack by R. Berks on Hill 60.	
6 p.m.	Major Didion's Batteries fired on C17 D25, a point at which the enemy was seen to be establishing asphyxiating gas apparatus. During the night "D" Battery fired on the roads in its sector between the Canal & the Railway, to stop later on enemy's German attack.	AS
May 8th. 7.30 a.m.	Major Didion's Batteries again fired on C17 D25, as on May 7th. —	
6 p.m.	Major Didion's Batteries lay out night lines beyond the British trenches in C2R — C15. "D" Battery searches the roads, footbridges & huts in its sector at irregular intervals during the night.	AS
May 9th. 2.30am	Major Didion's Batteries fired on the German trenches in C17 owing to the rearrangement of the British front the sector allotted to Major Didion's Batteries was changed to-day from Battery at C1a22 to I10D20 to a line from Battery to I10B30.	APPENDIX IX
10a.m.—12 noon	Major Didion's Batteries swept the woods in I6S.	AS

WAR DIARY or INTELLIGENCE SUMMARY

Army Form C. 2118.
(27)

Hour, Date, Place	Summary of Events and Information	Remarks and references to Appendices
May 9th 10 a.m.	Wire received that the withdrawal of H.Q. 2nd Div. was possible. The 2 Batteries resting in position in H.16.c. were to change their position to H.29.c.63 - So as to bring them to Div. area.	
3.30pm	A German prisoner reports that a German H.Q. Staff was established near "K.27" in square O.6.a. "R" Battery fired at this point.	
3.p.m.	Orders Major D. Doris Batteries again except No. 6 in I.6.6.	
3.25pm	This Battery continued its ranging shots.	
4.45pm	The Battery obtained its range by 200 metres.	
3.25pm	The other of Major Didio's Batteries opened fire on the wood in I.12.6.	
5.15pm	Both Batteries ceased firing.	
6.20pm	Fire again opened on wood in I.6.6.	
6.30pm	The 2 Batteries fired on a wood in I.12.b & to the other in I.6.b.	
	The firing of the battery was directed on a line through I.6.d.3.6. to the wood in I.12.b.	
	During the night R. Battery fired on the roads in its sector.	
6.30pm	The 2 Battalions (Col. Cunard) stating its position in H.16.c. ordered.	
	The position of H.29.c.68 which was reached at that hour to a 6-gun Battery of the 3rd Div.	AS.
May 10th 8.30am	Major Didio Batteries again address to open fire on the line through I.6.d.3.6.	AS

WAR DIARY
or
INTELLIGENCE SUMMARY.
(Erase heading not required.)

Army Form C. 2118.

Instructions regarding War Diaries and Intelligence Summaries are contained in F.S. Regs., Part II. and the Staff Manual respectively. Title pages will be prepared in manuscript.

Hour, Date, Place	Summary of Events and Information	Remarks and references to Appendices
May 10th		
10 a.m.	Reports soon came in from Infantry that the Belgian Batteries were firing right in to our Trenches & the Artillery was stopped. Report regains from Infantry that wished to holding a Liax to N. of the line through I 6 d 36, as had been supposed, the actual position of our infantry was E. of this point. So that R > Belgian Batteries had been actually firing (ammunition) at our own trenches. This mistake was entirely due to lack of information from the Infantry as to the line occupied.	C.B.
10.30 a.m.	Report rec'd. from Capt. Current that his Batteries was in pos'n at N37 c 88, with telephone lines laid to 2 Observation Sta - one for the 'Switch' line, one for G.H.Q. 2nd line.	
2.30 p.m.	Major DiVis'no Batteries (28 E Div'n) orders to turn observation on line I6d36 - last E of CHAPELLE in T 12 F.	
3 p.m.	Major DiVis'no Batteries established after Barrage in this line to Ypres Ln.	
4.50 p.m.	Renewed German attack to the N. of ETANG de BELLEWAARDE. Major DiVis'no Batteries fires on the Northern point of the Wood in T 12 G 8.3. - Rapid Rate. of fire at first. then Range decreased by 100 x. Slow rate of fire kept up until	
7 p.m.	When Batteries cease firing. During the night B'Battery fired on the Road in it's Sector on Scheme No. 6.	C.B.

(9 29 6) W 4141—463 100,000 9/14 H W V Forms/C. 2118/10

Army Form C. 2118.

WAR DIARY
or
INTELLIGENCE SUMMARY.
(Erase heading not required.)

Instructions regarding War Diaries and Intelligence Summaries are contained in F.S. Regs., Part II. and the Staff Manual respectively. Title pages will be prepared in manuscript.

Hour, Date, Place	Summary of Events and Information	Remarks and references to Appendices
Aug. 11th 10.30am	Information received that the Germans had reoccupied our first line trenches in I.12.a.8.3 which had been previously evacuated owing to heavy bombardment from the French & Germans advancing files on trenches to N.W. – even when given at first the Germans 30 in the woods in I.12.6 ran when the mounted attack got into our trenches. Major Divine Batteries opened a rapid fire on these woods.	
12.5pm	Report from Infantry that the firing of the Belgian Batteries was very effective, very accurate. Rate of fire reduced to 1 round every 2 mins.	AS.
12.15pm	85th Inf. Bde. requests Major Divine Batteries to fire on the woods in I.12.6 to N.M.W. & the Strong pt BELLEWAARDE - Rapid Rate.	
1.40pm	Ceased firing all ammunition having been expended.	
2.7pm	G.O.C. 2nd Corps requests 9.O.C.5th Corps to hand over another 1600 rounds to the 2 Batteries. but 28th Div? - to the 2nd & Div? More such valuable work this pressure was given to the munition was sent up.	AS.
7pm.	During the day Regt. HQrs. were was from H.14 6.45 to P.9.d.0.39 in order to turn the sector of the 5th Div? - Sketch showing bridges on canal S. of YPRES Recing. Communication with reference to haplor not Received	APPENDIX IV APPENDIX

WAR DIARY or INTELLIGENCE SUMMARY.

(Erase heading not required.)

Army Form C. 2118.

(30)

Hour, Date, Place	Summary of Events and Information	Remarks and references to Appendices
May. 11th 7.15 p.m.	Major DiDino Batteries registered on the German trench in Ibc, crossing the Railway, particularly at R of ROULERS - front 400 x telephone wire breaking, registration is incomplete.	A.
May. 12th	"D" Battery again fired at the "Ferme Olm", reported to be occupied by a German H.Q. - The Battery also fired at a farm E of house.	C.B.
6 p.m.	Major DiDino Batteries complete their registration of 11th 7.15 p.m.	
May. 13th 7.15 p.m.	Major DiDino Batteries fire on the trench registered.	
8.30 p.m.	Rate of fire increased to 1 round a minute per Battery	
11 a.m.	" " " " 1 round every 4 minutes	
9 p.m.	Batteries cease firing	
	C.R. DiDin, accompanied by Capt Bragg, proceeds to H.Q. 2nd Army to take (sent) J.O.C. 2nd Army to envoys of H.Q. to take have C.in.C of ST OMER to meet Col. Bellecour, commanding the training Regt of Belgian Art -	
11 p.m.	Order receives to send a further 300 rounds to Major DiDino Batteries. These rounds were taken from Cdt Courvots Batteries in action in G.H.R.27 line - leaving him without ammunition.	
11.25 p.m.	Major DiDino Batteries order to be ready to open fire should heavy attack firing to begin in case the infantry are not there.	C.B.

Army Form C. 2118.

(B1)

WAR DIARY
or
INTELLIGENCE SUMMARY.
(Erase heading not required.)

Hour, Date, Place	Summary of Events and Information	Remarks and references to Appendices
May 14th	"B" Battery fired at KLEIN ZILLEBEKE.	CB.
May 15th	2nd Belgian Art Regt (Col Dechesne) arrived at POPERINGHE	APPENDIX XII
May 16th 9 a.m.	Two Group Cos. 27th Regt arrived to arrange relief of Dujardin Regt. O.C. 1st Group to take over from Group pits V.S. Div. - O.C. 2nd Group to be but huprank to 26th Div. with his 3 Batts to relieve Major Didion's 2 Batts. - The O.C. 1st Group with his B.C. proceed to H.Q. 27th B30. R.H. - The O.C. 2nd Group with his B.C. to H.Q. 28th Div.S. - It formed from Belgian Arsenal arrived with 4 guns to complete Regt. 4 Ysport try to be attached to Regt for after tonight	ad
6.30 p.m.	Relief carried out as follows: - 1sec "A" Batty by 3rd Batty, - 1sec "B" Batty by 12th R.P.A. - 1sec of each of Major Didion's Batts by 4th & 6th Batts. - 1sec "C" Batty by 129 R.P.A. in H.Q. B.52 - O.Cs Groups 27th Regt & 2nd Batt. replaced 1sec G 124 R.P.A. - O.Cs Groups 27th Regt establish themselves near their sections.	CB.
May 17th 11 a.m.	1st Batty commenced constructing emplacements at H.29.B.10.5.	
3 p.m.	Col Dechesne & Regt H.Q. replaced Col Dujardin at G.34 D.63 - Col Dujardin went to BILLCO near POPERINGHE where his sections immediately. The M.T. Regt. Arm. & Col A (Spinning) with Lt. Vanderliggen proceeded to ABEELE where it was attached to 3rd Arm Park.	CB.
6.36 p.m.	The Relief (as above) was completed. 1st Batty occupied its new emplacements at H.29.B.10.5. - Col. Command Batts. arr. withdrawn to POPERINGHE.	CB.

Army Form C. 2118.

WAR DIARY
or
INTELLIGENCE SUMMARY.
(Erase heading not required.)

(33)

Instructions regarding War Diaries and Intelligence Summaries are contained in F.S. Regs., Part II. and the Staff Manual respectively. Title pages will be prepared in manuscript.

Hour, Date, Place	Summary of Events and Information	Remarks and references to Appendices
May 20th 3.30pm – 5.30pm	2nd Battery fired at the German Trench app. 27.	
5.27pm–6.30pm	3rd Battery fired on Transport in O2d + O4b to S.E of Canal at N.E of J.O.C.Rd.	
6.45pm – 7.30 pm	3rd Battery 3 Salvos at Trenches pp. 27 + 28.	CB
May 21st 10.45am – 2pm	1st Battery fired at Sep Hd I.34 d.2.3.	
6pm–6.30pm	1st Battery fired again at Hero Sep Head.	
5.30pm – 8.30pm	1st Battery fired at farm I.34 d.3.3.	
	3rd Battery fired at Trenches app. 28.	
9.25 am – 10.15 am	3rd Battery fired a road in O4d + O4c.	
10pm – 12 mn	24 E. Div'l Battery fired at a German machine gun shelter + knocked it out. – In the evening they fired at small columns	
May 22nd	of reliefs + dispersed them.	CB

Army Form C 2118.

(34)

WAR DIARY
or
INTELLIGENCE SUMMARY.
(Erase heading not required.)

Instructions regarding War Diaries and Intelligence Summaries are contained in F.S. Regs., Part II. and the Staff Manual respectively. Title pages will be prepared in manuscript.

Hour, Date, Place	Summary of Events and Information	Remarks and references to Appendices
May 2nd 10.30 am – 11.30 am	1st Battery fired at Sapkrad I 24 D 23	
6.25 pm – 6.37 pm	— at Trenches in I Bey I 24f.	
9.38 pm – 9.47 pm	— opp. 32 E	
6.05 pm – 6.14.9 —	3rd Battery fired at Trenches opp. 27.	
10.10 pm – 10.15 pm	3rd Battery fired at Trenches in S.E. corner of square O 3 E.	E.S.
May 23rd 4.035 pm – 4.48 pm	3rd Battery fired at Trenches opp. 27 & 28	
7 – 10 pm – 7.15 pm	Do.	
7.35 pm – 7.54 pm	Do.	
9.10 pm – 9.20 pm	1st Battery fired at about 200 x to S.E. of corner of German Trench opp. 32 a	E.S.

Forms/C. 2118/10

WAR DIARY or INTELLIGENCE SUMMARY.

(Erase heading not required.)

Army Form C. 2118.

35

Hour, Date, Place	Summary of Events and Information	Remarks and references to Appendices
24 May. 3 a.m.	2nd Group (28th Div) ordered to open fire on MENIN ROAD & to establish a line of barrage in the enemy's support & reserve trenches.	
3.15 a.m.	2nd Group ordered to establish the barrage on the ROULERS Railway	
5.25 a.m.	Order received to fire in E, I 6 D, & on the Railway	
5.55 a.m.	— on the 6 division and Battery on the French S.E. of Railway	
9.28 a.m.	B.M. Battery ordered to fire in I 12 C & H.N.W. of ETANG DE BELLEWAARDE & towards a Battery 4 rounds per minute.	
9.39 a.m.	B.M. Battery ordered to increase their Range by 100ˣ	
10 a.m.	During the above series several guns of the group dropped out of action in the Jamming of the Breech mechanism. The breech of one of the guns of 4" Battery was damaged by the discharge of a H.E shell. No 1, one gunner badly wounded.	
10.10 a.m.	The Battery was subjected to an accurate fire of shells apparently fired — one N.C.O. of 4" Battery wounded. The effects of the asphyxiating gases was specially felt in the 5 guns which gave much pain & sickness. No vapours seen.	
1.15 p.m.	Group ordered to fire at the small wood I.11.b.10.4. on the bars & I.6 Square 11.6.17.a. — Information received that British troops were not crossing in I.11.6.	
2.15 p.m.	Group ordered to fire with one Battery on the wood in I.11.6.63 south the other Battery on BELLEWAARDE FARM I.11.d.79	
5 p.m.	B.M. Battery ordered to fire on the wood N.E. of ETANG DE BELLEWAARDE	

WAR DIARY
or
INTELLIGENCE SUMMARY.
(Erase heading not required.)

Army Form C. 2118.

Instructions regarding War Diaries and Intelligence Summaries are contained in F. S. Regs., Part II. and the Staff Manual respectively. Title pages will be prepared in manuscript.

Hour, Date, Place		Summary of Events and Information	Remarks and references to Appendices
May 24th	7 pm	A second gun of "F" Battery put out of action by an explosion in the chamber. 3 gunners wounded & one slightly burnt.	
	11 pm	Battery ordered to cease firing at this time owing to the accidents above mentioned & to the jamming of the breech mechanism only 2 of the 12 guns were able to fire.	
	12 mn	2nd group orders to have their 2 guns in action ½ w. towards the ferme to the sugar line.	
	11.5 am–11.50 pm	1st Battery fired at guns on Francheo opp. 31.	C.S.
	11.50 am–12.10 am	– – – – 32.	
	9.25 pm–9.40 pm	3rd Battery – – – 28	
May 25th	12.30 pm–12.37 pm	2nd Battery fired at Château O.4 D.	
	5 pm–5.15 pm	– – – Trenches in O.4.a.	
	9.37 pm–9.57 pm	3rd Battery – S.E. corner of guns O.4.a.	C.S.
	4 pm	D.A.D.O. 2nd Army & O.C. Ammn. Train STRAZEELE came to examine Belgian Ammn. & and to see whether the Red & Yellow H.E. shell could be used in the Portuguese guns. They at the same time examined the	

Army Form C. 2118.

WAR DIARY
or
INTELLIGENCE SUMMARY
(Erase heading not required.)

32

Hour, Date, Place	Summary of Events and Information	Remarks and references to Appendices
Mar 25th (cont)	Howitzer guns & informed He gunners that the damage cannot have possibly been due to a faulty exploring of the H.E. Shell (filling) which was unnecessary to the guns.	
Mar 26th 3 a.m.	A new gun having been received from the arsenal at CALAIS it was sent up to replace one of the damaged guns of 2nd Fort.	
9.27pm – 9.29pm	1st Bethe fired at Trenches ref. 32 f 33	13.
9.27pm – 9.37pm	— — 31.	
10.30pm	Orders received from S.O. Dirk.Art for the positioning 1st Group Batteries in the event of a withdrawal to switch W.H.R. 2nd line.	
Mar 29th 9.30am	Above orders communicates to O.C. 1st Group.	
12 m.d.	O.C. 1st Group reports to Col. Strong R.S.A. when when orders he was to receive in the event of a withdrawal – in order to receive instruction as to his sector &c.	APPENDIX XVE
3 a.m.	A second messenger having been received from CALAIS it was sent up to 2nd Group & placed in action. By the opening 11 guns of 2nd Group are fit to shoot. W. James	

Army Form C. 2118.

WAR DIARY
or
INTELLIGENCE SUMMARY.

(Erase heading not required.)

Instructions regarding War Diaries and Intelligence Summaries are contained in F. S. Regs., Part II. and the Staff Manual respectively. Title pages will be prepared in manuscript.

3B

Hour, Date, Place	Summary of Events and Information	Remarks and references to Appendices
May 27th	Going thus' inclusive having put out the jammed Breech Mechanism right & the 2 Damaged guns having been replaced as ordinates :—	CB.
May 28th	O.C. 1st Siege ordered to prepare a position for 3rd Battery in I.31.G.3.8. whence it can to work from KRUISSTRAAT on gun of 3rd Battery moved up to this position afterdark.	CB.
May 29th 11.58am – 12md	This gun at I.31.G.3.8. registered its Zone.	See APPENDIX XIV
1.50pm – 2.22pm	3rd Battery fires on German Trenches 5/6.28	CB.
May 30th		
May 31st	Orders received that Sector of 5th Divn Billets changed	CB.

Appendix X

Secret.

Bridges

8. Inf. in fours any traffic
9. Road Bridge.
10. Road Bridge.
11. Inf. only footbridge
12. Inf & light transport.
13. Road Bridge.
14. Earth Bridge (any horse traffic)
15. Footbridge (Inf. only)
16. Earth Bridge (any traffic)
17. Inf. only
18. Road Bridge.
19. Inf. only
20. Trestle. Inf. only.

YPRES

Military Maps. Trace for use with Artillery

APPENDIX IX

Identification Trace for use with Artillery Maps.

10

YPRES

Battery
Diary

APPENDIX XI.

Copy

SECRET.

Belgian Artillery

D.S.C. 154.   11/5/15.

It is reported there is no more telephone wire in the country. It is therefore of the utmost importance that all units redouble their efforts to reel in or pick up unused wire as none will be forthcoming from D.A.C. or ordnance.

5th Div. Art.
9.45 a.m.

APPENDIX XI

?ᵉ Régiment d'Artillerie.
Ordre de bataille au 20 Mai 1915

État-major du régiment	Dechesne	Colonel AEM. comdt le régiment.
	Aerts	Capne comdt AEM ffons d'Adjudant-major.
	Bridge	Capitaine (armée britannique) adjoint
	Grégoire	Lieutenant adjoint.

États-majors des groupes.

1er groupe		2e groupe	
Bon Greindl	Major comdt	Sevrin	Major comdt
Tamsy	Capne adjoint		
Blyckaerts	f/f Sous-Lieutt adjoint	Pulz	Sous-Lieutt adjoint
Loriers	Médecin de bon 1re cl.	Casman	Médecin adjoint
Créteur	id auxiliaire	Gustin	id auxiliaire
Olivier	Vétérinaire 2e cl.	Fagot	Vétérinaire 1re classe
Vander Elst	id auxiliaire	Hazette	id auxiliaire
Moureau	Sous-Lieutt payeur	Hombert	Sous-Lieutt payeur
Peeters	Aumônier adjoint	Belpaire	aumônier adjoint

Grades	1re Bie	2e Bie	3e Bie	4e Bie	5e Bie	6e Bie
Capne	Samson		Ct Dumonceau de Bergendael	Demuenynck		De Cuijp
Capne en 2d		Duvret			Tiberghien	
Lieutenant	Godeaux		Mauss	Levecamp		Leurquin
Sous-Lieutt	Stroleus	Servais De Man	Cluts	Jacostie	Castadot Seeley	Coutilier

Services auxiliaires

Corps de transport	Col. M. 2e actif	P.A.M.A.	Col. auxil. amb. blessés	Train de vivres
Hotelet	Rodelet Lieutenant	Vandebragen Sous-Lieutt	Alexander médecin	Daoust Sous-Lieutenant
Evely			Godeau médecin	
Wenmaze			Dumont aumônier	
François Sous-Lieutt payeur				

Appendix XIV

Identification Trace for use with Artillery Maps.

7th Belgian Art Reg att. 5th Div.

o Observation Stations
--- Telephone lines
a. Position prepared for 3rd Batt, of 1st group.
b. New Position occupied by 3rd Battery 30/1/15
I 66 07

FURNES.

I 68 50.

4th Bt
O.C Group
1st Bt

VLAMERTINGHE
2nd Group

To G.O CRA 24th Div.
O.C BzeR.Pd.

YPRES

Menin Road.

1st Line Wagons.
3rd Bt

1st Line Wagons
1st Bt
2nd Bt
O.C Group
3rd Bt

1st Group
2nd Bt

4th Inf Bde

1st Batt
2nd B O Bellegarde
O
2nd Bt

2nd O
2nd Bt

1st Bt
2nd Bt
3rd Bt

NOTE.—(1) These traces are intended to facilitate the communication of information as to the position of targets, which have been located on a squared map.
(2) The squares on this trace are 1,000 yards in length on the 1/20,000 scale, and 2,000 yards in length on the 1/40,000 scale.
(3) The squares on the trace are fitted to the squares of the map showing the targets, which are then drawn on the trace. Sufficient letters and numbers must also be added to enable the recipient to place the trace in the correct position on his own map. A little detail may also be traced, but this is not essential. The name and scale of the map to which the trace refers must be always given. The trace can be used for either the 1/20,000 or 1/40,000 scale.

G.S.G.S. 3028

Tracing taken from Sheet................
of the 1:................ map of................
Signature................ Date................

Appendix XV

Front of 5th Divn on G.H.Q. 2nd line.

A — B. front crosses
Belgian Battude

B

31

A

Identification Trace for use with Artillery Maps.

O.B. 1st Group

3rd H.A.
Battn. 29

2nd Battery

Etang de
DICKEBUSCH.

121/5971

MO3

5th Division

Belgian Artillery Reps.

Vol IV 1 — 30.6.15

Confidential

War Diary

June 1st – 30th 1915

for

2. Belgian Field Artillery Regt
attd. 5th Div.

Kept by
Capt. C.D. Bridge R.A.

Army Form C. 2118.

(39)

WAR DIARY
or
INTELLIGENCE SUMMARY.
(Erase heading not required.)

Instructions regarding War Diaries and Intelligence Summaries are contained in F.S. Regs., Part II. and the Staff Manual respectively. Title pages will be prepared in manuscript.

Hour, Date, Place	Summary of Events and Information	Remarks and references to Appendices
June 1st 7 am	Wire received from 2nd Div. A.A. that the Batteries of 2nd Group were to have under orders of 3rd Div. Art. from this date & not under orders of 6th Div. Art. as had been previously arranged.	
10 am	O.C. 2nd Group reported at H.Q. 3rd Div. Art. to receive orders. Orders were arranged that 2 Batteries were to keep their same Zones of fire but that the O.C. Group was to work under 3rd Div. A.A. H.Q.	See APPENDIX XIV. N.S.
11.30 am	Communication received from 6th Div. Art. that Batteries of 2nd Group were to pass under their orders. As it was agreed that O.C. 2nd Group should maintain telephonic communication with Bde. Cdr. at I.2.B.2.4. in B/m — & await further orders.	
3 pm	Visit of Col. Loiselet & Capt. Laurin from Schauendwoerke. They report that the Front guns had been examined & that it was found out that the Turrets & the jaws of the Breach Mechanism were soft due to the nature caoca — towards the use of cast. iron cases wrought to the guns which prevents the proper engaging of the threads of the Breech Screw with those of the Breech Ring.	See Page 35.
4.30 pm	Report Despatched to H.Q. S. Div. A.A. explaining that the 7015 rounds of 7 inch H.E. shell (painted as ordered) in a truck at ABEELE would not be sent by the guns of 3rd Belgian A.A. Regt. & requesting that Orders would be given for their return to HAVRE where they could be exchanged	

Army Form C. 2118.

WAR DIARY
or
INTELLIGENCE SUMMARY.
(Erase heading not required.)

Instructions regarding War Diaries and Intelligence Summaries are contained in F.S. Regs. Part II. and the Staff Manual respectively. Title pages will be prepared in manuscript.

Hour, Date, Place	Summary of Events and Information	Remarks and references to Appendices
June 1st	Exchanged Fire Control table M.E. provided by Belgian govt.	
June 2nd — 2pm	1st Group succeeded in taking up present occupied position this 2nd Lieut T. moved into 5th Div's area as follows:- 1st Battery H.25.D.6.2. 2nd Battery H.26.C.65. 3rd Battery H.26.C.2.9. O.C. group remained in Farm H.27.D.8.4.7. Also reports that 2nd Group were to be attached to 6th Div F. 6th Corps remaining in its present positions - & being under the orders of its O.C. 2nd Bde - W.O. relieved by Bdr. Cov. R.20. & 2nd Div F. at H/12. D.7.4. 2nd Group registered trenches in area (6th Div A.) Zone. between VERLOREN HOEK & WIELTJE ROAD. Shell Street. 2nd Group H.Q. = J.1.C.15. Killing 4 men & wounding 1.	AD. AD. CB. CB. CB.
June 3rd 8.20pm	2nd Group H.Q. established at H.11.F.8.3. —	
June 4th 8pm	Regrouping of 6th Div'l Batteries. 2nd Group passed under orders of O.C. 2nd Bde R.F.A. - when Hd Qrs at I.1.D.0.5 - G. 6th Div'l sector greatly enlarged it was arranged to bring 3rd Batty of this group up into action - pos't already constructed at I.1.C.2.10. The first 3 Batteries to be Dutchies are withdrawn of 6th Div's front from first evening in I.1.B. to one tour in C.15.C.	
June 5th —	Report sent to 5. Div R.F.A. Hd Q". 7" Bdg. Art Rey Deficient of one gun.	CB.

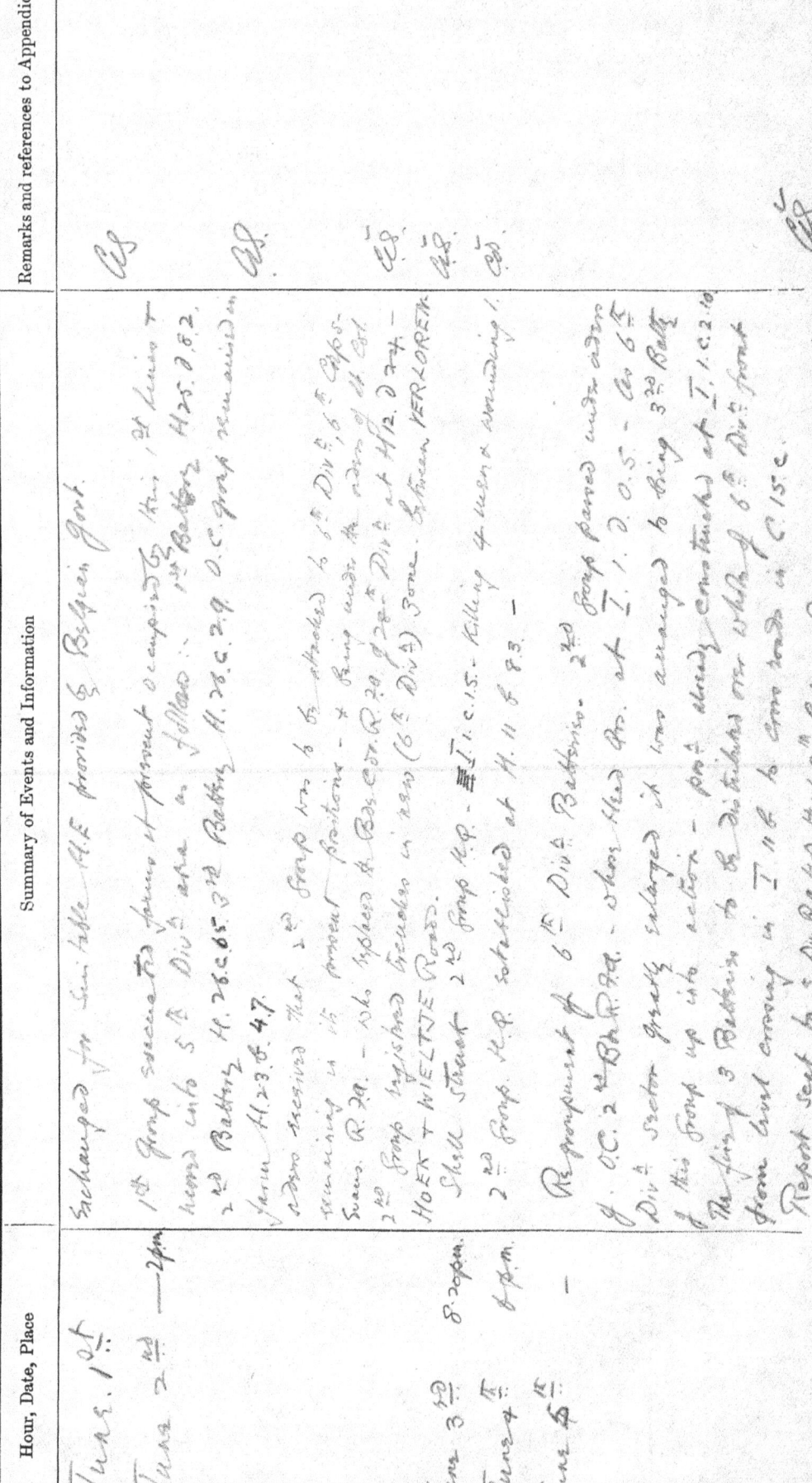

Army Form C. 2118.

WAR DIARY
or
INTELLIGENCE SUMMARY
(Erase heading not required.)

Instructions regarding War Diaries and Intelligence Summaries are contained in F.S. Regs., Part II. and the Staff Manual respectively. Title pages will be prepared in manuscript.

Hour, Date, Place	Summary of Events and Information	Remarks and references to Appendices
June 6th —	1st Group fired at Trenches opp. 30 & 31 & at house O4 & E. Third Battery of 2nd Group (only 2 guns available) went into action in I.1.c.2.10. — Batteries of Group fired few H.E. at Trenches in this sector. 2nd Group H.Q. moved up into Dug-outs in rear of the Batteries.	
June 7th —	Authority for move of Div cav. to G.S.D. & 4th Regt. missions for use of towers Tilephnisto.	C.S. C.S.
June 8th 12.30 pm	A gun of 6th Battery 2nd Group was put of action by a partial blowing out of the Breech Block. A second gun of this Battery put out of action by a jammed Breech & a third gun withdrew from action owing to it giving up fumes at the Breech. Report sent to H.Q. R.A. 3rd Div. that 4th Regt. was short of guns. Also that 2nd Group was only to fire shrapnel. Parts of projectile that caused jupting Breech mechanism & those used lined guns found about 700 yards from the guns. The shells (H.E.) appeared to have exploded in the guns & blown parts of scoring & rifling barrel.	C.S.
June 9th 10 am	2nd Group organised with 3 guns in action in rear of 1st & 2nd positions & 2 guns in action in 3rd position. 1st Group fired during day H.E. at Trenches opposite 28 & 31.	C.S.

WAR DIARY
or
INTELLIGENCE SUMMARY.
(Erase heading not required.)

Army Form C. 2118.

(42)

Hour, Date, Place	Summary of Events and Information	Remarks and references to Appendices
June 10"	1st Corps fired at Trenches opp. 32a. 32a. 33 & 27.28 also on support trenches in J 32 & 9.	C.J.
" 11"	1st Corps fired at Trenches opp 31. 32a. 33 & 28 also # trenches in O.24 av F. & also in Bridge 02.F.	C.J.
" 12"	1st Corps fired at Trenches opp. 27 & in Bonel line Trenches I 3 & 9.	C.J.
" 13"	1st Corps fired at Trenches opp. 31. 29.30 & 27 & 28 & also at a HE Sta. at O.4.a.9.8.	C.J.
" 14"	1st Corps fired at Trenches opp. 27.28.29.30 & 7th Gurkhas in 57.a. Phone & rec. received from 2nd Corps that 2nd Corps are prep. for Bdes to advance with 5th Divn & that it be a storm H. Region 15 inst.	C.J.
" 15" 2 am.	1st Corps (3rd) at house I.34.9.6.6. O at Trenches opp. 27 & 30. 2nd Corps came at Jackson & opposed Regt going in to Attack at BORSCHEPPE L 15th Battery advance R.5.C.39.45. & inform R.5.C.99.	Rd.
" 16 "	1st Corps fired at Trenar opp. 27	Rd. Idet 27 P.N. C.J.

Army Form C. 2118.
(43)

WAR DIARY
or
INTELLIGENCE SUMMARY.
(Erase heading not required.)

Instructions regarding War Diaries and Intelligence Summaries are contained in F.S. Regs., Part II. and the Staff Manual respectively. Title pages will be prepared in manuscript.

Hour, Date, Place	Summary of Events and Information	Remarks and references to Appendices
Jan 17th 1.45–3.40pm 4–5.4pm 11.32–11.55pm	3rd Batty fired at "projectors" in the Trench opp. 29. 1st Batty fired at M. mortar in front of 32 B. —	Cet.
— 18th 10.38–4.38 pm	1st Cont fired 3 series at Trenches opp 32, 63 & B & M. mortar opp. 6, 32 B.	R.
— 19th 9.1pm–9.15 pm	2nd Battery fired at trench opp. 29.	R.
— 20th 9.8pm–9.23 pm	1st Battery fired at Mortar + Trenches opp. 32 & 31	Cet.
— 21st 6.57pm–9.34pm 9.52pm–10.17pm	1st Battery fired at mortar opp. 32. — Trenches 31 & 30.	Ces
— 22nd 4.35am–4.41 am 12.16pm–4.14 pm	1st Battery fired at Trenches opp. 31. — opp. 29 & 30.	Cet.
— 23rd 11.58pm–12am	1st Battery fired at Trenches opp. 31.	Cet.

Army Form C. 2118.

44

WAR DIARY
or
INTELLIGENCE SUMMARY.
(Erase heading not required.)

Instructions regarding War Diaries and Intelligence Summaries are contained in F.S. Regs., Part II. and the Staff Manual respectively. Title pages will be prepared in manuscript.

Hour, Date, Place	Summary of Events and Information	Remarks and references to Appendices
June 25th. —		
— 26th. —		
June 26th 10.14am – 10.23am	Orders received for Retaliatory barrage & 2 group by sections night 28–29th & 29/30th inst. Group HQ to be reason tert completion. 1st Battery shelled Trench opp. 31	
10.40 – 10.58am	2nd Battery field S. of Canal A O4.F.	
11.3 – 11.10am	Sec. 3 Battery shells shr(B) O4.F.	
11.12 – 11.20am	3rd Battery shells(B) O5.G.55.	
11.28 – 11.30am	3rd " Battery shells) S.of Canal in O4.F.	
11.36 – 11.40am	1st " Battery shells) O6a.43	
2.17pm – 2.35pm	2nd Battery shells) S.of Canal in O4.F	
5.43pm – 5.58pm	2nd Battery shells) opp 27	
June 27th 11.57am – 12.12pm	1st Battery shells) Trench opp. 31	
12.37pm – 12.46pm	3rd Battery shells) Howr. O4a.7.9.	
1.27pm – 1.37pm	2nd Battery shells) Howr. O6c.33	
5pm – 5.47pm	3rd Battery shells) opp Trench R27.	

Army Form C. 2118.

WAR DIARY
or
INTELLIGENCE SUMMARY.
(Erase heading not required.)

Instructions regarding War Diaries and Intelligence
Summaries are contained in F.S. Regs., Part II.
and the Staff Manual respectively. Title pages
will be prepared in manuscript.

Hour, Date, Place	Summary of Events and Information	Remarks and references to Appendices
June 28: 11:38 – 12:46 pm	3rd Battery fired at Entrenchments opp. Trench 27	G.S.
2 pm – 2:12 pm	2nd Battery fired at same O.4 C.5.3.	
5 pm – 5:45 pm	1st Battery fired at home O.7.A.9.4.	Ed.
	R. section of 4th, 6th, 15th Batteries... 2nd Group ordered on section of	
	1st, 2nd & 3rd Batteries inspecting. — R. section of 1st Battery	
	proceeding to ROES CHEPPE in reserve.	
June 29. R. 12 md – 12:39 pm	2nd Battery shelled canal Trenches O4a. 10. 5 – 8. 5.	
12:45 – 12:55 pm	" – opp. Trench 28.	
2:45 – 2:57 pm	1st Battery – " 31.	
4:15 – 4:7 pm	" – canal bridge O.4 B.16.	
4:55 – 5:15 pm	2nd Battery – opp. Trench 28.	C.S.
5:13 – 5:25 pm	1st Battery – opp. Trench 31.	
	Remaining sections of 1st, 2nd, 3rd Batteries retiring to section of	Ed.
	2nd Group – 1st Group assembled at BOESCHEPPE.	
June 30. R.	2nd Group occupied in registering their Zones with shrapnel.	Ed.

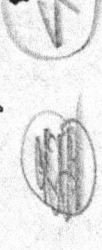

5th Division.

Belgian Inf.: Reg.

Vol V 1. — 31.7.15.

137/6231

Confidential

WAR DIARY.

7th Belgian Field Artillery

atto. 5th & 3rd Divⁿˢ

&

L.G. Artillery - 3rd Divⁿ

1st - 31st July/15

kept by
Capt. C.S.D. Bridge
R.A.

Army Form C. 2118.

(46)

WAR DIARY
or
INTELLIGENCE SUMMARY.

(Erase heading not required.)

Instructions regarding War Diaries and Intelligence Summaries are contained in F.S. Regs., Part II. and the Staff Manual respectively. Title pages will be prepared in manuscript.

Hour, Date, Place	Summary of Events and Information	Remarks and references to Appendices
July 1st	2nd Group registered its zero.	C3.
July 2nd	— continued registration	C3.
July 3rd	4th Battery shelled German trenches opp. 31.32 v 33.	C3.
	6th Battery — " — " — " — O4+7 & O4+7.5	C3.
	5th Battery — " — " — " — opp. 28	C3.
July 4th	4th Battery registered opp. Trench 29 & shelled opp. 31.	C3.
	5th & 6th Battery registered opp. Trench 28	C3.
July 5th	—	
July 6th	6th Battery shelled wirpbridge a Ficreul	C3.
July 7th	6th Battery again shelled a footbridge which has been repaired.	
	at night	
	4th Battery shelled a horse continuing a Farmhouse	
1.40pm – 1.50pm	4th Battery shelled German (Read) line Trench in H3 a J.2.5.	C3.

Forms/C. 2118/10

WAR DIARY
or
INTELLIGENCE SUMMARY
(Erase heading not required.)

Army Form C. 2118

Place	Date	Hour	Summary of Events and Information	Remarks and references to Appendices
	8/7/15	6.30pm	4th Battery shelled a French worker opp. Trench 32 & I 34.d.57	CB
		6.40am		
		7pm	Orders issued for Group in Reserve to make all preparations for occupying position H.28.c	APPXVI & APPXVII
			S9. (See page 37 - Map 26 + app.XVII) - Memo Dispatched in consequence to O.C. 1st Group. Memo issued for 1 section to proceed to ST OMER 11th inst. for trial. 1 section of 1st Group selected to go & memo Dispatched in consequence to O.C. 1st Group.	CB
	9/7/15	10.2am		
		11.7am	6th Battery shelled shelters near I.33.c.78. (12 H.E)	CB
		10.45am		
		10.50am	4th Battery shelled 2nd line trenches opp. 31+32 (12 H.E)	CB
	10/7/15	5.25am	4th Battery shelled opp. Trench 32. (10 H.E)	CB
		5.30am		
		6.3am		
		6.15am	Shelled a gun & I.35.a.3.1. (10.H.E)	CB
		11.55am	— opp Trench 33 (9 H.E)	CB
		12.02pm		
		12.20		
		12.30pm	— — 30 (sshrap)	
		2.19pm		
		2.30pm	5th Battery shelled Château O4 D.17 (6H.E 6shrap)	CB

Army Form C. 2118

WAR DIARY
or
INTELLIGENCE SUMMARY
(Erase heading not required.)

Instructions regarding War Diaries and Intelligence Summaries are contained in F. S. Regs., Part II. and the Staff Manual respectively. Title Pages will be prepared in manuscript.

Place	Date	Hour	Summary of Events and Information	Remarks and references to Appendices
H	1/9/15	3.35 – 3.41 am	4th Battery shelled opp. Trench 31 – (12 HE)	
		3.42 – 3.48 am	6th Battery shelled a mortar at I35 D 0.2 – I35 D 30 (12 HE)	
		4.57 am	— opp. Trench 27 – (10 HE)	
		5.9 am	— Shelled a mortar at 04 c 39 (1 HE)	
		5.10 am		
		7.30 am	1 section 1st French H.A. BOESCHEPPE to WIZERNES under command of 5th section	see previous 27/7/15 Ry HAZE to BOESCHEPPE
		3.30 pm	accompanied by Capt. DEWAET & Capt. Burg. R.a. The section arrived at WIZERNES	
		11.9 am – 11.11 am	4 Battery shelled opp. 30. (8 HE)	
		11.28 – 11.30 am	— — 31 (8 HE)	
		3.58 pm	6th Battery — opp. 29 (10 HE 6 Shrap)	
		5.17 pm	5th — house 04 c 02 (8 Shrap)	
		5.59 pm	— — 04 c 54 (8 Shrap)	
	2/9/15	5.23 am	6th Battery — Trench opp. 28 (6 HE)	
		5.36 am	— — Trench — 27 (8 HE)	
		6.4 am	— — 29 + 30 (20 HE)	cont.

1875 Wt. W593/826 1,000,000 4/15 T.R.C. & A. A.D.S.S./Forms/C. 2118.

WAR DIARY or INTELLIGENCE SUMMARY

Army Form C. 2118

Place	Date	Hour	Summary of Events and Information	Remarks and references to Appendices
	12/7/15	9.3 am	Section 1st Sept. Randy arrived near LONGHENESSE on STMR Rifle Range – carried out trial short with tracer Rest fellow H.E. shell. with Perbigen Shrapnel. Planes of Trial shown that Pencil shell gave accurate results + that the Perbigen Shrapnel gave shorter range Sect [?] – Trial carried out at Range of 3150 yds. firing towards (E) SETQUES.	1st 100,500 HAZEBROUCK S.A.
		1.30 pm	Section Returned to Billets at WIZERNES.	[?]
		10.25 am	6th Battery Shelled Bridge 04 a 97 (10 HE + 5 Shrap.)	2B.
		11.19 am	" Battery Shelled Trench opp. 31 (8 HE + 5 Shrap.)	
	13/7/15	10.11 am	6th Battery Shelled Bridge 04 a 77 (14 HE + 2 Shrap)	Eg. Og.
		4.41 pm	4th Battery — opp. Trench 32 (12 H.E.)	
		7.30 am	Section left WIZERNES to repair S.th Divt.	7/5
		3.30 pm	Section reached BOESCHEPPE	
	14/7/15	6 pm	Major received that 1st Group was to take up position of 27th Bav. R.F.A. on night 16th–17th to consist of O.C. 9th Bav Ypres Art. Reg. taking command of "left group" 5th Div. Art – 15 consist of 13th, 4th, 5th, 6th Batteries of his Regt. – 1 Section 65 H (Heavy) Batty 1st Mountain Art. + 1 Trench Morter Battery.	5th Div. Art. operation order 14/7/15.
		6.30 pm	Major Baron Freund (in absence of Lt. Dickson) Capt. Bridge visited Lt. Col. [?]	[?]

WAR DIARY
or
INTELLIGENCE SUMMARY

(Erase heading not required.)

Army Form C. 2118

Instructions regarding War Diaries and Intelligence Summaries are contained in F.S. Regs., Part II. and the Staff Manual respectively. Title Pages will be prepared in manuscript.

Place	Date	Hour	Summary of Events and Information	Remarks and references to Appendices
	15/7/15	9 am	Major Brown firmed accompanied A.C.C.T. Higginson in to 14th Inf. Bde. HQ to make arrangements for the Relief of one battery.	Pz/49
		12.45 pm	5th Battery shelled a pair at Oberge (12 HE, 7 in.)	ea.
		10.15 pm	6th Battery shelled Canal Trench (20 HE 2 shrap.)	
		11.2 am	5th Battery shelled houses T34 C71 (20 HE)	
		11.30 am	5th Battery shelled houses Trench opp. 28 (20 HE)	
		4.10 pm	5th Battery shelled Trench opp. 28 (16 HE)	
		7.57 pm	4th Battery shelled House T34 B51 (12 HE 3 Shr.)	ea.
	16/7/15	11.3 am	4th Battery shelled House T3# B.61. (25 HE)	
		5.30 pm	1 section each of 1st 2nd 3rd & 4th arrived at CHATEAU H23 & to take over from 119 & 120 & 111 & Batteries.	
		9.20 pm	Relief of one section of each of the Batteries completed.	BZ
	2/7/15	11.30 am	2nd Battery (Right Group) Registered Trenches 28 supp.0. (27 shrap. oz HE)	
		11.35 am	1st Battery Registered Trench 31 (9 shrap. 2 HE)	
		2.15 pm	3rd Battery Registered HOLLEBEKE CHATEAU (13 shrap.)	
		3 pm	1st Battery fires one salvo on Register 3c.	
		(M.u.DDq)	had a Great firemat arrived at CHATEAU H23 & took over command of left group.	fat.

1873 Wt. W503/826 1,000,000 4/15 T.B.C. & A. A.D.S.S./Forms/C. 2118.

WAR DIARY or INTELLIGENCE SUMMARY

Army Form C. 2118
(51)

Place	Date	Hour	Summary of Events and Information	Remarks and references to Appendices
			Section Mobile Artillery, Left Group & Centre Group formed into 2nd & 3rd Centre Group.	
	17/9/15	5.35pm	4th Battery shelled German hook at T.34.6.6.1. (38 HE) at request of 15th Inf. Bde.	C.S.
		7.30pm	6th Battery shelled 29 Register (4 HE) as a Test	
	18/9/15	11.55am	Arrangements made for indiv Relief of 1 Bund of 14th Inf Bde between S Battery & left Group, to take effect from 6am 19th	App XVIII
		2pm	Section 65th Battery R.F.A. registered on right protection in 29 Register (5.4 HE, 2 Shrap.)	
		5.34pm	6th Battery shelled 29 Register (12 HE) at request of Trenches	
		7.35pm	— point T.34.6.6.1 at request of 14th Inf Bde	
		9.50pm	6th Battery T.34 29 Register (4 HE) at request of Bn. 1 - 3rd, 4th Batteries fired Test Salvos	
		2.30 — 3.55pm	2nd Battery (Centre Group) Registered 26.25.B.3.4. (17 HE + 27 Shrap) (each + HE)	C.S.
	19/9/15	11.23am	4th Battery shelled 34 Register (34 HE) at request of Trenches	
		1.10pm	1st Battery fired 1 salvo (4 HE) at 32 Register at request of Trenches.	
		1.30pm	6th Battery shelled 2 nd line 29 Register (4 HE) at request of Trenches	
		5.40pm	6th Battery shelled 29 Register (20 HE) at request of Trenches	
		6.37pm	Section 65th R.F.A. fired 6 RF Lyddite at 29 Register at request of 14th E. Inf Bde.	
		6.37pm	3rd Battery fired 3 Salvos (12 Shrap) on Register 27 at request of Trenches	
		6.47pm	1st Battery fired 4 Salvos (16 HE) at Register 32 at request of Trenches	
		6.49pm	4th Battery shelled 33 Register (6 HE + 1 Shrap) at request of Trenches	
		2.50pm	2nd Battery (Centre Group) shelled 27 Register (1 HE)	C.S.
		3.42pm	— (1 HE)	
		7.10pm	— (1 HE)	

Army Form C. 2118

WAR DIARY
or
INTELLIGENCE SUMMARY
(Erase heading not required.)

Instructions regarding War Diaries and Intelligence Summaries are contained in F. S. Regs., Part II. and the Staff Manual respectively. Title Pages will be prepared in manuscript.

Place	Date	Hour	Summary of Events and Information	Remarks and references to Appendices
	30/7/15	1.38 am	4th Battery shelled 33 Register at report of B² (2.HE)	C.6.
		1.44 am	1st Battery — 29.30 Register. — (4 HE)	
		2.18 am	5th & 1st Batteries fired Test 27 & 28 Respectively (2 Sharps) at report of Bn.	
		12.6 pm	4th Battery shelled 3rd Register (4 HE) at report of Trenches.	
		12.50 pm	6th — 29.30 — (4 HE) as a Test	
		3.1 pm	1st — 33 Register (4 HE) at Report of 15 Bde.	B.
		3.40 pm	1st — (10 HE) at Report of Trenches.	
		3.57 pm	1st — (12 HE) — Wyse.	
		4.1 pm	4th — 33 Register. (12 HE)	
		4.19 pm	6th — 30 Register. (2 HE)	
		5.07 pm	5th — 27 Register (2 Sharps) in Test at report of Inf. Bde.	
		6.43 pm	6th — Fired 29 Sharps at 30 Register at Request of Inf. Bn.	
	12.30 pm	12th Battery shelled Trench 32 Register (40 HE)	Critic group.
		3.58 pm	—	
		5.07 pm	2nd Battery fired 148 at request Bn.	
		6.47 pm	2nd Battery fired Test 28 — (1 Sharp)	
		11.33 pm		
	2/7/15	12.59 am	1st Battery shelled Test 32 (4 HE) at request of B².	
		11 am	5th Battery — Test 29 (1 Sharp)	
		1.4 pm	3rd Battery — Test 28 (1 Sharp)	
		2.2 am	4th Battery — Test 33 (3 HE)	C.3.

WAR DIARY or INTELLIGENCE SUMMARY

Army Form C. 2118

Place	Date	Hour	Summary of Events and Information	Remarks and references to Appendices
H	21/7/15	11·44am	5th Battery fired 'Test 27' (25) at request of Bde.	
		11·53am	4th Battery fired 4 HE at 34 Register.	
		12·15pm	— Registers point opp 34. (3 HE)	
		1·17pm	6th Battery fired 6 HE at 27·20 Register at request of Trenches.	
		2·57pm	1st — Registers point opp 32 (6 HE)	
		4·40pm	3rd Battery fired 'Test 28' (4S) at request of Trenches	
		9 pm	5th Battery fired 'Test 27' (1S) — Bn.	
		9·4pm	3rd Battery — 'Test 28' (1S) — Bn.	
		11·24am	2nd Battery (Czehr Group) fired 12 HE at 23 Register.	
		4 pm	— — 'Test 26' (1S) met } Czehr Group.	
		9 pm	1st Div. Art. Obsvation ordrs No 2 Red — Relative Rds of 5th, 6th, 3rd Divs.	
		9.30pm	Necessary addnl ordrs issued to Sect 65th R.G.A. to PC 381 R.F.A.	
22/7/15		5·30am	Arrangement to 5 Divns.at 9P.cdrs. No 3 Res Delaying action till 9·45 24th-25th inst.	
		8·45am	Necessary addnl orders to G. for.	
		9.35am	addnl ords. Kit Account Park wait till transferred from S.A.amm. S. Park to 3rd amm. Sub Park on return of 5th, 6th, 3rd Divs.	
		10·42am	1st Battery shelled 22 Register (10 HE) at request of Trenches.	
		10·53am	— — — (12 HE) — — — Bde.	
		11·4am	6th — — 27·30 — (12 HE) — — Bde.	
		1·7pm	4th — — 34 Register (4 HE) — — Bde.	
		1·10pm	5th — — Fired Test 27 at request of Bn. 5 rounds.	
		1·55pm	3rd — — — 28 — 3 mins	
		2 pm	Sect 65th RGA Register Canal Ridge 05a4z (8Shrap 6 lyds) + 08turns 2Direct Hits

WAR DIARY
or
INTELLIGENCE SUMMARY

Army Form C. 2118

(54)

Place	Date	Hour	Summary of Events and Information	Remarks and references to Appendices
	22/9/15	2.24 pm	6th Batty. Registered Horne 7,3,4 & 12 (10 HE) at request of Franckes.	
		11.57 pm	1st Batty fired Post 33 (2nd firing) at request of 13ee (2 HE) 3 mins.	
		12 nn	1st Batty fired Post 27 at request of 13" - 5 mins. (5 sharp)	C3
			3rd Batty fired Post 28 " " - 3 mins. (3 sharp)	
	23/9/15	12.7 am	1st Batty Shelled 32 Register (4 HE) at request of 13".	
		12.10 am	6th Batty Shelled 29,30 Register (5 HE) - Rn. Post Posts 2 mins.	
		4.50 am	4th Batty Shelled 34 Register at Request of 13" (13 HE)	
		1.4 pm	3rd Batty fired Post 28 (1 sharp) at request of Franckes (1 min)	
		3.10 pm	5th Batty fired Post 27 (1 sharp)	
		3.37 pm	4th Batty registered Shells on line Trench opp B.Y.	(8 mins) - fire to Finckes being fired
		3.27 pm	3rd Batty fired Post 26 (1 sharp) at request of Franckes. - 1/2 min - at request of B" - (32 HE)	
		4.30 pm	5th Batty fired Post 27 (1 sharp) - - 1/2 min	
		4.49 pm	5th Batty fired Post 27 (1 sharp) - - 10 mins - one shell broken	
		6.30 pm	5th Batty fired 24,29,30 Register - - - Trenches (4 HE)	
		11.32 pm	5th Batty fired Post 27 (1 sharp) - - Br. (3 mins)	C.8
	24/9/15	11.24 pm	1st Batty fired 26,27,32 Register (4 HE) - - Br.	
		3.20 am	2nd Batty fired 24 at 23c Register (1 min) 1 sharp (Exeter group)	
		12 midnight	5th Batty fired Post 27 at request of Pa (1 sharp)	
		2.55 am	6th Batty fired Post 24,30 at request of B" (1 min)	C.4
		4.55 am	5th & 3rd Batts fired 15 HE rounds + 16 Sharp at 2,7 + 28 Register respectively at Request of 14" Div	
		7.45 am	14" Siege Bde opened fire (10) minutes) - - to relieve 33 S.P. D. 2	
		12 noon	1st Batty (Exeter group) fired Post 24 - Rounds timed Taken -	C.5
		6.37 am	- " " Shell 32 Register - (12 HE) - Exeter Group.	

WAR DIARY or INTELLIGENCE SUMMARY

Army Form C. 2118

(SS)

Place	Date	Hour	Summary of Events and Information	Remarks and references to Appendices
	24.7.15	11.55am	R.X. 65ᵗʰ R.F.A. shelled German work and Canal Barge 04a97 (6⅓ g Sharp.) 1 obtained 2 Direct Hits on parapet –	
		12.30pm	1ˢᵗ Bty. shelled working party opp 32/64 HE)	
		12.35pm	6ᵗʰ Bty. – 2ⁿᵈ Lieut 75. 04a.29 at request of 14ᵗʰ B'de (24 HE)	
		3.33am	5ᵗʰ Bty. fired Test 29 at request of Trenches (sharp) – 2½ mins.	
		4.4pm	3ʳᵈ Bty. fired Test 28 – – – (4 Sharp) – 1 min 20 sec.	
		4.2pm	1ˢᵗ Bty. shelled 30 Register at request of Bᵈᵉ (By HE) Made 2 trenches in parapet	
		6 a.m.	O.C. B.04ᵗʰ Bʸ Bde R.F.A. Made 2 trenches in parapet	
		11.45pm	1 sect B.81ˢᵗ B'de tour in action in new emplacements sect 65ᵗʰ R.F.A. Northwesterday	
		P.30pm	Rt. Half of 1ˢᵗ Kings Bde by 6ᵗʰ Bty Bde commenced –	
		10.40pm	2ⁿᵈ B'de. (Entire Group) shelled 26 Register. (9 HE + 2 Sharp.)	Cig.
		11.16pm		
	25.7.15	11.15am	R.X. 65ᵗʰ R.F.A. shelled work opp Trench 29 (by Sharp + P.4.33) – 1 Direct Hit	
		12.30pm	X. B'Bty. commenced Registering – Canal Barge 04 82.5	
		3.9pm	3ʳᵈ Bty. fired Test 28 at request of Trenches – 1 Sharp.	
		5.3pm	5ᵗʰ Bty. fired Test 27 – – – – 2 Sharp.	
		5.47pm	2ⁿᵈ Bᵈᵉ (Centre Group) shelled 28 Register. (2 HE + 2 Sharp)	
		5.00pm	2ⁿᵈ Sect. J.B.Bty. 87ᵗʰ Bde R.F.A. retired R.X. 65ᵗʰ R.F.A. at H.30.6.5.6	Cig.
		10.30pm	3ʳᵈ B4 received orders "S.O.S. Test 28" from Trenches. This order not being understood reply Bring on accordance an attack	
	26.7.15	12.34 am	With pre-arranged Code B.C. fired 4 HE at 28 Register 2 nights for an explosion – R.I. of 4 cars that was	
		8.55am	6ᵗʰ Bty. shelled working party in trenches to left of Trench 30 at request of O.C. Trenches (6 Sharp)	
		9.25am	6ᵗʰ Bty. shelled a cart arriving in front of 29.30 at request of O.C. Trenches. (2 HE)	
		5.36pm	4ᵗʰ Bty. fired Test 34 (3HE) at request of O.C. B 2. –	

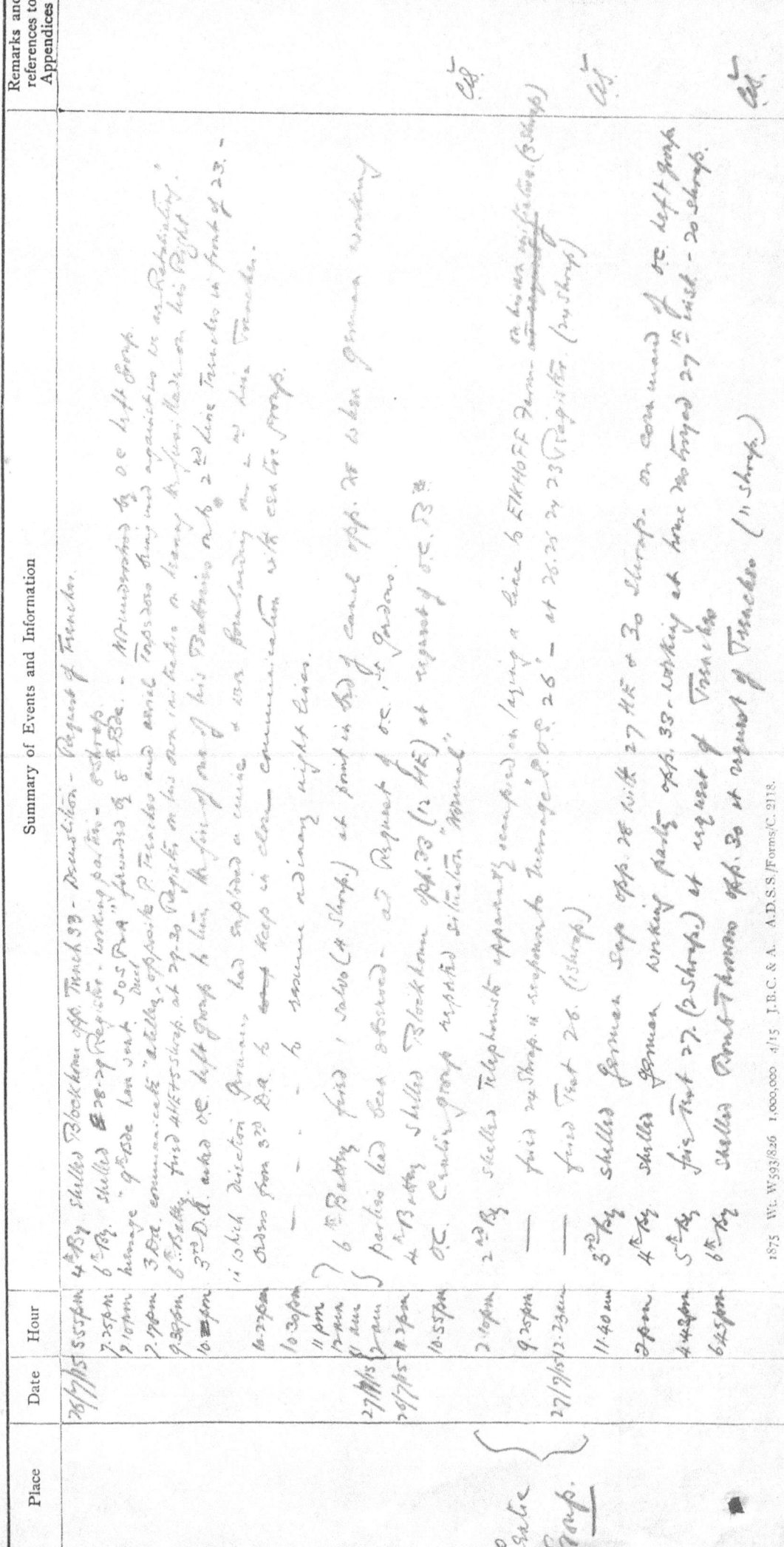

WAR DIARY
or
INTELLIGENCE SUMMARY

(Erase heading not required.)

Army Form C. 2118

(57)

Place	Date	Hour	Summary of Events and Information	Remarks and references to Appendices
	29/9/15	4.30pm	OC B/61 registered Redoubt opp 34 (Ct.fen 04D)	CS
	28/9/15	11.30am	2nd Bde. Registered 27 & fired 3 rds. Calib. Rnds.	
		12.59am	Report received that Germans were seen at work on canal bank opp 29.	
		1.33am	3rd Bde. fired 3 salvos (12 Shrap) at their working parties.	
		2.58am	— 1 salvo. (4 Shrap)	
		9.30 am	Arrow received that as this Trench had been taken over by 2/15 Inf. Bde, D.O.O of 2nd Bde. or to proceed to Bn. H.Q. R.I.R at night & not to that of Suffolks. Arrangements made for 4 VB 2 Bde to fire.	
			Plan of attaching Telephone communications sent to Div. Sig. Offr. to arrange for turning of lines. For no "Arrangements for opening of fire at request of Inf." circulated to Bdes.	APPX/X
		2.50pm	6th Battery shelled 2nd line Trench opp 30 (BHE+8 Shrap) at order of Inf. Brigadier in Trenches (Test)	
		3.30pm	5th Battery fired Test 29 - 3 shrapnel at request of O.C. Trench.	
		9.30pm	3rd Div. C/283 sent asking for explanations as to shearing of Test and sent B.L.O. 6 men 2?, ?- 6 men 29 ?- to destroy it. A Trench 29, 2 nm salvoes to 2" Inf Bde.	Answered 29 Sept
		11.55pm	3rd Bde. fired Test 28 - 4 Shrap at request of Inf.	
	29/9/15	12.4am	5th Dy. fired Test 27 - 2 Shrap. - at request of Trench.	
		1.35am	Road behind 2nd Bde. shelled. 3 rounds fell near Bty. - 1 man & Sig. Hy wounded.	
		4.5pm	1st Bde. fired Test 31 at request of O.C. Trench (11 shrap.)	Cf.
		4.15pm	1st Bde. shelled a house behind 31. Registers a Reprisal on request of Inf. (10 Shrap.) This permission asked from the Div.	Cf.
		10am	3 Shrapnel fell in 2nd Bde. wounding 2 men. One of whom died 5 later.	

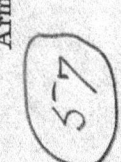

WAR DIARY or INTELLIGENCE SUMMARY

Army Form C. 2118

(Erase heading not required.)

Instructions regarding War Diaries and Intelligence Summaries are contained in F.S. Regs., Part II. and the Staff Manual respectively. Title Pages will be prepared in manuscript.

Place	Date	Hour	Summary of Events and Information	Remarks and references to Appendices
	29.7.15	4.30pm	6" By. shelled 2nd line trenches opp. Sqp. 29.6.30, at request of O.C. Trenches on Reserval (2nd H.F.)	
	30.7.15	12.40 am	3rd By. shelled Working party at o.4 B.39 (17 shrap), reported by 1st Gordons	
		3.45 am	Rapid notification - it appears that kills of 4" By. advises B. shell pond in T.3" along Dy. to S. of Caterpillar	
		4.0 am	4" Battery opened fire. Bde. Orr. to advise for preparing this short having Stuck cent direct to B.C. t not thro'	
			Group Orr. who on informing Bdon	
		4.0 am	Report received that battle Hdrs was at HOOGE 7.15 am. Situation Key 3 5.0 am.	APP. XXII 3rd Div. Diary
		9. am	Cd. tel. group report that 25 shp (3d[Be] approx.) y Bg. Shelling Hs tops opposite 2.9 at 11.30 am.	BM/127
		10 am	Tracing BM/27 giving Divisional Zones in course Withdrawal, received & communicated.	
		12.10pm	Orra received for from 3. Bde to arrange concentration the fire of our Battlers in poor shl. of	
			Left Group on Trenches 2.9 D.1 Arrangements made for 2.3rd & 5th 46 B Battles to fire there	
		2.12 pm	arr. Recd. from 3rd Div. let for aim a Bsan to open fire at 2.30 pm — for 30 mins (30.4.5 + 30 Shrap for 3rd)	
		2.20pm	Orr. Rec. for a passing 5 rounds at 2.30 pm. Fire Trenches 2.9 B.30 Register - aiming 15° R, 2.°, 30 Shrap	
			Fire Trenches. 2.9 B.30 Register- aiming 15° R,2.°,30 Shrap	
		2.30pm	Bn. opened as above	
		2.50pm	Pause	
		2.55 am	3rd By. fired 50 salvos of Shrapnel as above.	
		3.52 pm	5th By. fired Trench 27 at Request of O.C. Trenches.	
		6.40 pm	4" By. Shells 33 Register at request of O C Royal Scots as Reprisal (8.H.F.)	
		6.45pm	—	6.10 P.M. transferred Asst. from 3rd Div. H.Q. now from m.m.to 6.34.B.30 -
		10.30pm	B.M. 157 transfer from 3rd Div. Gp. as to Shelling by Day subject to Battns orders	(8.H.F.)
		12 mn	Orra to fire 5 effect rounds on Battnies	
	31/7/15	12.40am	1st By. fire Trat 27 (5 shrap) at request of O.C. Trench.	APP XI
		12.30 am to 1 am	All 5 Belgian Battries & 5/61 fired round subsequent stragglers to travel of works under various orders	
			It is acertain of the above orders	C.B.

WAR DIARY or INTELLIGENCE SUMMARY

Army Form C. 2118

Place	Date	Hour	Summary of Events and Information	Remarks and references to Appendices
	31.7.15	4 am	Reports received from 8th Bde that "gun supposed to be on armoured train was active again."	CB
		6.5 -	6th Batty shelled road in rear of German trenches. (1 shrap)	
		6.7 -	5th Batty — HOLLEBEKE XROADS. (2 shrap)	
		6.8 -	5th Batty fired Test "y" at N.E. of x Trenches.	
		8.50 -	1st Batty shelled working party opp. 31. (7 shrap) & N. of O.C.1. 9 a.2.	
		2 pm	4th Batty shelled a home at T.34 B.6.5 used as a M.G. observation station (32 HE)	
		5.17 pm	3rd Batty shelled back in canal opp. 29 & N.W. of O.C. Lg. Arh. (12 HE)	
		5.55 pm	1st Batty shelled 32 Regist. to Reprisal at request of O. 2nd B? (20 HE)	
			4th Batty — 32 Regist. to Reprisal (6 HE) at request of Trenches.	
		6.24 pm	— 1st Line Trench T.34 d.89 (6 HE)	
		6.30 pm	4th Batty — T.34 d.89 (6 HE)	
		6.39 pm	4th Batty — — — T.34 d.89 (6 HE)	
		9 pm	13/61 commenced shelling 012 B.4.9 & O5 B.6.8 at intervals with after rounds shrap	2 aeroplanes
			4th Batty shelled Road in rear of German Trenches. Its Road crossing road HOLLEBEKE to COURTRAI	U.K.BMI 157
			Railway. Th. woods in T.35 & 2 WARTELEEN. During the night	SD 2.7.15
			5th Batty shelled Road 140.91 & HOLLEBEKE village	App XX
		6.34 pm	Fired Test "y" (1 shrap) at N.E. from Trenches.	—
		6th Batty shelled Road behind German Trenches, during the night	
			1st & 3rd Batteries also shelled this Road during the night	
		10 pm	B.M. 176 (Secret) 3rd Div. Art Reco. as to relief of 7th & 15th Inf. Bdes by 52nd & 50th Bdes	APO XXI
			of 17th Divn respectively.	CB

APP. XVII

Secret
BM. 51
9/7/15

All units:

The different Switch lines and G.H.Q. 2nd line have been under Discussion today & the Brigadier has decided to cancel all orders originally given for these lines & substitute the following. Please therefore cancel my BM 41 of yesterday (not received)*

x C/S.

Ref. 5 Div S.G. 136/5 sent out to with my BM 207 of 25/6/15 para 3.

If (A) or (C) are held the grouping will be as follows:—

With Right Inf. Bde.   Lt. Col. Duffour   37 (How) Btty.
                                            146 Bde.
With Centre Inf. Bde.   Fitzmaurice   27 Bde.
With Left Inf. Bde.   Strong   15 Bde
                                            65 (How) Bde
                                            1 group Belg. Art.
                                            1 section Mount. Batt.

If (A) or (B) are held

With R. Inf. Bde.   Lt. Col. Duffour   37 (How) Btty
                                            146 Bde.
With L. Inf. Bde.   Lt. Col. Fitzmaurice 27 Bde
                                            15 —
                                            65 (How) Btty.
                                            1 group Belg. Art.
                                            1 sect. Mount. Art.

Div. Art. in all cases 29 Bde 9 heavy Bde 3 Siege Btty. 1 Group Belgian Art.

Group & Bde commanders will make all arrangements for the different contingencies in accordance with my HbM 247 of yesterday.

(Sd) H Bartholomew
Maj.

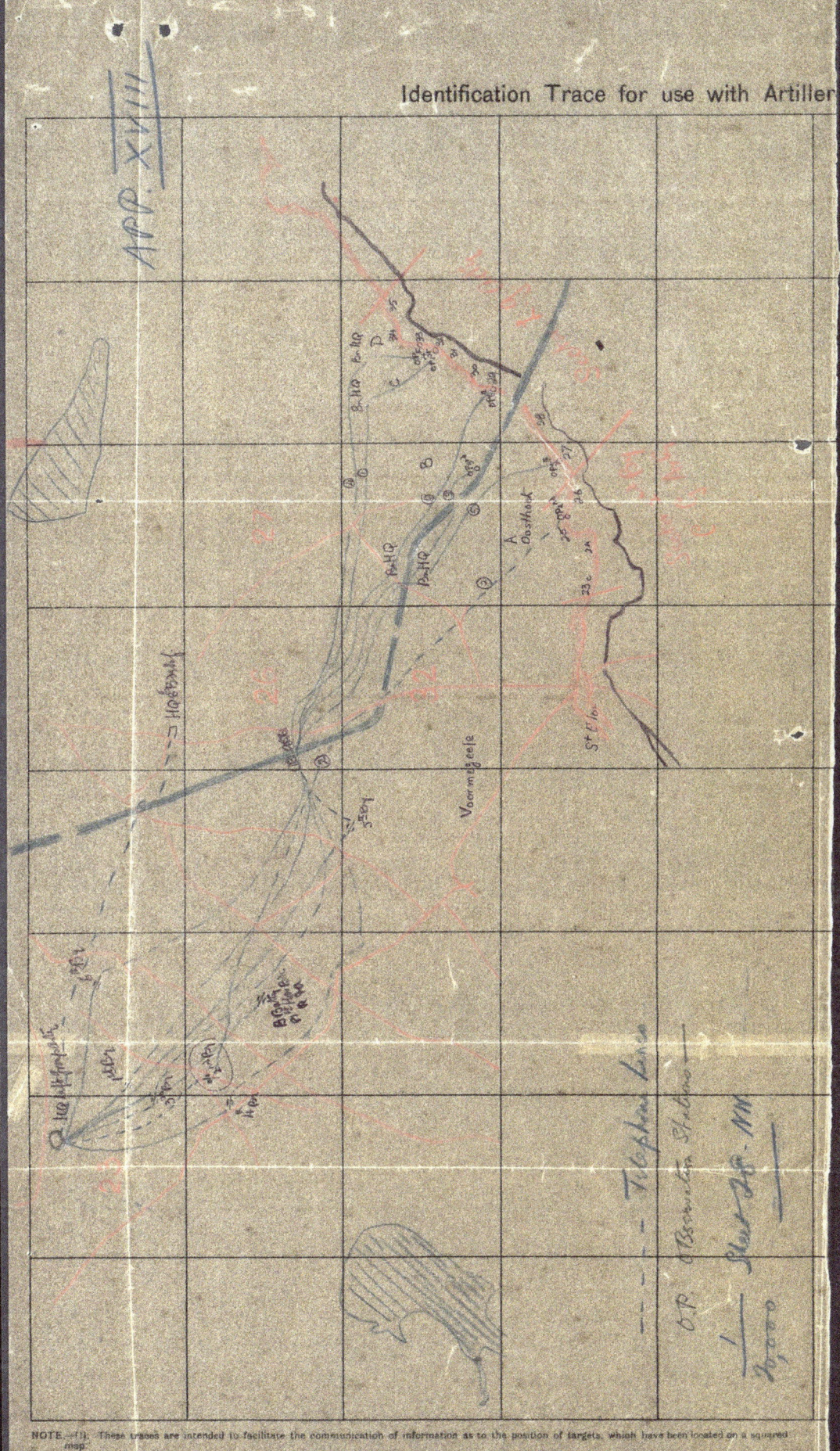

APP XIX

Arrangements for opening fire
on Request of Inf.

O. C.

During day.

Orders may be given direct from trenches to Battery in the following circumstances:-

"Test 28"

1. To carry out test, when the message "Test 28" will be handed to the F.O.O. and the general direction in which fire is required will be indicated on the map. The test will always consist of one round shrapnel.

"Reprisal 28.
04 a 5.5"

2. When a trench is being annoyed and retaliation is required, "reprisal" will be asked for from the F.O.O, and the spot on which fire is required will be indicated on the map, but the number of rounds and the nature of ammunition will be left to the discretion of the F.O.O.
Such orders will be immediately reported to Bde. H.Q.

"S.O.S. 28"

3. When fire is urgently required for defensive purposes the message S.O.S and number of trench will be handed to F.O.O., who will order his Battery to open rapid salvos of shrapnel distributed over the front of the trench named until he is handed the order to "stop" by O.C trench.

"STOP"

Immediately on receipt of message S.O.S the O.C. Battery will communicate with O.C. Left Group.

P.T.O

(continued)

In the case of Trench 28 where the F.O.O. is not actually in the trench a line will be run direct from him to the trench, and the message which would be handed to him if he were in the trench will be sent to him by telephone.

By night

All messages from Trench to Battery will be sent through Battalion H.Q. as hitherto. The F.O.Os return at night to Bn. H.Q. A series of tests will be carried out to see if this arrangement gives quick enough fire. If not it may be necessary to make some other disposition

W. Fraser Capt for Bde Major.
8th Infantry Bde

28/7/15.

APP. XX

R.A. Left Group.

BM 157.   30.7.15.

In order to harass the enemy CRA wishes you to consult your Brigadier as to the advisability of firing one or two rounds every now and then both by night & day on such points as C.Ts and places where works are under construction and frequented paths and roads & transport routes &c &c. One round occasionally will not draw any retaliation probably.

3rd D.A.
10.25 pm

App. XXI

Secret.

Left Group.

Bde 176 – 31.7.15

According to information recd. from the Divn. 9th & 7th Inf. Bdes withdraw from their present fronts on nights of 1/2 & 2/3 August respectively and are to be replaced by the 52nd & 50th Bdes respectively of 17th Divn. on the same nights.

G.O.C. 17th Div. will take over command of the front from VERSTRAAT-DICKEBUSCHE Road to road 03b107. on completion of relief of 7th Inf. Bde, & at the same time the command of the artillery covering this front will pass to 17th Div. Art.

Trench 27 will still be covered by 5th Belgian Batty as at present.

17th D.A.H.Q. will be at ZEVECOTEN huts (G35 c83) to which signal officers concerned will arrange cables from the two groups effected.

3 Div. & 3 D.A.H.Q. remain as at present.

Requests for fire of 3rd Siege section will be made from this H.Q.

Acknowledge

R. J. Finlayson
Maj. B.M.

9.45 p.m.

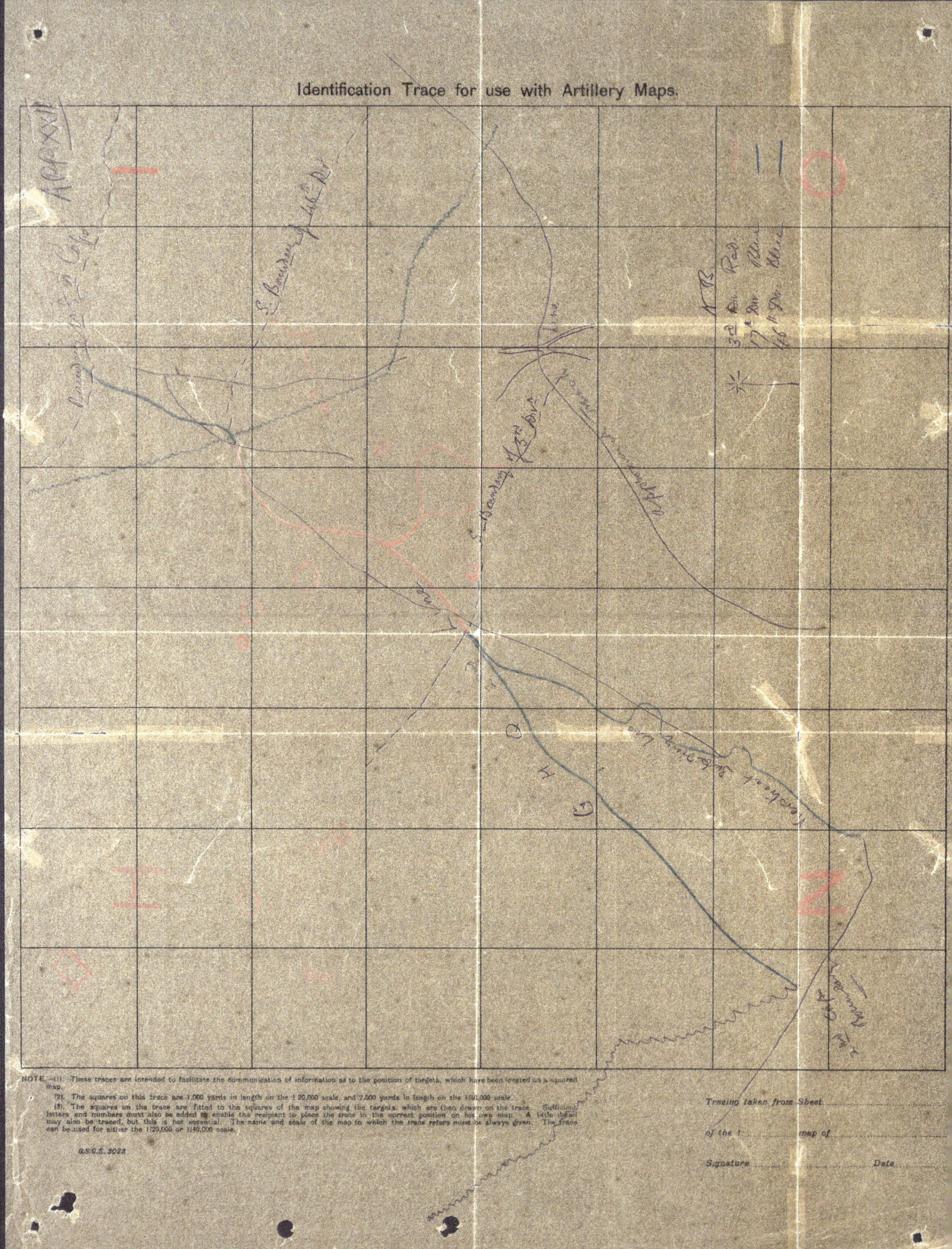